NOT FOR
OURSELVES
ALONE

Also by Jenny Robin Jones

Writers in Residence:
A Journey with Pioneer New Zealand Writers
Auckland University Press, Auckland

No Simple Passage:
The Journey of the 'London' to New Zealand, 1842 – a ship of hope
Random House New Zealand, Auckland

NOT FOR OURSELVES ALONE

Belonging
in an age of
loneliness

JENNY ROBIN JONES

SADDLEBACK

Published by Saddleback
175 Wilton Rd
Wilton
Wellington, 6012
www.jennyrobinjones.com

First published 2018

ISBN 978-0-9951025-0-7

Cover image:
"Symbolic image (loneliness, defencelessness…)"
ID 13127835 © Ruslan Grechka | Dreamstime.com

Book production, design and layout:
Quentin Wilson Publishing, Christchurch
wilson.quentin@gmail.com

Printed in Taipei, Taiwan by CHOICE Printing Inc.

For Piper, Riley, Nicolas, Carter and Matisse

CONTENTS

Non nobis solum nati sumus.
[Not for ourselves alone are we born.]
– *Marcus Tullius Cicero*

A human being is a part of the whole that we call the universe,
a part limited in time and space. He experiences himself, his
thoughts and feelings, as something separated from the rest... a kind
of optical delusion of his consciousness... Our task must be to free
ourselves from this prison by widening our circle of compassion to
embrace all living beings and all of nature.
– *Albert Einstein*

GENESIS

In New Zealand's great rugby encounters I didn't care who won and who lost. Daydreams instantly took over when sports reporters tried to claim my attention. The idea of keeping score so that a winner could be announced meant little to me. No doubt about it – I was not a true New Zealander.

When the time came for New Zealand to gear up for the Rugby World Cup 2011, my attitude was as usual – sooner over the better. I had been through the alienation many times since I came here in 1970 and I knew how to cope, though this time it was worse, the excitement in the country more intense than I ever remembered. The games were a constant topic of conversation, the ups and downs of progress towards kick-off were on everyone's mind, the untimely injury of someone called Dan Carter was front-page news. As usual when failure at inter-national sport threatened, 'the nation was gutted' and I felt very alone.

But we are all capable of change when circumstances and personal history collide in a conspiring sort of way.

After a week in Tauranga staying with my mother it is time to go home to Wellington. The airport is ablaze with reminders of the World Cup and of the All Blacks' projected victory. A big TV broadcasts news about the rugby and the person called Dan Carter. Booklets entitled 'REAL New Zealand Festival' outline the times and places of matches and tell visiting fans how to get the most out of New Zealand while they are here. I retreat into my head and bask in the pleasure of going home.

A flight announcement splinters my trance. 'All planes out of Tau-ranga are cancelled due to fog'. In few minutes, I'm standing outside in the rain with about thirty other people. We mill about, waiting for instructions. Reduced to our externals – sex, age, colour, appearance

– we are nonetheless linked as travellers watching our certainties vapourise.

The coach trip to Auckland begins well enough, until, a few miles out of Tauranga, smoke billows up near the driver. We evacuate and mill beside the road. Who knows what will happen, whether we will make it to Auckland safely, whether the 6.30 flight will take off from Auckland, when we will get home?

The man next to me is thirty-something, sports an Irish accent and is nattily dressed beneath a shaven head. We exchange names and more. Occupations even. Soon we are joined by Craig, a Tauranga businessman involved in the export of dairy products. When a taxi and a couple of minibuses arrive, it is James, Craig and I who score the taxi – James and me in the back, Craig beside Doug the driver. For the next three hours the four of us will be sharing confined space and everyone makes an effort, like a singles dinner where the point is connection. To the obvious externals of appearance, sex and age we add direction of travel. James and I are headed for homes in Welling-ton. Craig has to get to Los Angeles and then on to Madison. Doug is a Tauranga man and he's convinced everyone in New Zealand would like to live in Tauranga if they could. On to occupation. Doug asks James and Craig, but not me, what they do for a living. James doesn't let that pass, he tells Doug, 'You may have read about her in the paper because she's a writer.' Doug decides my face is familiar to him and that he has seen it on TV. I fantasise about my face being familiar; the others try to decide if I am a somebody. James exclaims with delight when he recognises a bridge we are passing, because he was involved in its construction. Moments later he dismisses his revelation as a piece of useless information.

Craig is anxious to make his connection at LA because he's travelling for business. We talk about Fonterra and I try to sound knowledgeable about export prices dropping. When we pass some stamper batteries near Waihi that I once explored on a walk, I mention cyanide and Craig backs me up with male certainty: 'Those were cyanide tanks.' I start to feel at ease.

My co-passengers are deeply interested in the taxi. They had hoped it would be swankier. I'm not sure if it's a Ford Focus or whether the Ford Focus was the one they hoped we would be driven in, but it doesn't matter – I'll experience this day for whatever it brings, even when it exposes shameful ignorance. The words 'Ford Focus' ring in my ears without meaning. Doug says 'it has the feel of diesel', referring to its 'low rev swerve'. It's done 140,000 kilometres. We're getting on well. Soon I'll know more about this car than I do about my own.

Doug asks me: 'And what do you write, Madam?' I suppose he is being polite but I hate 'Madam'. 'And what's your name, Madam?' I try him with Jenny but first names won't do. He wants the famous author.

Of course, there is considerable talk about the rugby. All the way up to Auckland we see flags flying for the participating countries and it's fun to identify them. The majority are for the All Blacks – or 'ABs' (stressed as in babies), as I discover they are referred to by true New Zealanders. That name, Dan Carter, comes up again.

At Auckland Airport it turns out that planes are indeed flying to LA and Wellington. James and I get to sit next to each other. The airline's safety instruction video has been newly minted to feature ABs giving the instructions.

Alone together, conversation turns personal. James divulges that staying bald requires shaving his head every two weeks. He has a wife and child in Wellington. He can't wait to see his little boy, who, he hopes, will have waited up for him.

Things feel cosy and safe so I ask James, Who is Dan Carter? He explains that Carter was New Zealand's great hope for a win. Suffered an injury in a training session and can't play for the rest of the World Cup. He says the country is now hearing the intimate details of the state of Dan Carter's groin. I like James a lot.

A week later I turn on the TV and watch the All Blacks play Argentina in a quarter-final. I have discovered I can be part of the Rugby World Cup. It isn't such a big step from there to realising that my whole life can be seen as a journey to belong.

So, what is belonging all about?

INTRODUCTION

In an age of loneliness, it sometimes seems as though self is all we have. Not so. This elastic, permeable marvel is our building block for belonging.

In earlier ages people took belonging for granted. It grew organically in their societies, bringing psychological stability and well-being. It endowed group life with meaning, purpose and effectiveness; it offered peace and security. Our age is different. The great must-have of the modern age is individual freedom. In its name we, the people, have fought revolutions and crossed continents. The idea of 'freedom' inhabits us like a religious tenet. Nearly everything capitalism can offer is groomed in its service. Above all else, our story goes, we are individuals.

But often lonely with it. Often depressed with it. Often badly adrift, often suicidal, often sinking into abandonment of that very self we cherish so highly. And sometimes willing to throw away 'freedom' for the sake of 'belonging'. Any kind of belonging, be it benign or sinister.

It doesn't take long to find headlines about loneliness: Loneliness in Old Age 'Deadlier than Obesity'; Loneliness 'Can Kill You', Scientists Say; Chronic Loneliness Affecting NZ Elderly; Loneliness Linked to Poor Sleep; Kiwis Under 30 Are the Most Lonely; Loneliness as Bad for Health as Smoking, Say Experts. Articles abound: Loneliness is a Very Deep Pain; Loneliness Can Hurt More Than the Heart; Neoliberalism is Creating Loneliness; Is Facebook Making Us Lonely?; Is This the Loneliest Generation? Research studies and surveys present a sobering list of dangers faced by lonely people: lowered immunity, higher blood pressure, disturbed sleep patterns, illness, cognitive changes, headaches, unhealthy stress levels, dementia, heart attack and stroke. An article by *Guardian* columnist George Monbiot sums it up in a headline, The Age of Loneliness is Killing Us.

Loneliness, which we may define as the perception that one's relationships do not meet one's social needs, is on the increase. The more modernised the country, the greater the loneliness. A leading expert on loneliness, John Cacioppo, a neuroscientist at Chicago University, found in a recent study that chronic and severe loneliness now affects 20% of Americans – about 60 million people. A 2006 study cited in the *American Sociological Review* found that in 1985, only 10% of Americans said they had no one to discuss important matters with, but by 2004 the number had risen to 25%. In 1985, 15% said they had only one such good friend, but by 2004 this had increased to 20%. In the United Kingdom, government officials have been ordered to find out exactly how lonely Britain's population is. The government's fear is that 'the most isolated generation ever' will overwhelm the national health service. Even in New Zealand, where community bonds are probably stronger than in the bigger countries, a government survey in 2010 found that 8% of older New Zealanders felt lonely all or most of the time, while a further 44% rated themselves as moderately lonely. Among younger people, 18% of those under thirty had felt lonely at least some of the time in the previous four weeks.

Another kind of suffering associated with lack of belonging is alienation. This phenomenon has accompanied the modern world from its beginnings but globalisation is making it a hallmark of our times. You won't find people marching down the streets crying, 'I feel alienated!' but when you analyse the reasons for the Occupy movement or the Brexit vote to leave the European Union, or the voting into the White House of Donald Trump, it seems clear that we are hearing the voices of thousands who feel excluded from the mainstream social, political and economic systems of their countries. Instead of being respected as intelligent, socially responsible citizens, we are treated as economic units called consumers, as if this is our only function in society; unless it's as production units. Increasingly we interact not with people but with algorithms and 'smart' systems demanding conformity to inhuman rules. The race is on to replace ourselves with robots.

Alienation is at the heart of modern terrorism. The Chechnyan-American brothers who carried out the Boston marathon bombing in 2013 and the Somali-British teenagers who became Jihadi brides in 2014, failed to develop a sense of belonging in the adopted countries of their parents. Instead, they turned to online groups that brought them in touch with think-alikes all over the planet. If only they could get the correct identity their lives would be meaningful and significant.

Then they could work out whether they were of the society around them or of the religion or the country of their parents. Was it possible to be a blend of all three? Wouldn't it be better to join a group with an internationalist vision and not bother with being part of a nation state at all? A radical Islamist group for instance.

Apart from that extreme reaction, thousands of young people fall prey every year to a need for belonging that is like a cri de coeur – with herd mentality and careless cruelty the result. Our challenge today is to help people develop a self comfortable with doubt and at ease in its surrounding society and in the world.

When belonging was simply part of the human condition, people belonged to families, families were connected to communities and communities were part of larger groupings such as region and country. You belonged because you were there. As humanity evolved from tribal organisation and consciousness, the concept of each person possessing an individual self developed to the point where belonging has become downright elusive. The Jamesian insight that uncertainty is the sharpest of human realities has never felt truer. That being so, those who cannot cope with uncertainty become a menace to society and themselves.

In a world of globalisation, belonging is more important than ever. We need it within our democracies, our economic structures, our nations. We need it to enable social cohesion without social coercion. And in these fraught days of climate change it's not just human society that we need to belong to. Try the botanical and sentient world, try the universe. Each of these strands for possible belonging sits on a continuum of self vs collective. How far is the self cherished at the expense of the collective and vice versa?

No matter how globalised the world gets, we experience it as individuals, so my approach with this book is to start with the personal and then relate it to the general. In addition to the autobiographical contribution, there are interviews with friends and family who were willing to speak candidly. The personal is also represented by the documented experiences of historical figures and literary characters as understood by their authors. In looking at contemporary theories of society and the dominant political and economic narratives of our times, I have included historical context to help illuminate what has been happening and how this has affected belonging.

At birth we have no sense of individual being. A foetus nestles totally secure in its mother's womb. Entry into the world heralds separation, insecurity and a lifelong challenge to belong again. Western societies demand that each human being develops a sense of self as a basis to achieve connection with others. Part I traces mechanisms for evolving this sense of self.

To emphasise the relative newness of a modern sense of self, medieval society is held up for comparison. In feudal times a person was considered identical with his or her role in society. As the economy slowly became more fluid a spirit of rebellion emerged. Catching the mood of the times, Martin Luther encouraged people to have a direct relationship with God and to base their actions on personal conscience/ the voice of God within. This new freedom brought unprecedented personal doubt and uncertainty. Protestantism offered people restored certainty through unconditional surrender to God.

But Luther had let the genie out of the bottle: the self once discovered can never be entirely effaced. Soon dissemblers would abound and playwrights such as Molière and Shakespeare became focused on disentangling truth from fiction. The best rule was, 'To thine own self be true.' Rousseau developed the idea, making it his mission to be entirely frank about himself and persuade others to follow his example. The Age of Reason gave way to the Age of Sensibility. Feelings were everything.

In Part II, as I start to connect with the adult world, I realise that personality and knowing myself are vital factors in finding a comfortable place in society. The essential thing in a job is for it to have meaning. I interview Glenys, who explains how the loss of work undermined her sense of belonging and how she found ways of restoring it.

And then there is the importance of place. As a young adult, I return from England to the country I departed at age three, and find the physical land calls to me profoundly. I see that Māori experience the land very differently. In early times and to a lesser extent now, 'place' is inseparable from the living body of the tribe. Much of this orientation to place has been lost in Western civilisation, but by looking at ways in which place is still significant in belonging, we can glimpse possibilities for our own age.

Since the teachings of Luther, marriage and family have attained the status of spiritual vocation. An interview with a couple married for four decades reveals the constructive accommodations they have made between their individuality and their married selves. People outside marriage and long-term relationships find alternative, often imaginative ways to experience belonging.

More interviews explore the changing face of community in the modern world: a New Zealander living in Luxembourg; a woman's struggle to find belonging in community rather than gaol; and the efforts of the old to maintain their sense of belonging when those who mattered most to them are dead or living far away. An Iraqi family living in New Zealand speaks frankly about learning to belong in their adopted country.

It turns out that the body is biologically predisposed for bonding with others. Social media rewire our brains with implications for belonging. Facebook enables everyone to find their group – or their conglomeration of individuals – with mixed results.

Everyone tries to develop connectedness. You spend time with family, I walk with a friend, she plays tennis, he joins the Labour Party. Whatever we do in our ever more fragmented units, if we are to survive then it is vital to take control of our own belonging, and vital that society assists us. As a society, we need to take heed of surveys that tell us what once we didn't need to be told, and work out how to respect freedom while offering sustenance through belonging.

Part III deals with the wider world and the arrival of the Age of Loneliness. Since neoliberalism became the prevailing ideology in many societies, what has happened to belonging in terms of the public space, the economy and the nation? As swathes of the population in country after country are excluded from a share in prosperity, and the cult of the individual reaches life-denying proportions, the sense of alienation has exploded. Modernity and then globalisation have made people desperate for certainty. Islamic extremism, Christian fundamentalism and Donald Trump appear to offer it.

Finally the Great Belonging. Throughout the ages, some people, especially in the East, have learned a profound sense of belonging with the entire universe. In the age of loneliness, and finding that climate change spares no one, we are rediscovering the ways in which we are interdependent, not only with each other but with every other organism. We glimpse how to retain our individuality whilst understanding uncertainty to be an intrinsic part of the territory. Doubt need not drive us to fundamentalism or climate change denial (or despair) but can be seen as a common predicament, mostly unwelcome, that binds us all together. A combination of acceptance of doubt and the imaginative act of empathy offer us an excellent basis for belonging.

PART ONE

GETTING STARTED

ONE

FOUNDATIONS

On emerging

Like every other human on this planet I am of woman born. My nine months' gestation was bliss. As I flipped from fish to amphibian to human, I never had to worry about a roof over my head or where my next meal was coming from. I never felt cold or hot or ridiculed or lonely. My mother was home, restaurant and companion in one. She demanded nothing, accepted all my metamorphoses, criticised nothing, and her body was mine to plunder: if I needed calcium her teeth gave it up; if I craved iron, her blood made the sacrifice. If something went wrong, if poison infiltrated her bloodstream and flowed into mine, we were one in our suffering. But with my first breath I found myself alone.

My mother came and went like a free person. In and out of my company she flitted and at night she left me alone in the dark. The darkness of the womb had been comforting and I'd never known light then. My new dark bristled with menace. As for my father, I hardly saw him. Siblings? As firstborn I had none.

From my first breath I had to work. To take in nutrients I was forced to purse my lips and suck. Within months of my arrival I had to enclose matter in my mouth and swallow. These nutrients were offered at set times and often contained things I heartily disliked. I was forced to sit in front of horrid green messes until I ate them. When hard white things pushed up through my gums, the nutrients came on a plate in chunks which I had to make disappear down my throat. Not only that but I had to eat in a certain way, with knife and fork, sooner the better. It was considered quite acceptable to keep me waiting until everyone was served, even when I was frantic with hunger. Very soon they didn't want me pooing my nappies but sitting on a cold pot and doing it according to their timetable. One day the roof over my head became someone else's. The family had abandoned it for another. I had to get used to another kind of light and another darkness.

There was constant pressure to get words right. Sometimes it was correct to get the past tense by adding 'ed', play – played, for instance, but other times it wasn't and you couldn't guess what it should be. If they heard you say 'buyed' they laughed at you. A lot of language was to do with manners. I had to say please and thank you and pretend I liked a present even if I didn't. There were words I was not allowed to use and feelings I could not find the words for, feelings that no one else seemed to have. I had to kiss people I didn't want to kiss and be squeezed half to death by people who called themselves 'Aunt'. I had to sleep in the dark with bogeymen threatening to burst through the window at any moment.

I didn't hate it. There was plenty to interest me, always new things to do and see, hear, taste, touch. Just getting to know my own body was a pleasure. To discover this bit and that bit and learn the word for it. To learn the words for everything. To find there was a whole world to find words for. Besides, I forgot the horrid things almost as soon as they were over. I assumed everything was going to be wonderful until it wasn't, and then I was in the middle of it and when it was over I forgot. Or thought I did.

But nothing took away the fact that togetherness was over. At the moment of my arrival, the connecting cord to my mother was severed. I emerged; my mother stayed where she was. Since then many years have passed during which I've had to learn how to live separately, to provide my own food, warmth, shelter and company. When old age and sickness arrive no one else will feel my pain and when death comes I'll make the journey solo. No one else can be me being born, me living or me dying. It's me alone.

It makes matters worse that I don't remember anything of my first three years. All the above is simply a reconstruction, there's no memory involved at all. If only I could remember those first critical months in the womb, that parental whoop for joy when I emerged, even the pain and suffering of sleeping alone and having to do as I was told. Then I'd have an unbroken line of consciousness, something I could refer to whenever I felt unsure of my existence.

And like everyone else on the planet I started with a further handicap: no memory of what came before the womb; no knowledge of what I was being born into. It all had to be learned or taught, and that could only happen if people bothered to keep handing down the memory.

I took an ordered society for granted. What I found was presumably what had always been – playgrounds with slides and swings and climbing frames, free books to borrow from libraries, Father Christmas at the department store handing out presents. I inherited civil society, with laws to enable children to have a happy childhood, and free doctors and dentists to make them grow big and strong. I had no memory of the act of taming or of the world before the civilising: rival aristocrats that locked child princes in towers, rich men who made children slave all day in coal mines, pressgangs who forced them to work on ships at sea. I did not realise that every advance had been fought for and that if you didn't keep fighting, the bad old days would return.

No, like everyone else I just found myself here and had to make sense of it. Evolution hasn't helped. There used to be a time when people lived in small groups or communities that were their whole world. We were much more one with our kind then. 'The other' meant one of three things: predator, prey or irrelevance. There was no need for 'society' or 'identity'. One just was, one belonged. None of this was clear to me. I knew, however, that by fair means or foul I must belong or perish.

When I was three my mother bore me a brother. This seemed at first a generous gesture. I was allowed to sit in an armchair with baby on my lap and alert my busy mama to his needs. I could put him in my doll's pram and wheel him round the garden. He made no objection; he was, after all, an optional extra. The rights and the toys were all mine, my parents adored me and were expressing it by giving me a brother. The situation began to feel normal and like most children I laughed often and without restraint. I noticed that my parents didn't laugh unless they had someone to laugh with.

So far so universal. My first big self-differentiating shock took place on an ocean liner. My parents, finding their little country short on opportunities, booked a sea voyage to the far side of the world. There my father would study for further qualifications and then we would all come home.

I soon noticed that my brother was an object of interest to many of the passengers on the ship. This was a puzzle. After all he was three years my junior, only six months out of our mother's womb and just beginning to crawl, whereas I was able to talk in sentences, use a knife and fork, the toilet and many other things considered vital in human society. My brother had only to smile and people fought for his attention. Then he won the fancy dress competition. My mother had dressed me as a lampshade; for my brother she fashioned a chef's hat out of one of the large starched napkins provided on ship, put another on his lap for an apron and added a loaf of fresh bread. The photograph taken of the winner on his mother's lap shows, at their side, a sulky lampshade to whom the unbearable injustice of life had just been revealed. Soon my parents dared not leave me alone with my brother lest I cause him bodily harm. By the time I was told this, it seemed incomprehensible – I no longer felt any desire to hurt him, but I continued to protect my rights as the longer serving resident on the planet.

The next great shock occurred when I was sent to school. My parents prepared me carefully and I looked forward to it. In the playground, some big girls came up and said hello. I exulted inwardly. Already I belonged to this brave new world of school where big girls came and talked to the likes of me. Such eminences recognised me as a kindred spirit. Soon I would be an eminence too.

'What are the initials for Girl Guide?' one of them asked. That was all right. I knew what 'initials' meant.

'G. G.,' I said.

'Can't you say horse yet?' Smirks of triumph. This was a lesson in belonging. The big girls were letting me know I didn't. They wandered off in search of new prey, leaving me bewildered and frantic. Here was the great challenge facing every new entrant to the human race: to acquire a self and to learn to connect.

The child takes a self

I soon realised I couldn't just belong. I had to *be* someone first. My mother helped by differentiating me from my three brothers.

'You were very determined,' she would say. 'I could always deflect the boys. Like the books tell you, get them interested in something else instead of just saying no. But if *you* decided to do something I could never persuade you out of it.'

Was that good or bad? It sounded bad that I wouldn't let my mother do what she wanted and it sounded bad that I was the odd one out in the family and it sounded bad that I defied the advice in grownups' books. Perhaps I should try to be less determined? Perhaps I had no right to do what I wanted, perhaps my judgement was wrong. On the other hand, to be determined made me feel different from the others and it felt good to possess something worth my mother's remembering.

So, was it good to be determined?

They started saying I was sensitive. 'You take things too seriously.' Was there any other way to take them? And then my mother relayed something from my headmistress: 'She thinks you will suffer a lot in your life because you're so sensitive.' At first I was pleased. My school's headmistress had taken the time to work out my destiny. But was my destiny any good? Or was it God's punishment? A life sentence perhaps. If I insisted on sensitivity, unending suffering (whatever suffering was) would follow.

So, was it good to be sensitive?

They said I was good at drawing. There was an old lady who lived down the road. Her name was Mrs Mead, she lived in one room with a poodle called Pompey and she always gave me drawing paper when Mummy and I came to visit. I loved drawing Pompey and I liked drawing Mummy and Daddy with me in the middle, but I had a feeling that drawing was something adults asked children to do when they wanted to deflect them. When my father's friends asked me what I would be when I grew up I said an artist or a writer. They wanted to know which but I couldn't decide. I began to realise that another of my attributes was 'indecisive'. Anyway, the things that mattered were running fast and wearing shoes the other girls liked.

So, was it good to draw?

Then there was winning. When I came last in a running race, my confidence plummeted but as a winner, I felt bad in another way. Once I won a competition for the best drawing of an object in an old church. The pastor came to school to give out the prize and all the children clapped, but I assumed every one of them had wanted to be the winner as much as I did. Was it me my friends were whispering about when we went out to play? Were they secretly saying I didn't deserve to win? Wouldn't they like me anymore? And did winning a competition for drawing mean I wouldn't be a writer? And if I didn't win the next competition would that make me a failure? Would it make me a fraud?

Was it good to win?

I questioned and answered myself: *Why do you see everything good or bad, marked out of ten, as it were?* I don't know, *Perhaps it's just in your imagination*, Yes, maybe, but it's like a voice, *Your brother doesn't seem to have it,* No, but he's got Ted, *The pink teddy bear he takes with him everywhere?* Yes, he laughs and jokes with Ted and Mummy talks about Ted as if he were real, *That's an imaginary friend, it's quite normal for a small child.*

This voice began to accompany me and it wasn't a friendly pink teddy bear. Wouldn't own up to name, sex or shape, more Grand Inquisitor than friend. I didn't like it but in a way it relieved my loneliness, for, even with loving parents and boisterous brothers, I often felt lonely. *What exaggeration! Surely you don't expect everyone to believe that,* Well, there's quite a bit of truth in it but maybe I forgot the nicer things, *You certainly did,* Were there lots then? *No, not that many really.*

My seriousness was such a worry to everyone that my grandmother and great aunt decided to give me a course on Acquiring a Sense of Humour. I didn't know this at the time, of course, thought I was just making a five-hour train journey in the company of strangers for a summer holiday with Nanna and Auntie Nellie – and it wasn't so painful, I was hardly aware of the Great Lesson. It was only afterwards that I realised how many times they had made me laugh at myself.

It was one of the most important things I ever learned. *So now you're taking your sense of humour seriously!* Touché, and by the way I'm smiling, but in any case, my grandmother and aunt were very proud of their achievement, *Well I hope you thanked them properly*, No, I can't say I did, *How ungrateful!* Well by the time they told me what they had done, it felt like it was me they were describing, *How do you mean, you?* I mean my sense of humour didn't feel like something I could turn on and off like a tap. It was part of my core, *But you learned it in the first place from them*, That's true, but then it became part of me, *Well it wouldn't hurt to show a little appreciation.*

Appreciation, gratitude, consideration, generosity. The dreaded word selfish. When my father was angry with me, he would declaim, 'You are utterly selfish!' He spoke with such vehemence that other attributes vaporised. There was no room left for 'determined' or 'sensitive'. Selfish defined me utterly.

And there were still some kinds of jokes I didn't get. Like when I told my father I got 99 out of 100 in a test and he said, 'Why not 100?' *It's true you are too sensitive,* He only talked about the 1%! *But with love and pride written all over his face,* I never thought of that, *But it's true, isn't it?* I don't know, after that I always saw 99% as a failure, *That's crazy, your dad was paying you tribute,* I never thought of that, *Your sense of humour was a bit new, that's all.*

Impersonations

You might not think a child's life is a matter of impersonations but it soon is. For society, it wasn't enough to call me determined or sensitive and then leave me to grow into that kind of person; there were dozens of scripts to learn and they were all part of developing a self. It didn't feel natural at first – but it was fun.

I was put in a room with other children and we had to stand up when the teacher came in. She had to say, 'Good morning, Class' and we had to say 'Good *morning*, Miss *White*'. When we all said it together, it came out like a chant, which was rather surprising but we couldn't help ourselves. It got us in unison.

Then we had to sit down and wait until the teacher told the class what to do. If one of us wanted to say something, we had to put up our hand and wait. If we wanted to go to the toilet or to interrupt when she was writing on the blackboard and had her back to us, we had to say, 'Please, Miss'. I became so good at this that my end-of-year report read 'unfailingly polite'. Was it good to be unfailingly polite or did it mean I lacked the courage to be rude?

At home my mother sometimes sent me to the grocer's up the road. 'Walk quickly, no detours, and return with the right change.' At the shop I had to queue up behind other people. The grocer had to say, 'What can I do for you?' And I had to say, 'I'd like some butter, please.' When the grocer said, 'That's a shilling,' I had to hand him the money. If he said, 'And how is your mother today?' I had to say, 'She's fine thank you,' even though her back was sore. The grocer didn't want to know the ins and outs of my mother's well-being; he just wanted to acknowledge my mother as a regular customer. Then I had to take the butter home to my mother. I had successfully impersonated a person on an errand. It made me feel part of things.

I also learned to impersonate actual people. It was called fancy dress and my mother kept a trunk full of her old clothes for the purpose. My favourite was a ball gown of pink taffeta. I and my friends clumped about in high-heeled shoes, playing fine ladies, princesses, kings and queens. Fine clothes signalled eminence. Sometimes I dressed in rags, pretending I was a poor girl in the forest. A prince would find me and instantly recognise my loving heart and distinctive breeding. We would fall in love and get married and then I'd dress in fine clothes, feeling sure that my inner beauty matched my outward opulence.

In time, I took on the personas of lovers with paired names: Henry and Henrietta, Victor and Victoria, George and Georgina – soulmates who couldn't be parted once they had overcome initial difficulties. Eventually I became brave enough to suggest to my friend Angela that we could play the game together. As Classroom Monitors we had jobs to do in the classroom during some playtimes and I found it wholly entrancing, in the midst of sweeping the floor, tidying up the desks and changing the water for the tadpoles, to sing whatever words of love came into my head. Angela giggled but entered into the game enough to return my love. Still the Grand Inquisitor took me to task: *Imagine if someone had come into the classroom and found you doing it!* I don't remember that ever happening, *But the possibility must have been in your minds,* Yes, we knew we might be caught exposing our raw selves, *How could you be exposing your raw selves when you were pretending to be other people?* The emotions were very real and very intense, *You can't speak for Angela, can you?* True, *So, are you saying you loved her?* No, but I was pouring out true intensity.

I learned to present myself to my mother as a risk taker who had adventures. I learned to tell her about my day in a way that aroused her interest. I knew when to pause for the meaning to sink in, when to grin, when to leave her dangling with suspense – and my success made me feel larger as a person. It didn't work so well when her friends came for tea. With strangers who didn't listen to the end, I was diminished. I would rather have watched them to gauge how they would like it told, but when my mother said, 'Tell them, dear', I had to play my part on cue or let my mother down. She was often too excited to wait until the end and hustled the story on in her own way. Next time I saw her friends I'd try to give that sort of presentation from the start.

Where Princess Anne goes

It turned out there was a lot more to being human than the necessities of food and shelter. I wasn't just arms, legs and head with a few internal organs thrown in, I was also things not strictly necessary to survival: ideas and strivings, joy and suffering, being accepted and rejected, being worthy of attention and then not. I had ideas about 'who' I wanted to be and made daily attempts to impersonate them. I was supposed to be like other people, and wear shoes the other girls liked. But I was also supposed to outdo them, to win races and pass exams to show I was special. If I wasn't special, I didn't count.

Some people were special because they had special fathers. My father was special in a way: at the hospital he wore a white coat and the nurses and patients spoke to him as though his words counted more than theirs. But the children at school didn't know that, so it didn't count. Their fathers were special by virtue of running the local butcher's or being the bus conductor or having fought in the war. At Girl Guides, the fathers who were special were rich and their families had double-entrance driveways. If someone's father was so famous that the guides had *heard of him*, that made him special and no questions asked.

When people came down from London for my parents' parties, they asked me if I wanted to follow in my father's footsteps. I didn't, because then I'd be him and not me. It was bad enough that he was a great man in a white coat. I doubted I was really his child.

I learned that when Lady Gower asked me where I went to school she expected it to be somewhere posh and well known. Lady Gower frowned because she hadn't *heard of it*. Afterwards my mother explained that Lady Gower's daughter went to Benenden, 'where Princess Anne goes'.

Even when people were obviously special they could still be lonely. You might think that kings and queens belonged because their power was recognised and admired by everyone, but they were often lonely just because they knew no one as special as they were. Their advisers knew the dangers of getting their heads cut off, so instead of being honest they said whatever they thought the king or queen would like to hear.

My own parents seemed outside all this. They had come from a little country thousands of miles away and they didn't care about having a big driveway or sending their daughter to Benenden. But then a new girl came to school. She was very pretty and she played the harp. At the school concert, she sang and played on stage all by herself and my mother was very taken with her. But I found Loyola rather difficult. She talked a lot about her father, who was super special, and one day she asked me what my father did. I said he worked in a hospital. At home I repeated to my parents that Loyola's father was 'a knight of the realm' and had wanted to know what my father did.

'What did you tell her?'

'I said you worked in a hospital.'

'As if I'm a cleaner or something!'

This was confusing. I was being brought up to respect every person as equal and to respect the work they did, but my father was angry because someone might think he was a cleaner. Jesus of Nazareth, whom I was learning about at Sunday School, wouldn't have minded. I liked the idea of quietly living my life while word went around about how wonderful I was until I woke up one morning to find myself saint or genius. *You are taking a big risk there, you know,* How? *You have developed a persona of self-deprecation,* What's wrong with that? *People may take you at your own valuation,* But surely they can see my worth if they look, *That's the trouble, people nowadays don't look, they go by who shouts loudest and what other people say,* But it's so demeaning to have to sell my own wares, *If you want to be a success you have to* pretend *you are a success,* What do you think I should do then? *You could try to be more of a saleswoman, you could tell people how great you are, that's quite all right nowadays,* Oh but I couldn't, it's not in my personality, *You make your personality, don't forget,* Yes, but there are limits, *I see, you want to be Jesus of Nazareth in disguise,* You make it sound as if I consider myself above everyone else, *Like everyone else, you don't want to be ordinary.*

Limits to transparency

At Sunday School they said God could see me wherever I was and whatever I was doing. I pictured him looking at me on the toilet and from there it was a short step to his seeing me whenever I was naughty. Perhaps everyone else could too.

Some people routinely present themselves as cleverer or better than they are. They pretend to loyalty they don't feel and a lot of other things too. The womblike connection between Henry and Henrietta seemed desirable, but real life was about learning how to connect with people on a self-to-self basis and total transparency was not much use. Boundaries were better. I needed to be able to lie.

My mother wanted me to go to an exercise class to improve my posture, which was deteriorating as bumps became breasts. The teacher was a middle-aged woman and the participants were middle-aged too. My mother insisted I attend once a week and gave me the bus fare. In protest, I decided not to pay. Other kids cheated so it seemed like the thing to do. When I gave my mother the change she asked how much I had paid and I lied. After a few weeks, I could barely face the bus conductor or my mother. I could barely face myself.

I felt even worse when my mother said my posture was improving. *One wonders if you gained anything at all by lying,* At least I lied without self-delusion, *Rubbish, you're just like everyone else,* Give me an instance, *You just provided one,* How? *You persuaded yourself it was okay to cheat the bus conductor,* I told you it was a protest, *Exactly, that's what you told me, but in fact you were looking for an excuse to lie,* Do you really think so? *Yes, I think you admired those other kids and you wanted to test your courage and prove you could lie.*

TWO

A SHORT HISTORY OF THE SELF

In feudal times, it was easy

At school, we learned that the Feudal System gave every person a worth decreed by birth. To be born was to belong. The king was at the top, then the nobles, followed by the knights, the clergy, the tradesmen and, at the bottom of the heap, the peasants – or villeins as they were called in England. To be poor might be unpleasant but everyone knew it was not your fault and that your contribution mattered as much to the working of the whole as that of the baron or the monk. In any case, there was no chance of moving on. Your place was your place for the whole of your life.

It was easy to figure out another person's place – you just had to look at their clothes. A man in silk, velvet or damask with fur linings and trimmings was a noble. A headdress shaped like a heart or a butterfly indicated a nobleman's wife. You would hardly miss a knight's chain mail armour – it took five years to make, could weigh between 20 and 30 pounds and sometimes had up to 200,000 rings. The clergy had their own hierarchy: a man in a tall pointed hat or mitre was a bishop; if he wore a long black gown he was a priest; a brown gown with a woollen hood and a rope around the waist housed a monk. You could never mistake the wimpled nun with the cross around her neck. The villeins, who made up about nine tenths of the population, wore rough wool or linen with thick leather clogs and their colours were brown, red or grey.

I drew pictures of the baron in his manor house and the villeins in their shacks. There was a cooking fire in the middle of the hut and a hole in the roof to take away the smoke. The villeins grew vegetables and hardly ever ate meat. It didn't occur to me, and no one ever mentioned, that the people we were learning about hadn't much sense of self. Not nearly as much as I had at age nine. A person was identical with his or her role in society: a peasant, an artisan, a knight, never someone who might currently be a knight but could later become a peasant. Peasants and knights were different in kind – and the clothing proved it. They had absolute security of belonging. Even if they sinned against God, they could be forgiven by buying a piece of paper called an Indulgence. God inspired confidence and love rather than doubt and fear, and their part in the natural order could not be taken away.

I arrived on the planet too late to know God as Identity and even now it defies my imagination, like infinite space or 21 trillion dollars. I've been acquiring a self ever since I arrived, so how could my medieval forbears have managed without one? Perhaps Chaucer misled me. When my schoolmates and I studied *The Canterbury Tales*, we were fascinated by the pilgrims, who were self-serving, avaricious or vain. Naturally, we were drawn to the bad ones – they displayed personality and we could identify with them more. Chaucer examined each pilgrim in terms of occupation, rank and dress, then asked whether they were what they seemed and whether they actually lived by the tenets of their occupation. Those who only pretended were the baddies we so enjoyed but, good or bad, each character had absolute security of belonging. Society was unchanged since the day they were born and would remain so until the day they died.

My school friends and I did not look upon society as unchanging, so it came naturally to us to set about creating our own. Secret, of course. Making up the rules as we went along.

Rule 1: Like Each Other

Rule 2: Be Polite

Rule 3: Keep Promises

Rule 4: Don't Tell

Rule 5: Do your homework, especially Physics

We believed our rules helped each of us do better and that by following them as a group we all became stronger against our foes. We started a newsletter, *Gang's Gossip*, which we plastered with our motto, Share and Share Alike. We sprinkled it with jokes about our teachers and other pupils, but mostly we filled it with stories designed to express our group identity as adventurous rule-breakers. Through our insistence on democratic process and regular rotation of roles, we learned the basics of belonging to a changing society. No feudal child, no matter how imaginative, could have done so.

Ambushed by doubt

Our lessons on feudalism did not include delving into the minds of our forbears. I assumed that though their customs were different their minds were the same. I would have been shocked to hear that between them and me a revolution in thought had turned our heads upon our heads.

Once the drawings were done, once we knew what our feudal forbears wore and what they ate and who was powerful and who was not, our lessons on feudalism came to an end. We never knew that after a while feudalism began to disintegrate. That economic and other changes allowed people to see themselves as masters of their own fate who could move around independently and get wealthy. Nor was it pointed out that these changes came at the price of terrifying insecurity. Monopolies were on the rampage, a craftsman couldn't belong to his guild without capital, and the new marketplace, no longer a place at all, was unpredictable. People were freer but more alone because now everything depended on their own effort. The voice in their head told them, Work harder – and harder still; make better use of your time; be efficient; get richer. To which they prevaricated, But what does life mean? How do I belong now? What do I count for anymore?

Christianity was part of our culture, my parents said, so we children should know what it was about, but at church the Anglicans didn't tell me what it was about, just the bit about believing. They didn't say that, even without believing, I was Protestant in my very bones. I know now that it is Protestant to be constantly aware of the clock ticking, to divide the days and hours into parcels of time in which things must be done and goals achieved. It's Protestant to see family life as a vocation. Protestant to locate the voice of God not in a monastery but in every human being. Protestant to protest against unjust authority. When my mother declared, as she often did, that she was a bit of a rebel, I had no context for her claim. Whenever she was told to do or think something, her reaction was, 'I'll make up my own mind'. It seemed to me she was just being Mum, but she was also being quintessentially Protestant.

The revolution was painful of course. The middle classes raged impotently while inwardly they succumbed to insecurity and anxiety, but the poor expressed their disgust with oppressive authority by joining peasant uprisings and urban revolutionary movements. Eventually even the Catholic Church came under threat. An hour came when an obscure monk called Martin Luther rebelled against its domination of people's lives from baptism to burial. He denounced the church's exploitative hawking of Indulgences, and set loose a torrent of protest which gave its name to a new religion.

Indulgences didn't work for Luther. Despite carrying out his allotted penances, his inner voice admonished him, 'You fell short there. You weren't sorry enough. Oh no, you sinned again.' His mind was in turmoil when he re-read some words from Paul's Epistle to the Romans: 'He who through faith is righteous shall live.' It was a Eureka moment. No longer should he passively accept what his priests told him; no longer should he rely on Indulgences to see him into heaven; through *faith* he and every other human being could have a direct, personal relationship with God. On 31 October 1517, Luther nailed a petition to the door of a church in Germany, declaring his radical proposition.

The idea of freedom from the power of the church struck a deep chord. People escalated their resistance to religious authority into a fight against all unjust authority, much to the distress of Luther himself. But the most profound effect occurred when they began to interpret the Word of God for themselves, becoming self-conscious and individual in a way not previously dreamed of. The trouble was they could never again be sure they were getting it right. Was the voice they heard the true voice? Could it be Satan? Unfortunately, Luther's answer to this was to replace the authority of the church with something even more tyrannical. 'Faith' meant unconditional surrender to God. Human beings were unworthy sinners who could only find favour with an angry god if they put their newly-minted individual selves in his power.

Didn't anybody ask, What is this? Why are we surrendering our individual selves before we even started to enjoy them? To what kind of god are we surrendering? What kind of belonging is this? I know now that Erasmus did. The most famous intellect of his age, he set his face against all forms of fanaticism. A person had a right to his own opinions; absolute independence of mind was essential, but no one should present his truth as the only truth. Especially not from pulpit or university chair. Sadly, people didn't want the thoughts of a quiet man.[1] The fiery rebellion of Lutherans or the authoritarianism of Catholics was more to their taste.

Nearly five hundred years after Luther's rebellion, the Anglican church taught me about my unworthiness, using instructions published in 1549. There was no health in me, said the *Book of Common*

Prayer, I would do the things I ought not to do and leave undone the things I ought to do. Was there any way out? I promised God I would not turn on the hot tap, then I did. Water spurted out amid ascending clouds of steam. They were right, *I would do the things I ought not to do and there was no health in me.* Yet they said God would love me under certain circumstances: if I gave myself to him; if I surrendered my self in all its badness. I promised again, failed again. That awful self inside me made me do it. I started doing everything three times. Opening doors. Shutting doors. Everything times three. If I ran my fingers unconsciously along a hedge and then realised, I'd do it twice more in expiation. Surrender of the Self. It restored certainty.

On to pretence

Much like me, many people found it intolerable to exist without knowing if they were 'saved'. Another tortured person, John Calvin, averred that nothing even a pious person did was sure to pass muster before the strict judgement of God. If, on the other hand, you were chosen by God for salvation, then nothing, no matter how bad, could change that. The problem was, how could you know if you were chosen? Calvin had the answer: Why, your own prosperity was all the proof you needed. The more you prospered in life the more obviously you were 'elect' for heaven.

Gone was the idea that poverty endowed the bearer with virtue; now wealth was the thing and the time-piece was ticking. Soon every town had a town clock overlooking a public space and every act was measured against time taken. Fame became compulsively desirable. The greater the number of people who rated you highly, the greater your certainty that your life was meaningful and significant. And now that the station you were born to wasn't set in stone, you had a chance to achieve it. A person of no account might become influential and even rich. But first you had to convince those around you that you merited their regard.

One of the first consequences of the evolution of selfhood was an explosion in pretence. The hypocrite-villain began to feature in literature as people struggled to tell the difference between the person and the persona. My mother told me, 'To thine own self be true. If you do that, everything else will follow naturally.' I didn't know then that the words were Shakespeare's and that they were in reaction to the preceding era of widespread pretending to be someone you weren't.

The question 'Is he what he seems?' bothered nearly everybody and

Shakespeare's characters ask it again and again as they try to disentangle whether Iago, Cassius or Hamlet's new stepfather are telling truth or lies. Shakespeare's advice, spoken through a character in Hamlet, became a useful rule of thumb, 'This above all: to thine own self be true... Thou canst not then be false to any man'. I learnt the lines and they reverberated through my brain but once again I had no historical context for them. No more than I had for Molière, whose plays I also studied at school. Across the English Channel and fifty years on from Shakespeare's time, Molière found similar things happening to the relationship between the person and the persona. The central character in *Tartuffe* is described in the dramatis personae as 'a hypocrite', and the interest of the play lies in how far he can triumph over society by means of deceit and insincerity. In *Le Misanthrope*, Alceste decides that compromising truth for the smooth functioning of society is an impossible price to pay. He upbraids his friend Philinte:

> My God, you ought to die of self-disgust.
> I call your conduct inexcusable, Sir,
> And every man of honour will concur.
> I see you almost hug a man to death,
> Exclaim for joy until you're out of breath,
> And supplement these loving demonstrations
> With endless offers, flowers, and protestations;
> Then when I ask you 'who was that?', I find
> That you can hardly bring his name to mind!
> Once the man's back is turned, you cease to love him,
> And speak with absolute indifference of him![2]

Disgusted by the corrupting influence of society, Alceste abandons it altogether, but Molière tells us that although Alceste has avoided insincerity, his obstinate pride has obstructed the wisdom and ability to love that his true self would have made possible.

And then confession

A century later, Jean-Jacques Rousseau, whose views would see off the Age of Reason and welcome in the Age of Sensibility, desperately wanted Alceste and not hypocritical Philinte to be the hero of *Le Misanthrope*. Rousseau made it his passionate goal to be entirely frank about himself and to persuade others to follow his example. In *Confessions*, he admitted his callous abandonment of his five children soon after each was born, and argued that there was 'no human breast, however pure, that does not conceal some odious vice'. Rousseau had a friend who was also fascinated by the way people constantly flattered each other for their own ends. Denis Diderot realised he was not seeing 'the real person' and explored the problem in a famous dialogue, which he called *Rameau's Nephew*. The nephew of the famous musician castigated himself for being poor when he could easily have been rich.

> A thousand silly little wits with no talent or merit, a thousand little creatures devoid of charm, a thousand dull wire-pullers are well dressed and you go naked! How can you be such a fool? Couldn't you flatter as well as the next man? Couldn't you manage to lie, swear, perjure, promise, fulfill or back out like anybody else? Couldn't you go on all fours like anybody else? Couldn't you aid and abet Madame's intrigue and deliver Monsieur's love-letters like anybody else?[3]

Rameau's nephew says that everyone in society 'dances a vile pantomime' in order to attain their goals:

> He began impersonating the admiring man, the supplicating man, the complaisant man, right foot forward, left foot behind, back bent, head up, looking fixedly into somebody else's eyes, lips parted, arms held out towards something, waiting for a command, receiving it, off like an arrow, back again with it done, reporting it. He is attentive to everything, picks up what has been dropped, adjusts a pillow or puts a stool under someone's feet, holds a saucer, pushes forward a chair, opens a door, shuts a window, pulls curtains, keeps his eyes on the master and mistress, stands motionless, arms at his side and legs straight, listening, trying to read people's expressions.[4]

Rameau's nephew hated this demeaning activity so much that he taught his son to value money as an alternative to supplication, and Diderot quite liked this:

> In all this there was much that we all think and on which we all act, but which we leave unsaid. That, indeed, was the

most obvious difference between this man and most of those we meet. He owned up to the vices he had and which others have – he was no hypocrite. He was no more abominable than they, and no less. He was simply more open, more consistent, and sometimes more profound in his depravity.[5]

The idea was the same as Rousseau's – what mattered was to be open and frank with others about who you were, even if that meant exposing ugly warts. Their ideas rippled through decades to come and eventually underpinned the ages of Sensibility and Romanticism – ages I came to revere during secondary school days.

Brave authenticity

Growth and development take strange turns at times. For a while all was fine. I grew strong and straight. Delighted in arithmetic, geometry and algebra. Was entranced by oceans and coal mines, rivers and cities. Understood these things were the basis for civilisation. Treasured my mind for its ability to connect with the world's wonders. Then the Age of Reason gave way to the Age of Sensibility. I turned to the world within and beheld a stranger. Nothing was more important than knowing and taming this usurper, this wolf in sheep's clothing devouring me from within. I lost all sense of belonging and went through the options for suicide, imagining how deeply everyone would mourn their loss when it was all too late.

This was nothing on the real Age of Sensibility. When the twenty-something Goethe published his first work of narrative prose, *The Sorrows of Young Werther*, in 1774, it took Europe by storm. Goethe had been having a difficult time coping with his love for a young woman who was engaged to another, and decided to fictionalise the terrible bind he had found himself in. In a tumult of unguided feeling, young Werther began to lose himself.

> Can religion, must religion mean the same thing to every man? When you look at our vast world, you see thousands to whom it does not mean these things, thousands to whom it never will, whether it be preached to them or not. Must it therefore mean these things to me? What else is it but the fate of man to suffer his destined measure and drink his full cup to the end? And if the cup that the good Lord in heaven has put to his lips be too bitter, why should I put on airs and

pretend that it is sweet? And why should I not feel ashamed in those dread moments when I tremble between being and not-being, when the past shines like a flash of lightning above the dark abyss of the future and everything around me sinks down and the world comes to an end? Is mine not the voice of a man cowering within himself, a man who has lost himself, hurtling inexorably downhill, who must cry out from the innermost depths of his vainly struggling forces, 'My God, my God, why hast Thou forsaken me?' And why should I be ashamed to thus cry out...?[6]

In Shakespeare's time, when God was a less complex force, Werther's inner voice would have guided him in terms of right and wrong, but the *god-given* aspect of self had apparently shrunk to a shadow, and what remained for Werther's sense of morality was little more than being in touch with his feelings. When Lotte became unavailable, he suffered an engulfing loneliness that robbed him of all sense of connection. Untamed nature could express his feelings, but offered no comfort. One night there was a sudden thaw and Werther found that the river had overflowed its banks, all the streams were swollen, and his beloved valley was inundated.

What a terrible spectacle, to see the turbulent flood in the moonlight, pouring down from the rocks to cover field, meadow, and hedgerow! Whichever way you looked, the broad valley was one stormy sea in a howling gale. And when the moon came out again above a black cloud, and the flood rushed by me with a dull roar in its gloriously fright-ening reflection, I was overcome by a great trembling and, once more, a yearning. With my arms open wide, I stood facing the abyss, breathing down, down, and was lost in the bliss of hurling my torment and suffering into it to be carried off foaming, like the waves...[7]

As Werther ceased to feel any real connection with the cycles of natural and social phenomena, the whole of life began to feel like 'a repulsive burden' and finally he committed suicide.

After completing *Werther*, Goethe felt unburdened and free again, but for his young readers, the new subjectivity obliterated all other reality. Many young Germans identified with Werther so completely that they too committed suicide. A ripple effect ran through the novelists of the day. Parisian life, with its emphasis on manners and insincerity, threw the new phenomenon into stark relief and set many a writer alight with the desire to expose society's corrupting nature. Stendhal, Balzac, Flaubert and in England Austen and Sterne all concerned themselves with sincerity.

In England at the beginning of the nineteenth century, rules of formality and etiquette had reached peak stranglehold on polite society. Immersed in social circles where it was all about defining oneself in terms of class and wealth, Jane Austen insisted that it is what goes on inside a person that matters. In novel after novel her heroines make mistakes, but not those of insincerity as they take their stumbling steps towards a new consciousness in which sensibility is pivotal. Though Austen punishes her heroines for their excesses, she admires their brave authenticity. In *Mansfield Park* she goes a step further. When the young people in the Bertram household embark on amateur theatricals, Fanny Price remains steadfastly against impersonations. Through Fanny, Austen suggests there is something dangerous about pretending to be someone else, especially when, like Maria Bertram, you are pretending to be a young lady in love with a young man – and especially when in *real life* you are engaged to someone else and the young man *on* stage has been paying you welcome attention *off* it. Fanny's instinct for the danger is proved correct when Henry's off-stage attention to Maria ceases with the end of the playacting and he quits the house without a backward glance.

On his next visit, he finds 'wonderful improvement' in Fanny and decides to give himself two weeks to make 'a small hole in [her] heart', making use of all, as Austen puts it, that 'talent, manner, attention, and flattery can do'. Just another piece of role-playing for Crawford, but when he falls sufficiently in love to propose to Fanny, her beloved uncle, Sir Thomas Bertram, expresses deep disappointment at her refusal of the agreeable young man with a good estate. For him, it's not a matter of authenticity but filial docility:

> I had thought you peculiarly free from willfulness of temper, self-conceit, and every tendency to that independence of spirit which prevails so much in modern days, even in young women, and which in young women is offensive and disgusting beyond all common offence. But you have now shown me that you can be willful and perverse; that you

can and will decide for yourself, without any consideration
or deference, for those who have surely some right to guide
you, without even asking their advice.[8]

Fanny insists that it's impossible for her to do otherwise: 'I am so
perfectly convinced that I could never make him happy, and that I
should be miserable myself.' Finally, Austen allows her to marry the
man of her choice, thus reassuring her readers that sincerity should
carry the day.

Eternal security

I managed to escape from the Anglican church when I was twelve
and my parents let me try out other denominations. I went to the
Quaker church for several years but when I joined the other Friends
in silence at Meeting, my mind went AWOL from God, filling with
considerations of what I should wear, what new clothes I needed and
whether the way so-and-so caught and held my eye meant more than
it seemed. In the end, I sought an answer of a different kind, the kind
that evangelical Christians called 'eternal security'. My friend Nancy
introduced me to the Open Brethren and I started attending at Oak
Hall. The youth group had its own bus called Rudolph, which it used
for outings to things like Billy Graham crusades and 'bearing witness'
in other churches. The teens were energetic, friendly and welcoming
in a way I had longed for. Their faces radiated certainty and the wish
to share it.

The Brethren said their religion was simple: you just had to believe
what the Bible said. All you had to do was accept Jesus as your personal saviour and you would be saved. Once saved, always saved. It
had started with Calvin, of course, but the Brethren said that God's
grace extended to *everybody* who accepted salvation through faith.
I was really more interested in having a 'social life' and if possible
a boyfriend, but I was curious about the big questions and the easy
certainty of my new friends was attractive.

Soon there was a boy who commanded my attention. I became
familiar with every muscle in his face and could locate him instantly
on entering Oak Hall. I treasured every word he threw in my direction
and I suppose he couldn't resist throwing a few more. When he was
leaving for a trip to Portugal he told me with a grin that if I wrote him
a seven-page letter he would send me a fourteen-page one. If only I
had realised he was a flirt by nature, but no, I began composing my

seven pages immediately. Christopher kept his word but there wasn't a single mention of love except at the end: 'With you in the love of Christ'.

As time went on things got serious about the need to be saved. They said unless I was converted I would go to eternal damnation. My new friends kept asking if Jesus had spoken to me and I began to feel like a fraud. There was a sense of urgency, a feeling that the waiting and watching must reach a denouement soon. I saw that if I didn't get saved I couldn't finally belong. The pressure was also getting to Nancy. She too needed saving and she had gone very quiet.

Billy Graham was coming to the end of his month-long London crusade and his final event was going to pack the Wembley Stadium. Billy Graham was our hero. He hosted the Billy Graham Crusades on American television and bailed Martin Luther King out of jail. He was spiritual adviser to a succession of American presidents. We all went up in Rudolph to join with a 94,000-strong multitude and soon Billy Graham was inviting us to accept Jesus Christ as our personal saviour. He wanted us to come up to the stage and give testimony that we believed. As the evening drew to a close he used his favourite call to the altar, the hymn 'Just as I am'. For a lost teen, the words are powerful:

> Just as I am – though toss'd about
> With many a conflict, many a doubt,
> Fightings and fears within, without,
> – O Lamb of God, I come!

Hundreds in the audience made their way across the aisles and up to the stage. I wanted desperately to be one of them. On the bus home, though I sat next to someone and laughed and joked with the group, I felt sickeningly alone.

A week later our church service included baptism. Nine young people ready to be saved stepped into a warm bath and were pushed backwards in the water until it covered their heads. The congregation was ecstatic about receiving the new recruits into God's church. Afterwards Nancy told me she felt terrible when they sang another of those powerful calls to the altar, 'Almost Persuaded': 'Almost cannot avail; Almost is but to fail! Sad, sad, that bitter wail. *Almost, but lost!*' Nancy said she didn't know how much longer she could bear the loneliness of not accepting Jesus Christ.

I felt lonely too. Sitting in my bedroom reading the book of St John I closed my eyes and entreated God to send Christopher as his messenger. On opening my eyes, the first words I saw were 'All or Nothing'. Over the printed page the leaded panes of my bedroom window had formed the sign of the cross. Faith poured into me.

At the meeting that night Nancy made the decision. Everyone was thrilled for her. I left to catch my bus home but I couldn't bear it. 'All or Nothing' I thought, and ran back to the hall. Everything unfolded as I had hoped. Christopher gave me instant and full attention when I asked him to minister to my religious confusion. He told me I could take the entire Bible literally. The devil was a real devil – not at all symbolic. When we had doubts about Christianity, this was Satan making us impotent as Christians. He said, 'Pray and cast Satan from your thoughts.' Although I was madly infatuated, I couldn't quite.

Christopher walked me to the bus stop but the last bus had gone and I had to call my parents to come and pick me up. It was very late and when they realised there had been no assault, not even an accident, they were fairly acid. 'Who's the boyfriend?' asked my mother. How dare she think this was about boyfriends and not about finding Jesus? It was Jesus or my parents and I chose Jesus.

The aftermath was a bit of a disappointment. As one of the saved I no longer merited special attention and Chris got a regular girlfriend. A few months later I started at university, where I learned in anthropology about people in Africa who had never heard about Jesus and had their own kinds of gods. My questioning mind began to reassert itself – what kind of god would condemn them to hell and what about the children that died before they grew up? The devil and original sin slipped quietly out of my repertoire.

It was much the same for Nancy, but my friend Monica was not so lucky. She was in my class at school and about the same time as I started at Oak Hall, she started with a Brethren church near her home, but at university she took up with a stricter sect. She had been a clever girl, always top of the class in maths. Now she sat in the library thinking about the young people around her who hadn't been saved and would be damned if they didn't repent. She put on weight. Her skin became greasy and pimply. When I visited her in hospital her hair was cut short and her wrists were bandaged. There was a glazed expression in her eyes. She couldn't talk about anything except people who weren't saved and would go to hell. Tears began to fall down her cheeks and she said she wasn't worthy.

'The Brethren write me letters and say I'm damned because I tried to commit suicide. And before that they said I was frivolous and God wouldn't be able to make use of me...'

Outside the hospital ward, Monica's parents were waiting. They asked me to explain how the Brethren could have had such an effect on their daughter, but I had no idea why Monica had taken this brand of Christianity so much to heart, while I sloughed it off without a backward glance. I only knew that certainty was not the answer after all. The Brethren's eternal security was no security at all.

PART TWO

WORLD FACE TO FACE

THREE

ADULTHOOD

Leaving home

Like everyone else on this planet lucky enough to survive childhood, I grew up, or rather, became a young person. In other words, I developed a workable self and began to choose my spheres of belonging.

The first big decision facing me as a young person was career. My teachers said we had to know our strengths and weaknesses, our interests, our motivations – we had to know ourselves. It seemed unambiguous that I should go to university and take English literature, but the study of literature was not what called me. There was a new subject on offer called sociology, something my father couldn't have done, or my mother. It was the study of people in groups and this did call to me. In sociology, I would learn about tribal life in far-off places, the evolution of societies and their underbellies, how villages and towns and cities worked, Utopian societies, class struggles, the sociology of religion, marriage and the family.

Even when I was eighteen, I see now, my choice of subject reflected my search to belong. *That's a bit self-aggrandising isn't it?* How do you mean? *You're fitting your life to your current agenda – post hoc, ergo propter hoc,* Sorry? *The cock crows before sunrise therefore the cock causes the sun to rise, you don't know your Latin,* I loved Latin – and it helped me feel part of a community! *You're joking,* Only partly, learning Latin was like joining a community of scholars, joining up the dots between the ancient world and the world today, especially when I realised how many Latin words were part of the English language today, *You've got this bug seriously,* I grew up without a community, *You went to school, you joined Girl Guides, later on the Brethren,* But they never felt like communities, or at least not communities that I really belonged to, *What would a community you 'really belonged to' look like, Utopia?*

I must admit, I'm interested in utopias, *So how come you didn't belong to the communities you joined?* Perhaps I didn't understand the rules or perhaps I wasn't the kind of person they wanted.

Exeter University was a three-hour train journey from my parents' house. It meant, in effect, leaving home. I was allocated a room in an ivy-covered student hall and soon two more students joined me. The three of us became all-in-together girls. We put money in a kitty to buy coffee, milk and biscuits, and talked for hours about boys – who we liked and who might like us and how we should go about 'getting them'. We had to decide whether to have sex, whether having sex meant we were more – or less – likely to keep the boy. Was it okay for a girl to ask a boy out or must she wait until he asked her? How much make-up to wear? Too much was tarty; not enough and you were a frump. If he had a girlfriend at another university, was it still all right to go out with him? If you did and he kissed you, how could you tell if he liked you? How could you tell anything? Was it essential to be afraid of spiders and no good at mechanics and map reading? Should you always lose the argument?

And yet, we were supposed to be intelligent. Students watched each other for signs. If someone 'had to work' in order to get good grades, that meant they weren't really intelligent. We were good at detecting students who only pretended they didn't have to work. How much time did they spend socialising, how often were they seen in the coffee bar, how often at the library? We never discussed whether we ourselves had to work. None of our ideas were to do with being our natural selves; they were all about roles and impersonations. Rich pickings for Diderot and Jane Austen.

Until I went to university I hadn't had much to do with alco-hol. At home, it was treated like a kind of food; we were taught to respect the people who grew the grapes and those whose expertise turned it into wine. But at university alcohol was for getting drunk. Young men at dances boasted to me about how drunk they had got the previous Saturday night and expected me to be impressed. They seemed to think that losing their powers of discrimination enabled them to reveal themselves without responsibility. People who got drunk together thought there was something bonding about ridiculous behaviour. Next day when they couldn't remember anything about it, they wanted someone to say, 'Oh, you were hilarious last night.' That told them they had acted outrageously and proved them greater than they seemed.

There are new techniques now. The University of Melbourne's annual induction for arts students keeps standards up by running competitions to make you vomit. Without the Strat. Vom. (strategic vomit), where you stick your fingers down your throat and make yourself sick, you can't drink enough to make the night worthwhile. Facebook has been described as 'an archive for wild nights out'. In the evening people blog, 'Who's going out?' and next morning, 'I'm so hung over – why did I go out?'[9] Apparently, the average Facebook user is drunk or drinking in 76% of the pictures they post.[10] Over the past fifty years, alcohol companies have become adept at selling the idea that their brands help foster a sense of togetherness. Jill Stark's book about her year without booze describes how a leading beer brand ran a 'Belong' campaign featuring a flock of starlings, recreating the word 'belong' in the style of its logo, while a brewery advert claimed that 'communities are strengthened through the unique, everyday bonds our beer creates'.[11]

As a sociology student I spent a lot of time studying the bonds of social class. My room mates and I knew about class – each of us had been brought up in one. Now we had excellent sport identifying which subclass of class we and other students belonged to: upper, upper middle, lower middle, upper working, lower working. We learned to read the telltale signs: what students wore, their names, who they hung out with, the status of their car. There was a girl in our hall whose surname was double-barrelled, whose father was an earl and whose boyfriend picked her up in a BMW. Indisputably upper class, indisputably not interested in us.

My room mates and I shared the minutiae of our daily lives, our setbacks and victories. We planned to share a flat together for our third and final year. But it seemed as though my brain could not function clearly during conversations in which clichés and the sayings of our times were used as shortcuts. Every idea had to be offered in summary, to be received with instant understanding. The beginning of a sentence was a race against someone else finishing it. More and more of my thoughts remained unspoken. And my friends came into my head, monitoring and censoring whatever I thought about. *That's exactly what Rousseau said*, Oh I thought you'd gone away, *No – I'm part of how you get to know your self and you're not done yet so I'm here to stay,* Oh, so remind me what Rousseau said*, That the sociable man knows how to live only in the mental processes and opinions of others*, But that was 200 years ago, *He happened to hit on something* *that was true of living in society,* Well he was right, my consciousness was not my own, *Yet you were still an individual,* One without a voice, *No one was stopping you from speaking,* Oh I talked, but nothing felt as if it came from me, *You were still an individual,* Actually I felt as though I had as many different selves as there were social demands, I liked that poem by Matthew Arnold,

> Below the surface stream, shallow and light,
> Of what we say we feel – below the stream,
> As light, of what we think we feel – there flows
> With noiseless current strong, obscure and deep,
> The central stream of what we feel indeed.

I'd lost contact with the central stream, *You were still an individual,* Yes, but one with nothing inside, *Because you had no connection with the outside.*

When my dilemma about flatting with my friends deepened into depression I followed instinct and knocked on the door of my anthropology lecturer. By the end of *that* conversation we had canvassed the whole question of listening to one's voice within. Nothing was clearer to me than that I should not go into the flat, that my 'homosexual thoughts' were not wrong, that it was vital to follow what made one feel real and present, that if we were to withstand the pressure for conformity, we had to accept our own inner nature, that I need not worry about belonging because society was in my very bones and one day I would *feel* what I could not see.

I did not go into the flat, I did not become gay, I did have an affair with that married man, which, had it become known, would have seen us both cast out in disgrace. This was how I learned to take my place in society.

Approaching work

They said the world was my oyster so I supposed that the pearl would be my dream job. 1969: plenty of jobs for the taking and it was true that with a degree I had a wide range of choice. Somewhere under the surface rumbled a vague inclination to write, also an inkling that I might enjoy social work. But trainees under twenty-eight were not eligible and I had no idea how to be a writer. I also wanted to go back to the place I was born, the place I was said to come from. Of these ideas, none could be actioned immediately, but another hankering was to learn how to manage information, and a book I'd read on the social psychology of industry had got me interested in large organisations. How they worked, whom they benefited, what it felt like to be an employee. So I took a job as a clerk with an insurance company.

Two thousand employees, many of them recently transferred from London, occupied a purpose-built office complex on a large, semi-rural site which included a swimming pool, dozens of leisure activities and clubs, in addition to cheap food at the canteen. I learned how to file pensioners' dossiers for easy retrieval, how to check the merits of a claim for lump sum or pension, and the advantages of colour coding. Unfortunately, I wasn't much good at learning how it felt to be an employee, or at least how it felt to be an employee other than myself. The 'girls' in my section performed their tasks contentedly enough but without enthusiasm. The highlight of their working day centred around lunch in the cafeteria. They invited me to join them, but participating in the conversation was one of the hardest things I'd ever tried to do. The girls wanted to talk about washing their hair, buying a new lipstick. If they had been to a movie, the fact of attendance was enough, with the name and perhaps a male actor thrown in. To analyse was to break a taboo. Of course, the girls probably talked about the state of their relationships with boyfriends, but not when I was there. After about three weeks, they secretly changed the time they took lunch and then I ate alone.

I had joined an institution where I must subordinate all individuality to an external power. A large mahogany clock hung high above the section leader's desk. We 'clocked in' when we arrived and out when we left. Tea and lunch breaks were at set times and we weren't to take too long in the toilet. At the end of the working day a loud bell reverberated through the building. Immediately, all of us downed tools. For the final quarter-hour we had only been 'marking time'.

I amused myself by working up stories to bring home to my parents. I told them about the bob-each-way parents who called their son, born during the war, Adolf Winston. I told them how I wrote to someone about his deceased mother, explaining what would happen to her Paid Up Benefit, only to hear by return post that the 'deceased' was still alive and the son distressed by my letter.

'What did you do?' asked my father.

'Nothing. The bell went!' I laughed. It had felt like an act of solidarity with my fellow workers; now it felt tawdry. 'You have picked up the very worst attitudes of the British worker,' said my father.

Every day I worked there I felt less myself. I couldn't engage with the work and I failed to connect with anyone in my section. Things turned around when I played a nervous old maid for the company's drama club. My opposite number, a grumpy old bachelor, turned out to be an eligible, kindly and witty young man in the actuarial department. By the time the play was performed G and I were considered 'an item' by the rest of the actors.

My next job was in New Zealand. It had always been my dream to return one day to my homeland and since I had not yet found my niche in England I began looking for ways to return. I discovered the government, desperate to procure more secondary school teachers, was offering free flights and a short teaching course in return for a three-year contract. I didn't want to leave G so soon after we had met, but he encouraged me to go and agreed to wait for my return or possibly to join me there. After completing a three-month course, I got a job in a small farming town.

Habits of my father began to infiltrate my working life: compulsive striving for perfection, relentless commitment to the workload, ambition to be outstanding. I loved many things about teaching. At nights and weekends, I read voraciously around what I needed to teach. The Boers' early history in South Africa, for instance, and their interaction with the indigenous Hottentots, followed by the Apartheid racism that ruled black South African lives and was still ongoing.

After a few months G joined me, sloughing off actuarial ambitions like an outgrown skin. We got engaged. The pupils, especially those in my home class, were excited. One day they presented us with a large box. Inside we found a handsome set of coffee mugs. I treasured the lines they had written on the card,

> Our social studies teacher
> Teaches us about Life.
> Our social studies teacher
> Will soon become a WIFE!

I believed I had found my métier. G and I made friends among the more progressive teachers, becoming a tight-knit group who went to one another's houses, where we discussed our visions for a brave new world in which children left school brilliantly prepared for life in a changing world. All I remember now of those discussions is G saying, 'It's a moot point' and someone else saying, 'No it's not' and G saying,

'Well, I would like to moot it' and everybody laughing and me feeling proud to have such a clever husband.

One of these Young Turks told G I had all the skills required to make a superb teacher. He didn't know about my dread of performance, the way deadlines controlled my mind, the straitjacket of imposing discipline, the terror of standing alone in front of pupils who didn't want to learn, the inner fragmentation of being bombarded by many personalities at once, the dreams on Sunday nights that had become ordeals of terror.

One day a pupil who was late for class appeared at the window and asked if he could come in that way instead of taking the much longer route via the door. I hesitated. If I said yes, he would be with us in a jiffy and I could get on with the Hottentots' ability to store water in their bottoms. If I said no, there'd be another interruption when the boy finally appeared at the door. A no-brainer. Then the headmaster appeared, red in the face and out of breath, having seen a pupil climbing in the window. He grew apoplectic when somewhere beneath his storm and bluster he heard me explain that I'd given the boy permission. That was the day he decided to get rid of me, and quite right too. I saw complexity where there was none. Windows are not to be used for entering a classroom. Windows are not to be used for entering a classroom. Windows are not to be used for entering a classroom...

Pregnancy and children took me out of the workforce for a while. When money was short I would sign on for casual labour, which served to remind me that I can't work in a job without meaning. After one day on an assembly line for sorting strawberries, I developed such a migraine that I never returned. On another job, I spent a whole day checking that figures in two columns were the same. I still remember it as the longest day of my life.

As a teacher I had found some meaning through introducing children to some of the wonders the world has to offer. It would be many years before I discovered a deep connection of belonging through work.

I was delighted recently to come across Marjolein Lips-Wiersma and Lani Morris's insightful book *The Map of Meaning*, which offers a research-based formulation of where the need to belong fits into people's work requirements. The Map of Meaning model postulates that meaning, which Wiersma and Morris describe as the element in work *most vital* to human beings, comprises four components: developing the inner self, expressing your full potential, service to others and unity with others. The unity-with-others component comprises belonging, working together and shared values. According to the map, each of the four elements in the circle is equally important in achieving meaning – the primary motivation in our lives.

The Map of Meaning

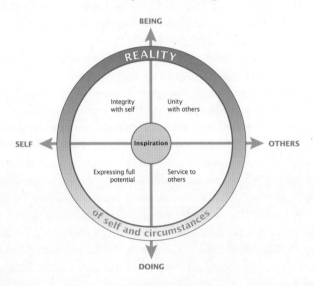

In later life, not long before my marriage ended, I had a job which gave me many of the things the participants in Lips-Wiersma's workshops associated with belonging: feelings of generosity, warmth, being part of, being at home among, acceptance, not having to justify, celebration together, feeling embraced, community, coming home. I was working with a small number of people, carrying out research into dependency and exploitation between developed and underdeveloped countries. The aim was to promote development through joint action on well researched issues. My new colleagues cared deeply about humanity and our carefully built networks made us feel less like lone crusaders. I fervently believed in the work and had total respect for my colleagues, who were committed, intelligent, thoughtful and principled. They were fun to work with and believed in treating each other as beings worthy of respect. I began to exhibit the traits I longed to possess – kindness, generosity, compassion, willingness to sacrifice myself for justice, being socially and environmentally responsible. This was J.E. Dutton's 'virtue perspective' in joyous operation.

But as usual there was a snake in paradise. Basically, my job was to do the 'administrivia' that the others didn't want to do. The staff had been dealing with it in rotation, thereby squandering their specialised research and campaign skills, so they compromised by advertising for another person to be paid at their own hourly rate. The job was part-time and I thought it would fit well with my writing, but after a few months it began to make me ill. My overwhelming desire was to stay home and sleep. Sometimes I was physically incapable of getting to work. As usual I berated myself: *You've found the perfect job, the perfect people to work with and you're still dissatisfied*, I can't help it, all I do is vet endless pieces of paper, *But you're earning money and you're able to write in the mornings*, But I need a job that leaves me free to think or observe, *Don't you ever think what it's like for the majority of people in the world?* I do, I do, *You're incredibly narrow in what fulfills you*, At least I'm doing good in the world.

One day I read that as a result of humanity's increasing use of chlorofluorocarbons (CFCs), the ozone layer between us and the sun was being seriously depleted. The statistics just kept getting worse and the industry resisted change. My natural pessimism regarding the destructive force of a world hooked on the profit motive and unbridled consumerism led me to despair. *Actually, you were outraged*, Well, yes, *While you had been doing work you loathed in order to increase world happiness, other people blithely made profits out of destroying the planet*, Yes, and now I couldn't sit in the sun without risking cancer! *You could spend the rest of your life doing work you hated and the world would still be a mess*, Absolutely – I felt alienated from the human world and the way it worked, *It's imperative to do work you love.*

Glenys

Glenys Anderson faced extraordinary challenges when her working life abruptly ceased. During my teaching years, I had developed a very close friendship with her and, later, as mainly stay-at-home mums, we developed a passionate love of gardening. Glenys went on to become the highly respected manager of a council nursery. She loved the work but after a few years was diagnosed with Crohn's disease, a type of inflammatory bowel disorder for which there is no cure. After a day at the nursery she had to choose between cooking dinner or having a shower, followed immediately by falling into bed. During one exceptionally stressful year she developed shingles and then a frozen shoulder, which she had to endure without painkillers. Eventually she had to resign her job. It wasn't until I asked to interview her that I realised how hard it had been for her to claw back a sense of belonging in society.

'I fought giving up work for months, until in the end I got so many things wrong with me at once, I couldn't go on. My friends were saying, For God's sake, Glenys, when are you going to listen to your body? How many more things are you going to get before…?

'Giving up work was very difficult. It takes a long time to get used to. The first month was quite good, like having a holiday, but then I started feeling like I wasn't very important, society was going on perfectly happily without me.'

Crohn's was unpredictable. One minute Glenys could be feeling fine, the next she couldn't leave home because of pain and needing the toilet. It made any kind of commitment a source of deep anxiety. A planned bus trip to Wellington could suddenly become impossible or, worse, the symptoms might come on when she was already on the bus, where there would be no toilet at the ready. While she was working, she had a place in society and meeting new people was fun. Without work, things were very different and Glenys found herself struggling with her sense of identity.

'I was known as the person who ran the council nursery and when I no longer did that, I was left thinking, Who am I if I don't run the nursery? I used to be known as a wife and then the-children's-mother and then I was Glenys-who-ran-the-nursery and suddenly I was none of those things because I was divorced and the four children had grown up and I'd lost my job. In a strange way, the same thing happened years before when the house burned down and suddenly there was nothing that belonged to me, nothing from the past. If you think about it, all the things you have around your house build a picture for you and for other people of who you are, and suddenly there was absolutely nothing apart from the clothes I wore. So I was left with, Who am I? Losing my job was like that, though not so devastating.

'After a while I realised that work isn't really what someone is about, it's an *expression* of it. It's *partly* what they're about, but if that's gone it can't *possibly* be all there is to you. I thought about all the people who don't have jobs or who hate their jobs. For them the last thing they want to do is be defined by their jobs.

'I started thinking, no we're not defined by our jobs. We are creatures of all sorts of interests and passions. It was hard work because
it's the first thing people want to know about you and sometimes
when you say you're not working they lose interest and you can easily
imagine the silence means disapproval.

'I don't like telling them about my illness – it's a very unsexy disease – but if you don't, they can't understand why you're not working.
And you get into feeling, Oh well, now I suppose they think I'm a bit
useless in society. Sometimes I tell them I used to run the council
nursery, and then wait for people to say, "Used to? What are you
doing now?". But some people pick up on the council nursery and
then that's fine.'

Financially, of course, Glenys's life changed entirely. She had been
earning a reasonable salary and felt secure knowing that if she worked
till sixty-five her super scheme would yield a good payout. She looked
forward to travelling after retirement. Now she had to come to terms
with living on an invalid benefit and her life plans were out of reach.
It felt like getting divorced.

'I absolutely loathe telling anybody I'm on a benefit and I try very
hard not to. It's an extremely sensitive area; you're just waiting for
the disapproval. Then you feel like you have to explain what having
Crohn's is like. The whole thing is very unpleasant.'

Glenys began to feel valued again when her son and daughter-in-
law asked her to help out with minding her grandchildren while they
were working.

'It was a huge boost to me because until then I was feeling completely unnecessary to anybody. It made me feel connected again in
society because I was making a difference to some people's lives. Then
Rachel around the corner needed me. She's finding it hard to cope
with her two kids because her husband has Asperger's and isn't much
help. She relies on me and I know I make a difference to her. I have to
be honest and say I'd love to be paid! But she can't possibly.

'I also tried voluntary work. I worked at the hospice shop for a
while but I hated it. I couldn't work at the counter in case I had to
rush away in the middle of serving someone, so I said I'd work out the
back. There are always two or three others out there, but apart from
saying hello they just carried on their talking and laughing with each
other and I was absolutely on the outer. I'd go home exhausted after
standing all the time and be too tired to cook tea. On hospice days I
started waking up with a sense of dread.

'Every now and then I'd think of looking for more voluntary work, but then something else would go wrong with my health. With prednisone treatment, I ended up with blisters all over my face and slitty eyes, so for a whole year I felt like an alien to myself and I behaved differently personality-wise. The following year I got an awful skin problem that was all over my face, I looked like I'd been burnt. Next year my eyes packed up. They felt like burning coals, bright red and raw and weeping. The whites were very red and all round my eyes got worse and worse. With each visit to hospital the nurse got more and more shocked. Basically, year after year after year my face was a mess and I didn't want to go out in society. I was amazed at how my self-confidence plummeted.

'The years went by. Sometimes I'd think, *Now* maybe I can look for work. Then the Crohn's would flare up again and I'd be tearing off to the loo at any old time. I can have a second's warning sometimes. I can be sitting here talking to you and then five minutes later I'm doubled over and miserable.'

Obviously Glenys couldn't commit herself to a time frame or fronting with people, but she thought of potting up and selling plants – before confronting another obstacle.

'I've always found it really difficult to take money – I'd love a life where we just swapped things and they gave me eggs or whatever and I gave them plants. Or say I'm good at growing zucchinis and not much good at tomatoes, how about I grow these and the sweet corn and you grow the tomatoes and lettuce and then we swap? I like that idea.

'My friends want to pay me when I give them plants, but I can't let them and the trouble with people who aren't friends is that they *become* friends. The first time I'll take the money, but by the second or third return they've become friends and then it seems wrong – because you don't sell things to your friends, you *give* them, don't you? If it was strictly a stranger each time I could do it, but when they keep coming back it all seems wrong and everything is changed.

'I had the same thing years ago when I knitted Aran jerseys while the children were young. By the time the jersey was finished, I had become really good friends with the person and I just couldn't take any money. It felt not just wrong, but sinful. It's violating the relationship and I can't live with it. So that's why it's never worked for me and yet the idea of making money out of growing plants appeals because that's what I'm really good at. I just want the stranger aspect to remain. When I was part of the nursery, it was the system and I had no problem, no matter how many times they came back.

'In the last few years I've given heaps of plants to the Esplanade, where I used to work. I would love it if the council gave me money, but of course they're not going to do that because they're hard-up and their gardeners aren't allowed to buy anything anymore. I had a little fantasy that they would say, "Glenys has given us so many plants, we'll give her a little gift voucher or something". Then I realised, of course that's not going to happen, that's not how councils work. But I have felt entitled to go and say to them, I want a couple of cuttings from the glasshouse, can I have them?

'Reading and gardening make me feel contented. The reading gives me a sense of connection with other people, because it makes me realise the commonality among people. We all have the same concerns, problems and joys and you realise there are plenty of people like you in the world. Whoever you are, you're never the only one who feels a certain way. I absolutely adore discovering books where people express thoughts and feelings I've had and I think, *You* must have had that feeling, I thought I was the only one. It was C.S. Lewis, wasn't it, who said, "We read to know we're not alone". It's certainly one reason to read.

'The garden is pivotal. It helps me connect to the world itself, to nature, to be part of the whole cosmos, it is one huge reason I do it, I feel more connected there than anywhere really. I have to garden with gloves now, but I wish I didn't because I like the feel of the soil. I like to lie on the ground, it makes me feel very connected, to lie on my back looking at the sky and the trees and feeling the earth underneath. That's why I keep a patch of lawn. Some people tell me to gravel it. But I need a little bit of grass, of something green, not a rug, that I can lie on, because I want that connection. It would be absolutely lovely without clothes on! With plants as well, I never ever stop marvelling at the beauty and the intricacy and the design of plants. I am in awe of them, every single one I look at.

'The internet is fantastic for giving you a feeling of connection. I started looking up plant websites where people would often list their favourite plant blogs. Now and then I would click on one of them and someone would be enthusing about their garden and the wonderful plants they've grown. There was a blog I loved run by someone in America who installed a plug-in on her website so she could see the plants in *our* gardens and what was giving *us* a thrill. So now we can upload photos from our garden and they'll go onto the website. The Net is a great way of finding people of like mind, like passions. It helps you realise who you are regardless of whether you have a job.'

The doctor knew his stuff when he told his patient that after a couple of years she would come to terms with the fact that she had to live with Crohn's. It took Glenys longer than that to find meaningful substitutions for the job she had loved, but finally she regained identity and self-worth arising from active citizenship. Ironically her former employers have a part to play.

'By my giving the council so many plants, I have changed their gardens and I feel like I've got back a sense of belonging. One of the things I liked about my job was making the city more beautiful and now my plants are flowering in the Esplanade and they look fabulous. So I can still have a hand in something that's giving joy to the public. One day my friend David was raving to me about a particular plant at the Esplanade. He didn't know I'd given it to them. He was saying it looked magnificent, this huge pink something with a purple smoke bush behind it. I went to have a look and it did look fabulous. It gave me enormous pleasure that a member of the public had been enthralled and I knew that if *he* felt like that, there would be others.

'Otherwise the park just stagnates because they're not allowed to spend any money. It's supposed to be ever-changing and enthralling the public and I can make that happen. Suddenly I feel like I used to at the beginning of my job. I'm creating beauty for the city and I can make people happy this way. That's more important than getting money. I can walk through the Esplanade and think, I grew that tree and these plants. It's almost like I've got the old feeling back again, the sense of doing something important.'

Look it's an HSP!

This self I've been beavering away at, trying to create something that other people will find interesting and lovable, sometimes I think it's not coming out as planned. It won't join in, it stands apart, especially at parties.

Nowadays the spectrum from introversion to extroversion is tirelessly researched by psychologists, not because it's new in the history of human evolution, but because it illuminates personality in a way nothing else can. In the minds of many people, extroversion is the more desirable trait, the better predictor of wealth and happiness. When Susan Cain was researching introversion for her book *Quiet*, she visited Harvard Business School to investigate how leadership related to hyper-extrovert traits. Students told her, 'Good luck finding an introvert around here,' and 'This school is predicated on extroversion. Our grades and social status depend on it.'[12]

Pressure to be extrovert is something Asian students living in America are acutely aware of. Hung Wei Chien, who came from Taiwan in 1979 to attend graduate school, expressed what many feel: 'At UCLA, the professor would start class, saying, "Let's discuss!" I would look at my peers while they were talking nonsense, and the professors were so patient, just listening to everyone... I thought, Oh, in the United States, as soon as you start talking, you're fine.'[13]

What Hung calls 'talking nonsense' her professors call 'class partic- ipation'. In cultures where extroversion is privileged over introversion, those who don't come across as exuberant or 'talkers' are liable to be undervalued – and to feel excluded – even though according to US studies they make up a third of its population. Cain says that many introverts solve the problem by behaving more like extroverts. They learn how to give hard-hitting, high-performance speeches or to be effective at selling a cause they wholeheartedly believe in, but if they play an extrovert persona just to impress others and be accepted as part of the group, then inauthenticity can exact a high price.[14] Denying and concealing our true self makes us feel alienated from those around us.

I have discovered that my kind of self has a name: HSP or Highly Sensitive Person. That sounds precious but apparently about 20% of the population is of this sort. Not all HSPs are introverts – about 70%, according to Elaine Aron, who published a ground-breaking book *The Highly Sensitive Person* in 1999. Our fine attributes are legion while our main enemy is over-stimulation, too many inputs in too short a time.

Recently I went to a party and tried to play my part. I talked to people and responded to them. I introduced myself again and again and took an interest in whatever anyone thought fit to say, trying to ignore the way my eyes seemed to rivet themselves on their face as if I would divine their personality from their eyes. I tried not to listen to the voice within that said, That was a stupid thing you just said, that wasn't a joke at all, it was motivated by your underlying hostility or your fear of rejection or of not being understood or just wishing you weren't at the party, can't you do better than that, that person's getting an entirely wrong impression of you, now they're asking you about your field of work and you're going to have to tell them … and they're going to look at you with glazed-over eyes because … and you're going to have to stumble on, trying to fire them up about the possibilities but really they don't want to know, it is not what they expected you to say, they just asked out of politeness, out of needing a topic of conversation, something to keep the words coming – and going, but now their glass is nearly empty and they can make an excuse about needing to fill it up and of course they won't come back, you need to introduce yourself to someone else and admire their blouse or ask if they've been watching the yacht race in San Francisco and make an interesting comment about the American skipper.

I came back feeling not like me at all. I couldn't bear the thought of noise or food and especially not of people's voices – I couldn't turn on the television or the radio even though there was news I wanted to hear. Although my mother had left a message on the phone I couldn't bring myself to call her. I sat by my empty hearth, not lighting a fire in case it delayed my going to bed. I was thinking, What shall I do, what shall I do? Shall I return my mother's call? No, better not, because I'd end up having a conversation about how much I loathed the party and she hates that kind of conversation, she wants me to be feeling happy. If only there were someone who could tune into me entirely, as if they were actually me, that would make the pain bearable, *There's no one, you know that*, Then all I want to do is disengage – disengage and feel nothing.

It seemed best to go and lie down in the dark with no noise or light, to lie on my back and be comforted by warm covers and the knowledge that no one was going to break into me. I wasn't depressed. I just needed time alone to recover, to feel myself again.

It comes back to being yourself, I couldn't be myself at the party, *You lost yourself in all the impersonations, all the presentations*, Yes I know, it was one presentation after another, not only my presentations but the presentations of all the people I talked to, *Actually it's about overstimulation, all that interaction and responding to other people's cues has got you overstimulated*, Oh yes, I forgot, the mark of the Highly Sensitive Person, *That's right, you just have to allow for it and give yourself time to recover*, Actually if it's true that 20% of the population is in the HSP category, then one in five of the people at the party must be highly sensitive, *Yes but then you have to take into account the people who invited them and whether they would have invited a true cross-section or, more likely, people who are not in the highly sensitive category*, Okay, okay, yes you're probably right, still there must've been a few there, *You should have thought about that at the time – you would have felt less isolated*, I wonder who they were and whether they came home feeling like I did.

I sobbed a bit in a half-hearted sort of way. I went to bed as soon as I dared and slept until the small hours when my mind started racing again with impressions from the day before. But as the small hours got bigger I imagined myself a normal person who was simply extra sensitive to stimulation. I started writing stuff down and I awoke next morning with a feeling of exaltation. *But you came home feeling desolate and you had spoken to nobody!* Yes, but I worked out how to speak.

FOUR

PLACE

Landfall

By age twenty-two I had achieved one of my goals – I was back in the land of my birth. Customs welcomed me, writing in my passport, 'New Zealander nineteen years overseas, returning'. New Zealander, that was me! In reality I was a mixed-up kid.

In England I had never felt English. Some of my most vivid memories were of my parents comparing the two countries, and of the yearning in their voices for that left behind. One day on a family drive, my mother spied a wooden house in the hills and cried out as if she had seen an accident, 'Oh, that reminds me of New Zealand!' What had she seen? My father treasured a collection of black and white enlargements of photos he had taken on weekend tramps. I stared at snow-clad mountains, wooden huts, cumbersome home-made skis and understood that our family's best qualities – ingenuity, practical resourcefulness, egalitarianism and impatience with class snobbery – derived directly from the land of my birth. I grew wildly proud of my middle name, an uncommon one in England, which heightened my individuality while extending a hand of belonging.

There was a contradiction. All my growing up had taken place in England. I felt at home with primroses and bluebells in spring, fiery autumn colours, centuries-old architecture, stone cottages, reverence for tradition, the Queen, high culture in music, dance, literature and art. I did not know the other country, the one I wanted to declare allegiance to.

Days after my arrival I took a coach trip from Auckland to Wellington. I saw hills as I had never seen or imagined them before. Raw mounds that gave no encouragement to human habitation descended in folds from great height, like a blanket dropped over the land. Totally unfamiliar, yet they spoke to something within me as though they had always been part of me, and from then on whenever I travelled away from New Zealand I would miss the hills and look forward to their embracing me on my return.

God given

In the days before self took centre stage, belonging in the world must have felt similar to being in the womb. In the mountains and rivers dwelt gods on whom people relied for meaning and security. Their relationship with the creatures of their spiritual world and with their ancestors was an unquestioned fact of life. We are lucky that some peoples with this way of looking at things survived long enough for those who had abandoned it to be reminded and, over time, learn to appreciate it.

The creation story of ancient Māori transformed the natural world into a vast pattern of kinship. The story begins in the void, a period of nothingness, known as Te Kore. From the void came a period of darkness and ignorance, expressed by the term for night, Te Pō. The earth was formed during Te Pō, personified by Papatūānuku. The sky also materialised, personified by Ranginui. These two clasped each other in tight embrace while their offspring gasped between them. Faced with imminent suffocation, the children pushed Ranginui upwards to his present position while Papatūānuku remained as earth. Each child became god of some aspect of the natural world essential to Māori survival. Between them they represented the forest and its inhabitants, the sea and its inhabitants, wind and weather, man himself, and items of diet essential for Māori survival: kumara and fern root.

Freed to wander upon the earth, the five brothers set about securing food sources. Tāne created trees, insects and plants. Tangaroa created the creatures of the sea. Tūmatauenga, or Tū, an ancestor of man (although not the creator of),[15] designed cunning snares and nets in which to trap these creations for food and medicine, and devised karakia (incantations) to his brothers to help produce plentiful offspring and therefore food security for man. Tū also offered karakia to conciliate Tāwhirimātea, the weather brother, who had bitterly fought the forcible separation of their parents. Tū called on his sky-father Rangi for fair weather and asked his earth-mother Papa to grant abundance upon the land.

The world was becoming a fit place for man but there was no place in it for woman. Finding his non-human couplings with trees, insects and plants unsatisfying, Tāne asked for help from his sky-father Rangi, who demurred that he represented only the realm pertaining to the permanent or undying. On his advice Tāne approached his earth-mother Papa, since hers was the realm of transitory things that are subject to death.

There were now three profound opposites: Sky and Earth, Male and Female, the realm of life and the realm of fate. Between them they provided the basis of organisation for Māori life. Everything to do with sky and the realm of life was tapu, a no-go zone or with restricted access; everything to do with earth and the realm of fate was noa or ordinary, with unrestricted access. Items that were noa should be kept separate from those that were tapu. Cooked food, for example, which was connected with the earth, should never come into contact with houses, which always contained a degree of tapu.

When the ironmonger John Nicholas visited New Zealand in 1814 he experienced tapu in practice. After a long day's journey in pouring rain, his Māori hosts told him he must not eat in the house.

> Unwilling as we were to provoke their resentment, by any violation of their customs, however absurd and ridiculous, we should either have gone without the potatoes, which were now very acceptable to us, or eaten them at the expense of a good wetting, (there being no shed for that purpose;) if very fortunately, a projection from the roof of the house, of about three feet, had not afforded us shelter, where we were enabled to take our repast. However, this indulgence was not suffered without many anxious scruples on the part of our friends, as they considered our proximity on such an occasion to the tabooed place, was highly impious. They watched us the whole time with the greatest care, lest we should be guilty of any egregious profanation; and whenever we wanted to drink out of a calibash they had brought us, we were obliged to thrust out our heads from under the covering, though the rain fell in torrents.[16]

Artist Augustus Earle, who came adventuring in 1827, was also perplexed by the custom:

> ...it is really difficult to walk without trespassing or infringing on some spot under this influence. All those who touch

a corpse are immediately taboo'd, and must be fed like an infant, as their own hands must not touch anything that is put into their mouths. In fact, as we strolled through the village at the time of their evening repast, it appeared as though some dreadful disease had suddenly struck the greater part of the inhabitants, and deprived them of the use of their limbs, most of them being either fed by their slaves, or lying flat down on the ground, and with their mouths eating out of their platters or baskets. The canoe that carries a corpse to the place of its interment is, from that time, taboo'd and laid up; and if any one by chance touches it, he does so at his peril.

... all those who worked upon their war canoes were similarly situated. Unfortunately for me, I one day took away a handful of chips from their dockyard to make our fire burn clearly. I was informed they were taboo'd, and upon my pleading ignorance, and sorrow for the misdemeanour, together with a promise not to renew the offence, I was pardoned. A poor hen of ours did not escape so well; she, poor thing, ventured to form a nest, and actually hatched a fine family of chickens amongst these sacred shavings! Loud was the outcry, and great the horror she occasioned when she marched forth cackling, with her merry brood around her. She and 'all her little ones' were sacrificed instantly.[17]

The land was part of the living body of the tribe. Inseparable from it were the spirit beings that gave the tribe its mana and helped protect its people from unpredictable humanity just beyond its precinct. Apart from the great ones, brothers Tānemahuta, Tūmatauenga, Tāwhirimātea, Tangaroa, Rongomātāne and Haumiatiketike, there were their descendants, or, as Eric Schwimmer put it in *The World of the Maori*, 'In some nearby tree lived a morepork who really was the chief's great-grandmother.' Schwimmer goes on,

With all these beings, intense relationships existed, manifested regularly through rituals and omens. They were simply part of the community, for the community, without its atua, was unthinkable and, indeed, already dead in spirit. Nor could these spirits be conceived apart from the land, apart from the places where people had always met them.[18]

In the two hundred years since Nicholas ate his potatoes in the rain, Māori, like other ancient societies, have relaxed most of the laws inconvenient to modern living, but their attachment to land, mountain and river remains part of their identity. When they introduce themselves on the marae, they still begin with geographical features of particular significance to their tribal area.

> Ko Waikato te awa
> Ko Taupiri te maunga
> Waikato is the river
> Taupiri is the mountain

They go on to name their waka (ancestral canoe) and their tribal kinship. The name of the individual comes last of all. When the Māori queen, Te Arikinui Dame Te Atairangikaahu, was buried on Mt Taupiri in 2006, Māori broadcasters often referred to the mountain as 'he'. The sense of intimate connection with the land in a particular place was palpable.

Eternal attachment

Even after the advent of Protestantism, regions of Europe survived for centuries where a sense of place as something permeated by God was paramount. In 1879, Robert Louis Stevenson chose the Cévennes in France for his travels on a donkey, partly because of his empathy with Protestants there who had rebelled against the prevailing Catholicism and remained loyal to the cause even under torture. By the time Stevenson visited, Protestantism had become the dominant faith. He met a wayfarer who had remained impervious to the change. What Stevenson saw in his face and heard in his words impressed him deeply.

> Out-door rustic people have not many ideas, but such as they have are hardy plants and thrive flourishingly in persecution. One who has grown a long while in the sweat of laborious noons, and under the stars at night, a frequenter of hills and forests, an old honest countryman, has, in the end, a sense of communion with the powers of the universe, and amicable relations towards his God... His religion does not repose upon a choice of logic; it is the poetry of the man's experience, the philosophy of the history of his life. God,

like a great power, like the great shining sun, has appeared
to this simple fellow in the course of years, and become the
ground and essence of his least reflections; and you may
change creeds and dogmas by authority, or proclaim a new
religion with the sound of trumpets, if you will; but here is a
man who has his own thoughts, and will stubbornly adhere
to them in good and evil. He is a Catholic, a Protestant, or
Plymouth Brother, in the same indefeasible sense that a man
is not a woman, or a woman not a man. For he could not
vary from his faith, unless he could eradicate all memory
of the past, and, in a strict and not a conventional meaning,
change his mind.[19]

Here, the unit is less an individual and more a whole people
melded with their countryside and their god. It would be impossible
to change their god without changing themselves fundamentally; nor
could they move from their countryside and remain intact.

Although by the nineteenth century England had largely lost
the sense of gods in its mountains and rivers, there lingered a sense
of ancestors as a living presence. As a young man in Southampton
Edward Tregear delighted in 'Pixy and brownie, sleeping princess
and fairy godmother, for the noonday visions; banshee and werewolf,
ghost and ogre, for delightful shudderings when the stories are told
in the twilight or by the winter fire.'[20] Coming to New Zealand in
1863, he found his new country bereft of such companionship, but he
noticed that for his Māori labourers and assistants the land was a far
from desolate place. They spoke of enchantment in their forests and
love-sickness in their mountains, while he walked alone. He realised
he had lost his psychic home and decided to create a new one. In 1884
he published *Southern Parables*, a booklet of thirty-two stories with
antipodean animals as characters – kiwi, tui, wood pigeons, kangaroos
and pukeko. What mattered was not that the country should be a paradise, but that 'every wood and hill, every lake and river is haunted
by beautiful or dreadful beings'. A collection of fairy tales[21] in which
he simplified the versions presented by Colenso, Grey and others,
attempted to create for young non-Māori a mythological heritage.

Since then many publications have helped keep alive the stories of
the mountains, plains and rivers around us. Some titles sailed across
the Pacific and Atlantic oceans wrapped as Christmas presents for my
family in densely populated Surrey, enabling me to grow up on tales of

taniwha that lived in deep water or under cliffs and rocks and brought death and destruction to Māori who ventured into their haunts. My uncle sent me the story of Hutu and Kawa, the 'bush babies' of the pohutukawa tree, who found guidance and succour in the spirits of birds and forest creatures. For someone who cannot undo the perception that she is a lone individual, these stories, still in print today, are little more than beautiful lullabies. They impart a fleeting sense of safety and order but they are not the stuff of which I am made. I arrived on the planet far too late to know the belonging that traditional societies took for granted.

The Māori world was designed to be unchanging, but its umbilical relationship with place-based spirits began to lose ground after my European forbears arrived. The ancestral spirits who had once protected them failed against muskets in the hands of unfriendly iwi and failed against the powerful new strangers who had taken up residence on their soil. Iwi had never known such insecurity. There loomed in front of them the self and all its challenges to communal life. There was little choice but to adopt or at least live by many of the European notions. The newcomers insisted on treating land as a commodity that could be bought and sold – and then sold on and sold on until all mana from the ancestors was lost. Māori could still work in whānau or hapū groups, but Pākehā paid their wages. Instead of utu, which exacted punishment on a whole tribe for an insult by one of its members, law courts held people individually responsible for their actions. Each step towards self-identity brought new insecurities and loss of the old markers of belonging. Some Māori found solace in the Christian god of love taught them by the missionaries. He seemed relevant to the new world they had to come to terms with.

When Māori began to move into urban areas this was further uncharted territory. Strangers had to be encountered every single day. Not as whole people but as impersonations playing different roles – shopkeeper, bureaucrat, schoolteacher – and spirit incantations did not help. Māori took up residence in the gaols out of all proportion to their numbers. If I were suddenly required to live in a tribal world and to abandon my sense of self, how would I get by? I think gaol might become my home too.

In the new, lonelier world, some familiar creatures lived on. In 2002, when the government proposed a major highway for a stretch of road straddling the Waikato River, Māori objected. It was the taniwha that had caused all the inexplicable head-on crashes, they said. Dr

Ranginui Walker, a former professor at Auckland University, said he grew up knowing never to swim at the bend in the river because the taniwha would get him.

The taniwha possesses eternal attachment to place. When somewhere as specific as a bend in a river was threatened with non-consultative change, the taniwha was able to express for the people their sense that once again, as so often in their modern history, Māori had not been sufficiently listened to. Dr Walker said that if there was more and earlier consultation with local elders, the taniwha would not rear its ferocious head out of the water nearly so often. Former Māori Cabinet minister John Tamihere suggested that over time and with the right handling the taniwha would evolve into a more docile creature, particularly if it was seen to stand in the way of progress for his people. 'Every culture will find a way to assuage these matters if it's for the benefit of the community.'

Fence lines

As a young man, Herbert Guthrie-Smith uprooted himself from England and spent the rest of his life making a Hawke's Bay sheep station his hallowed place of belonging. The depth of the symbiosis was so authentic and compelling that his written account, *Tutira*, became a New Zealand classic.

Although ill-equipped in either knowledge or experience to deal with the almost ineradicable bracken, Guthrie-Smith and an old schoolmate who together bought the 20,000 acres of land in the 1880s were filled with hope.

> I declare that in those times to think of an improvement of the station was to be in love. A thousand anticipations of happiness rushed upon the mind – the emerald sward that was to paint the alluvial flats, the graded tracks up which the pack team was to climb easily, the spurs over which the fencing was to run, its shining wire, its mighty strainers; the homestead of the future, the spacious wool-shed, the glory of the grass that was to be.[22]

As in the case of their predecessors, however, setbacks multiplied. After a short time, Guthrie-Smith and his partner were pressured by their stock and station agent to sell. When his partner buckled, Guthrie-Smith faced further heart-breaking rounds of labour and disappointment as ignorance and inexperience took their toll. Looking back on his first eight years at Tutira, he described himself as a failure,

> He stood, so to speak, on tiptoe, insecurely balanced on the piled carcasses of his predecessors, up to his lips in debt. Because he was young and foolish, and because he had not then lived as he has since done – to see wool at bedrock six times in 60 years and six times recover – he was filled with the gloomiest forebodings for the future, not only of himself and of Tutira, but of New Zealand; in his mature opinion the Colony was doomed.[23]

The piled carcasses of his predecessors. In this way, both the human beings and the thousands of sheep lost on the sheep station are joined together as Tutira's creatures. Thus, Guthrie-Smith learned to concentrate not on himself and his heroic or doomed deeds, but to take a different route altogether; Tutira entered his consciousness in its entirety and on its own terms. While doing his best to eradicate or at least control the unwanted elements, he cherished them all in his heart, even his former foe, the bracken, as it lost its battle with the Young Turk, mānuka.

> The bracken, crippled and weak, now endured the sufferings it had formerly inflicted on other plants; in the company of this virile newcomer it was squeezed to death, throttled, denied the right to air and light.[24]

As the author becomes more and more deeply attuned, he reflects that alien flora settling in New Zealand exhibit similar motivations to those of human colonisers: 'The scores of tribes of smaller living things are overlooked whose desire to multiply, whose lust for land, is quite as keen as that of man himself...' Each alien has to take prior inhabitants such as resident sheep into account.

> The grasses and clovers, for instance, bargain with him for the right to live; while providing him with food and raiment, they utilise his body as a distributing agent. Others elude destruction by enormous seed production, or nauseate him by their taste, or escape him on cliffs and rocks, or quietly withstand him and endure his perpetual crop and nibble.[25]

Guthrie-Smith felt a deep affinity for Māori and for him, as for them, the land was inhabited by spirits – in his case the spirits of the species living on Tutira. Even inanimate objects have a kind of spirit: 'A fence-line can be erected to the glory of the Lord as truly as a cathedral pile.'[26]

Uprooting

D.H. Lawrence once commented that, 'every continent has its own great spirit of place. Every people is polarised in some public particular locality, which is home, the homeland. Different places on the face of the earth have different vital effluence, different vibration, different chemical exhalation, different polarity with different stars: call it what you like. But the spirit of place is a great reality.'[27]

Lawrence travelled widely and thought a great deal about this spirit of place. In New Mexico, where he lived for several years in the 1920s, he often pondered differences between native Americans and the descendants of the Pilgrim Fathers.

As I read it, the overriding desire of those English emigrants was to preserve their identity, language and culture as a group. It wasn't just a case of escaping religious persecution. If so they could have continued living at their first destination, in Holland, where they were free to worship as they pleased. At first they were happy there, but Holland, as elsewhere in Europe, was a rising clamour of Renaissance innovation and imagination. One of the emigrants, William Bradford, recorded in his journal that as the children of the group grew older they were being 'drawn away by evil examples into extravagance and dangerous courses'.[28] Having taken one great step into the unknown, it was easier to do it a second time because, as Bradford remarked, 'they knew that they were Pilgrims and looked not much on those things, but lifted up their eyes to the heavens, their dearest country, and quieted their spirits'. So, in 1620, thirty-five members of the original group set out on the *Mayflower* for America. They did not imagine they would have an easy time there. For all they knew, the native people might be violent, there might be no source of food or water, disease might be rife and in any case the sea voyage would be hazardous.

The day before the ship arrived in harbour, some of the brethren were quarrelsome and the group found it necessary to 'combine together in one body and to submit to such government and governors as we should by common consent agree to make and choose'. The resulting Mayflower Compact laid the foundation for the political and legal system of the United States of America. The Pilgrim Fathers, as they later became known, promised submission and obedience to their 'civill body politick', which would enact laws, ordinances, acts, constitutions and offices. After landfall in Massachusetts Bay they began putting the compact into practice. Their beliefs developed into the characteristics of US democracy and government we know today: power-sharing, political checks and balances, trial by jury, town meetings, self-governance, the US Constitution.

The Pilgrim Fathers were puritans whose brand of strict, Bible-based Christianity and Protestant rebellion led their descendants to distrust state authority while cherishing inflexible notions of what it was to be American or un-American. Three hundred years later, Lawrence disputed the reality of the land of the free.

> This the land of the free! Why, if I say anything that displeases them, the free mob will lynch me, and that's my freedom. Free? Why, I have never been in any country where the individual has such an abject fear of his fellow countrymen. Because, as I say, they are free to lynch the moment he shows he is not one of them.[29]

As Lawrence saw it, something had gone badly wrong with the understanding of self brought over by the Pilgrim Fathers:

> ...there sits the old master, over in Europe. Like a parent. Somewhere deep in every American heart lies a rebellion against the old parenthood of Europe. Yet no American feels he has completely escaped its mastery.

Lawrence sheets the failings of the American Dream home to the failure to find true liberty, which he says will only begin when Americans discover 'the deepest whole self of man, the self and its wholeness, not idealistic halfness'.[30] The problem with trying to *escape* to freedom was that instead of obeying your deepest inner voice, you brought with you your prejudices and clung to them against all odds. 'Men are only free when they are doing what the deepest self likes. And there is getting down to the deepest self! It takes some diving.'

The migration of the Pilgrim Fathers to America was voluntary. They repudiated England and created their own society half a world away. How different it must feel to be exiled against one's will from the land of one's upbringing and choice – as happened to so many during World War II.

Stefan Zweig adored his homeland Austria and above all his home city of Vienna, in which, he wrote, it was a simple matter to enjoy life. By the 1930s he was the most widely translated living author in the world. His novels, short stories and biographies became instant bestsellers. But after Hitler's rise to power his books were burned and he was forced to leave Austria to seek exile in some other land. France could no longer offer refuge so he went with his wife to England, then the United States and finally Brazil. There was much he liked about all these places but nowhere felt like home and he fretted constantly about what was happening in Europe. In the months before he finally gave up the struggle, he wrote, 'I have been detached, as rarely anyone has in the past, from all groups and from the very earth which nurtures them.' Of a fellow exile he asked what was the purpose of continuing to live as a shadow. 'We are just ghosts – or memories,' Zweig said. For him, uprooting brought death by disconnection. He belonged nowhere.

Zweig saw the great problem of his time as how to remain free. When the Nazis turned destroyers of all he cherished, burning his books, forbidding him congress with friends and collaboration with fellow artists, he put all his energy into escape. His obsessive pursuit of freedom blinded him to the continuing importance of the need to belong. Fleeing from one country to another, he never cast in his lot with new compatriots but yearned always for Vienna and the life he had known. Terrified that Hitler would invade each new place of exile, he moved again and again.

In England he saw that people greeted the outbreak of war with far more equanimity than had the Viennese in 1914. Hard upon the declaration, Zweig found people outside his office so calm that at first he didn't think they could know what had happened. 'All was peaceful, the people were not walking at a quickened pace or in an excited manner.' But they did know. They bought the newspapers, read them and continued on their way. 'No high-spirited groups even in the shops, no anxious gatherings. And so it was week after week, each fulfilling his function placidly, without agitation, silently and replete with calm resolve.' Zweig thought that through gardening, the people gained a kind of moral constancy, 'a spectacle almost as great as that of nature itself'. Deeper than all else, he wrote in *Gardens in Wartime*, is 'the constant union with nature that transmits unseen a measure of its composure to each individual in a perpetual union, one on one'. Zweig was incapable of experiencing this for himself. Terrorised by fear of invasion by the Nazis, finally one day in Brazil he and his wife committed suicide together.

His sad story is in contrast to that of some of the other Jewish and anti-Nazi exiles, such as Thomas Mann, Albert Einstein and Bruno Walter, who made happy transitions to their place of exile. According to George Prochnik in his wonderful biography, *The Impossible Exile*, 'Bruno Walter attributed the secret of a happy exile to remembering the distinction between "here" and "over there"'. Zweig could never accept that 'over there' existed no more.

Embedding

The hills were only a beginning. For years I didn't know how to develop my feeling about them and also about the New Zealand bush into something strong and sustaining. The bush was dark and foreboding, marvellously energised by competition for light, but it was not until I read about William Colenso for a writing project that I began to understand it in a deeper way.

In 1844 Colenso's bishop sent him to a mission site in the Napier district. For their home, he and his wife Elizabeth found an unfinished raupo house on a swampy patch of toetoe, rush and flax. Their possessions arrived by boat in pouring rain and many of Colenso's treasured books were wet before they reached the shore. Bishop Selwyn himself described Ahuriri as the most disagreeably situated mission station in all New Zealand and paramount chief Tareha told Colenso it was 'the dwelling place of an eel', which was no compliment, but Colenso was undaunted. After just one month in the swamp, he turned his eyes to the Ruahine Range, which he could see from his study. Over the range lay Pātea, the most westerly village of his parish. He determined to cross the mountain chain.

With summer fast sliding into autumn, he set out with a Māori guide and porters, who told him it was really a bit late to be starting out. Tangled swamp vegetation and thick forest made progress slow and arduous. Heavy rain hampered them further, but they kept on climbing, wading through cold water, negotiating the bush and perilous ridges, enduring wet, chilly nights. Colenso made notes all the way, especially of sights that filled him with love, such as red mistletoe that sometimes gave the forest a reddish glare, especially in the rays of the setting sun. Finally, he stood on the snow-capped Ruahines, the first white man to do so. But his excitement was all to do with being a botanist on virgin ground, surrounded by a stupendous variety and quantity of flowers he had never seen before. Of course, he wanted to take some back with him.

> But how was I to carry off specimens of those precious prizes? And had I time to gather them all?... I first pulled off my jacket and made a bag of that; and then (driven by necessity!) I added thereto my shirt and by tying the neck &c got an excellent bag; while some specimens I also stowed in the crown of my hat.... That night I was wholly occupied with my darling specimens putting them up as well as I could, in a very rough kind of way, among my spare clothing, bedding and books; only getting about 2 hours sleep towards morning.[31]

Though a visitor in a foreign land, he felt an overpowering sense of connection with these unfamiliar plants, which made him happy to sacrifice any comfort for his specimens. They were like his children.

The guide and another Māori were sent on ahead to look for a settlement many miles to the west, in South Taranaki. They returned half-starved and exhausted, having found only an abandoned village. There was nothing for it but for the party to return home, which meant crossing icy streams another 108 times. Colenso's resulting sciatica would deepen into chronic rheumatism.

But he didn't care. In following years, he travelled seven months of each twelve, always carrying with him a few precious books, including his beloved English poets. His explorations in the bush enabled him to rise above the daunting trials of his life, and experience a sense of oneness with the natural world. His account of his Ruahine journeys shows Colenso at his happiest. Through his joy in the botanical delights of the country, he came closer to his God than ever he did in the company of mankind.

That god was not a creator of specific aspects of nature, like Tānemahuta or Tangaroa; he was the universal creator. Through the land, Colenso felt the presence of something he called the Almighty, which his beloved Wordsworth had described in 'Tintern Abbey':

> And I have felt
> A presence that disturbs me with the joy

Of elevated thoughts; a sense sublime
Of something far more deeply interfused
Whose dwelling is the light of setting suns,
And the round ocean and the living air,
And the blue sky, and in the mind of man:
A motion and a spirit, that impels
All thinking things, all objects of all thought,
And rolls through all things.

That was reason enough to include the poem as the concluding lines of *In Memoriam,* which remains one of the outstanding accounts of New Zealand exploration, but Colenso also hoped the lines might encourage in young colonists a greater love of poetry and of nature's works. He believed they spoke a universal language.

Out in the New Zealand wild he was able to love and be loved, free from anxieties about sin and egotism. The arguments he provoked throughout his life, the grudges he nourished, the self-righteousness he clung to, all melted away when he was exploring the bush or recapturing in words the awe he had felt in discovering a new fern, a new lizard or a new cabbage tree.

William Colenso became my companion. On paths through the bush he always went in front, inspiring me with the way he had coped with cold and wet and the joy he had found in the flora around him. I felt his sorrows and his consolations. Something in the love for the bush of this tortured and difficult man offered me a key to my own belonging of place.

Colenso was not a popular figure in New Zealand history: he fitted too well the stereotype of the fun-hating, body-hating, arrogant missionary. So I was surprised to find my father had retained an admiration for him. 'Oh, William Colenso!' he cried when I said I was writing about him. 'He was my hero.' It turned out that my father's study of botany had introduced him to Colenso's expeditions in the Ruahines and he too had responded to Colenso's love of the bush. During weekends of hard slogging through tangled supplejack and uninhibited tree roots, he discovered that every living organism was linked with all the others. He took that understanding into medicine, where his holistic approach enabled him to pioneer major advances in the prevention of eye disease. He returned to New Zealand in his old age. Too feeble by then to tramp or even walk far on the flat, he suffered many mini strokes and gradually grew quieter. One day we

were driving down the motorway out of Auckland when he suddenly
came to life.

'Oh, look at that!' he cried, pointing out of the window at the road,
which was lined with native plants.

'What, Dad?'

'The flax!'

He had come home.

By 1991 I was living in Auckland between the southern slopes of
Mount Eden and the volcanic hills named Three Kings. Through
studying the history of the city, I began to understand that what I saw
in front of me was never the thing in its entirety. Hidden from view
was both a past and a process of change. The more I learned about,
for instance, the mad race for land, the dominance of speculation and
absence of any overall plan of development, the more I belonged there.
Then I moved to Wellington, the city in which my forbears began their
New Zealand lives in 1842. That was so far back it meant nothing
to me until my father told me I was working in a building that once
housed the offices of his grandfather, a contractor who built bridges
and harbour piers and breakwaters as well as houses and apartment
blocks all over the city. Then my uncle, who was doing some family
history research, told me that my great-great-grandmother, who came
across from London in 1842, had her first baby in Wellington Harbour
the day after the ship arrived. He had worked this out from shipping
records and birth and death certificates. For months afterwards I never
looked at Wellington Harbour without seeing a woman giving birth on
a ship amid surging water.

I began to wonder what happened to her after that and what
happened to all the other passengers, especially the fifty-five married
couples who came steerage, labouring people whom the designer of
Wellington, William Wakefield, brought over in order to work for the
capitalist classes. Some families moved on to other settlements, but
most stayed in Wellington for a good number of years. My researches
again deepened my sense of belonging and resulted in another book,
No Simple Passage.

Landscape
At the forefront of ideas that burst into being during the Renaissance
was a new sense of beauty. Until then no one climbed a mountain for its
own sake. No one would have seen the point. But Francesco Petrarca,

an Italian scholar, poet and early humanist, decided in 1336 to climb the 1912 metres of Mt Ventoux in France and look at the view. It was the beginning of experiencing nature as a way of looking at the inner self. Nature could be seen as landscape and people could learn about themselves by studying its majesty and moods. Poetry found a new ground of being and offered people a deeper relationship with nature.

In his teens, New Zealand poet Brian Turner discovered the high country of inland Otago and of the South Island generally.

> It felt huge (sky, mountains, rivers, valleys) and grand. It still does. It was *my* place, *our* place, a place that 'belonged' to all of us that chose to live here irrespective of our racial background. I never felt daunted or suppressed by it, rather the opposite. Here I was engaged by and drawn to my country as never before. Here was an environment which made human pettinesses and the lust for power seem piffling, contemptible. Here was an environment which helped dissolve and wither the worst of me, gave me a better sense of what's enduring.[32]

Turner experienced becoming one with the material landscape. In 'The River in You' he described the process.

> *The River in You*
> (after W.S. Merwin)
>
> The first thing you want to hear
> is the river sound
>
> and then to see
> the source of that sound
>
> for it's never the same
> yet it's always something like
>
> what you think you remember
> from the time before
>
> and the one before that
> and when you reach the bank

though you no longer hurry
as you used to and look down

on the long reach that flows south
and curves east like a wing

light and sound are one
and you know the swirl

of having been there before
though it's not quite the same

as last time and the time
before that and you sense the pull

that draws you back is the river in you
racing to keep time with the river sound[33]

Like Turner, artist Grahame Sydney grew to love the majestic land-
forms of inland Otago's hill and tussock country during his teens. He
envisaged becoming an artist in Europe but found his muse deserted
him as soon as he left New Zealand shores.

As the silhouette of New Zealand's hills faded in the dis-
tance and slipped below the horizon, so, largely, did my
urge to paint. In the eighteen months away I did very little
work: nothing moved me enough, I was homesick, lonely,
and increasingly my London dreams were visited by star-
tling visions of Central Otago's clarity, the enormity of the
sky, its intense blues, the pervading silence, and wide, low
footings of parched landscape.[34]

Turner says the Otago landscape gave him a better sense of what
was enduring, echoing Eudora Welty's suggestion that perhaps we feel
such strong ties to place because, 'it has a more lasting identity than
we have, and we unswervingly tend to attach ourselves to identity'.
A landscape we know well brings us comfort, but danger lurks in
dependency because when we move away it stays behind, or as James
Wood put it, 'To have a home is to become vulnerable… to our own
adventures in alienation.' This can plunge a person into despair, as

Robert Louis Stevenson found in 1879. When he took a train across the Nebraskan plains to San Francisco, hoping to join the woman he loved, the landscape tested him to his limit.

> It was a world almost without a feature; an empty sky, an empty earth... The train toiled over this infinity like a snail; and being the one thing moving, it was wonderful what huge proportions it began to assume in our regard. It seemed miles in length, and either end of it within but a step of the horizon. Even my own body or my own head seemed a great thing in that emptiness... To cross such a plain is to grow home-sick for the mountains.[35]

The Black Hills of Wyoming were even worse:

> All Sunday and Monday we travelled through these sad mountains, or over the main ridge of the Rockies, which is a fair match to them for misery of aspect. Hour after hour it was the same unhomely and unkindly world about our onward path; tumbled boulders, cliffs drearily imitate the shape of monuments and fortifications – how drearily, how tamely, none can tell who has not seen them; not a tree, not a patch of sward, not one shapely or commanding mountain form.... here there is nothing but a contorted smallness. Except for the air, which was light and stimulating, there was not one good circumstance in that God-forsaken land.[36]

The journey continues for days 'through desolate and desert scenes, fiery hot and deadly weary', but one night Stevenson is awakened by a fellow traveller who declares they are in a new country. The train is temporarily stationary and, woozy with sleep, Stevenson registers tall rocks and dark pines. Somewhere nearby he can hear 'the continuous plunge of a cascade'. He returns to roost with 'a grateful mountain feeling at my heart'. Next morning, he finds a transformation in the landscape:

> I had one glimpse of a huge pine-forested ravine upon my left, a foaming river, and a sky already coloured with the fires of dawn. I am usually very calm over the displays of nature; but you will scarce believe how my heart leaped at this. It was like meeting one's wife. I had come home again – home

from unsightly deserts to the green and habitable corners of the earth. Every spire of pine along the hill-top, every trouty pool along that mountain river, was more dear to me than a blood relation...not I only, but all the passengers on board, threw off their sense of dirt and heat and weariness, and bawled like school boys, and thronged with shining eyes upon the platform and became new creatures within and without. The sun no longer oppressed us with heat, it only shone laughingly along the mountain-side, until we were fain to laugh ourselves for glee. At every turn we could see farther into the land and our own happy futures.[37]

New Zealander Eric McCormick thanked the hills of his native land for giving him the 'inland eye' that was part of his visual history of New Zealand, and culminated in his eminence as New Zealand's first important art historian. In his essay *The Inland Eye*, he refers to the 'inhuman loneliness' of his childhood landscape seen from the heights above the town of Taihape in the early 1900s.

The hills are indeed the striking feature of my birthplace. The town itself lies in a depression, half basin, half valley, descending to the river Hautapu. From almost any point in Main Street – more properly Hautapu Street – you see beyond the shop fronts, lines of hills rising to conical peaks or abruptly ending in precipitous bluffs. As you climb from the town, range upon range unfold until at length they stretch, an agitated sea of land, stemmed in the north by Ruapehu, to the east by the dark blue barrier of the Ruahines. Here and there you come across huge spherical boulders of volcanic origin, apparently hurled from Ngauruhoe in some ancient convulsion.

It may have been an ancient convulsion but on my arrival the striking fact was that such boulders were still so visible. In the New Zealand hills I saw youthfulness and a long exciting future. In England I had felt superfluous. There was no room for me in a land so overtaken with reminders of its human inhabitants. Everywhere I went I saw castles from an alien time trumpeting class privilege and warfare, churches redolent of authoritarian rule and hatred of the body. Political change was stifled by descendants of nobility in an 'upper chamber', judicial change was governed by the 'law of precedent', and the country was overrun with people – meaning queues for everything and much regimentation. Nature had been tamed. There was little forest left, the hills were worn down almost to nothing, like old people's teeth.[38]

As for me, nothing about my reaction to the New Zealand hills was objective; it was identification pure and simple. Not that the hills *were* me but they were, in Stevenson's words, my own happy future. The hills expressed what I wanted most in a country, the opposite of what I had known in England. They were what I could become.

Unity

In 1995 a journalist on Auckland's *Sunday Star* conceived a vision of a walking track the length of New Zealand that would connect the small towns, traverse the best landscapes and incorporate potent historical sites. There were fears at the time of New Zealand being taken over by the New Right and Geoff Chapple believed in action, not whining. His proposal would be an antidote to present woes, it would provide employment, work of dignity and meaning, there would be home and marae stays en route, Kiwis would meet Kiwis, foreign trampers would experience not only our nature but also our culture. 'It was a project for everyone. A landscape to dream on. A stirring of the country's blood'[39] – Chapple's imagination took flight. He managed to inspire hundreds of other New Zealanders and after many years of hard fundraising and hard work the trail became a reality. Now, hikers can do the entire trail in upwards of ninety days, or join and leave it at will. The Te Araroa trail resonates with New Zealanders as something intrinsic to their country and its popularity grows by the year.

For Chapple, it mattered to find unity in the trail. He was aware that the world's great trails – the Appalachian Trail, the Bruce Trail and the Pennine Way – were all trails along a single geographic feature. It might be an escarpment or a mountain range, occasionally a coast and sometimes even a man-made feature like the remnants of Hadrian's Wall, but there was always a unity binding it together. What would be the unity of the long pathway, Te Araroa, that he would design and oversee the building of? It would traverse the complete length of New Zealand but its unity must be more than 'the sunlit surface of its geography'. For a long time the source of unity was unclear to Chapple, but at length he found it under the ground.

Below New Zealand lie two opposing lithospheric plates,
and if you walk this country, you walk on land that has been,
on the back of those underlying plates, thoroughly tugged
about. The trail's unity is that singular force. Every basin
and range, every mountain and plain, every thermal pool
and volcanic hump exists because of it. The trail's unity is
its variety.[40]

Chapple found unity in a landscape that had been thoroughly
tugged about, but for the people of Christchurch who recently experienced that kind of tugging at first hand, there was disjunction rather
than unity and a lot of it was to do with buildings. Poet Jeffrey Paparoa
Holman felt unanchored when his familiar built environment could
no longer provide triggers to memory.

memory is
the braille of buildings
threading the labyrinth

how can I find
my way through myself
with the past torn down[41]

In *Shaken Down 6.3* he wrote that the buildings were more than
external memory banks, they were also 'an internal geography, our
shapes and roadmaps within'. He felt that in order to heal, people
needed to salute their vanished buildings and grieve for them.
'Memory is tied as equally to the place, the physical, as it is to the
personal, the human.'[42]

Buildings around us give us a sense of stability, we can depend
on them to be there tomorrow. They help communicate an identity
belonging to the place around us, an identity on which our own comes
partly to depend, so to lose them suddenly and without warning rips
the fabric of our belonging. In the first quake on 4 September 2010,
buildings fell but no one was killed. Resident and poet Fiona Farrell
wrote a poem about the randomness of ordinary life:

On beautiful mornings
the front of the bagel
shop falls down flat on

> the street. The pub
> slumps into the gutter
> and the church lays
> down its heavy cross.[43]

She felt as if the day 'could fly apart in an instant' and it was imperative to get the books back on the shelves and in order. Every few minutes the earth moved again, bringing ninety-eight aftershocks on that day alone and continuing into the thousands. Farrell found it necessary to set a glass of water on the windowsill. She needed to know whether the shaking was herself or the earth. If it was herself that did not matter so much. On that day, what happened outside mattered more than what occurred within.

When a cataclysmic natural event occurs, even people of the modern age tend to forget their hard-won self-identity as an independent decision-making person and regress to an earlier kind of consciousness. 'I thank God for saving me and my family' they say, as though he picked them out for special treatment while letting their neighbour perish. Or they lose faith because God let it happen at all. After the great Lisbon earthquake in 1755, Voltaire examined the entire notion of there being a god and found it wanting, but the ghost was never entirely laid to rest. After the Marlborough earthquake hit Wellington in 1848, the deputy governor proclaimed a Day of Humiliation and Public Fasting. Crowded congregations humbled themselves before the mighty hand of God and acknowledged his mercy in the midst of their tribulation. Even today, people thank God for saving them when a tornado or hurricane has struck, killing others but sparing them.

When buildings that have been part of people's lives for decades or centuries are destroyed, the question of what to do with them is often an agonising one. The early settlers of Christchurch began building their cathedral just fourteen years after the city was founded. It expressed their spiritual and civic aspirations and over time it became identified with the city itself. Twenty-first-century quake damage was so severe that the Anglican Church decided on demolition and replacement, but to many people the building was essential to the spirit and identity of their city. To lose it felt intolerable. Place displaced must be replaced. Place grown strange must once again become familiar, dependable and loved. The issue went to court and the dispute took six years to resolve in favour of restoration.

As Voltaire said, we all need to know, 'What am I? Where am I?

Where am I going, and where did I come from?' Is there no other way of answering these questions without the need to preserve the buildings that link us with our past? Part of Chapple's answer perhaps was that he wanted the Te Araroa trail to reconnect with ancient Māori tracks traversing the length of the country.

> I always saw Te Araroa's job as reinvigorating those trails that already existed. If they went on the coast that's where we go and if they crossed an estuary by simply waiting for the tide and walking, mud up between the toes, then that's the way we do it. And because you're walking the path of old Maori, you're back inside the experience and you should be able to get those landscape stories, all as a natural consequence of simply Papatuanuku (mother Earth), doing it slowly. There is a saying in the north, Te Ara Tawhiti – the trail of distance, Te Ara Roa – the long trail, and the last one, Te Ara Hou, which I think in that context means path of the spirit. And if you get those three things together then you're in a kind of, we won't say absolutely transcendent state, but you're on the way![44]

Te Ara Hou – path of the spirit. How often the word spirit seems the only possible way to describe what gives us a feeling of belonging with place. We no longer have gods embedded in mountain, river, glen – but we know that spirit is intrinsic to what we need and value in place.

FIVE

MARRIAGE AND FAMILY

Martin Luther finds happiness

In the world inherited by Luther, marriage had fallen into disrepute. Much of the available literature emphasised the depravity of woman-kind and the unhappiness of the estate of marriage.[45] A Roman official quoted by Luther in his treatise on marriage expressed the attitude: 'My dear young men, if we could only live without women we would be spared a great deal of annoyance; but since we cannot do without them, take to yourselves wives.' So poorly was marriage regarded that the famous twelfth-century lovers Heloise and Abelard chose not to marry, even when Heloise became pregnant. Marriage was merely to legalise weakness of the flesh and Heloise rated philosophers like her beloved Abelard far above that. She quoted St Jerome, who wrote of those great ones who had 'denied themselves every pleasure so as to find peace in the arms of philosophy alone'. To an ideal relationship, she said, marriage could add nothing of significance.

According to the official view of the Catholic Church, marriage and family life were sacred institutions, but everyone knew they were second to celibacy, and that the greater relationship was with God. Luther himself had taken a vow of celibacy, yet a few years after nailing the ninety-five theses, the force of his feelings led him to conclude that the estate of marriage was a thoroughly desirable, Christian vocation. God had created human beings male and female, therefore his divine creation should be honoured. God does not *command* anyone to be a man or a woman but creates them so; rather than order them to multiply, he creates them so *they have to*. In his marriage treatise Luther advised people who were unable to keep their vow of celibacy to acknowledge that they had promised what was not theirs to promise, and to marry without delay. He followed his own advice.

In 1525 he married Katharina von Bora, one of twelve nuns he had helped smuggle out of a convent in empty herring barrels. He was forty-one, she twenty-six. They moved into a former monastery and over the course of a happy marriage reared six children.

After his excommunication from the Catholic Church, Luther taught theology at the University of Wittenberg and Katharina helped make ends meet by farming the land and taking in boarders. Together they gardened and studied the Bible. Luther found the home as good a place of worship and of living by individual conscience as the church. Repudiating 'unnatural celibacy', he argued for domesticity as the healthiest and most sacred state. The family household became a kind of monastery, an estate which Dr Rowan Williams, former Archbishop of Canterbury, says we have inherited:

> What was true of the monastery – a disciplined household of prayer and work and service and mutual nourishment – all that is true of the family. This is where the monastic life is now... So the family becomes a place where vocation is real – God calls you into families and gives you responsibilities within that structure.[46]

Luther became an impassioned advocate of marriage: 'The greatest blessing God can confer on man is the possession of a good and pious wife with whom he may live in peace and tranquillity. To whom he can confide his whole possessions...'

He was at pains to make a distinction between merely being married and having a vocation for the estate. If you did not recognise the glory of the vocation, he said, you would find it a matter of bitterness, drudgery and anguish. You would be appalled by what you had to do. You would remonstrate,

> Alas, must I rock the baby, wash its diapers, make its bed, smell its stench, stay up nights with it, take care of it when it cries, heal its rashes and sores, and on top of that care for my wife, provide for her, labour at my trade, take care of this and take care of that, do this and do that, endure this and endure that, and whatever else of bitterness and drudgery married life involves?[47]

According to Luther, when a father washes diapers or performs some other menial task for his child, knowing that these distasteful duties are divinely approved, God smiles because he is doing so in Christian faith. Those who sneer at him for an effeminate fool, who see the task but not the faith, the practice but not the estate of marriage, are ridiculing God. In the true spirit of this estate all its works, conduct and sufferings become holy, godly and precious.

Not everyone has the vocation.

Myself as Cathy

Between Luther's ideal of marriage and mine there was the Age of Sensibility. When I was seventeen my father gave me Emily Brontë's *Wuthering Heights.* Two comments here: (1) it's a work of genius and (2) Brontë died unmarried at age thirty-two. I was overwhelmed by the love between Cathy and Heathcliff, which is about returning to the sense of oneness we all enjoy in the womb. I must have been attracted to the idea of merging my self, that self I had been working so hard to bring into being, with another. Like Cathy.

> My great thought in living is [Heathcliff]. If all else perished, and *he* remained, *I* should still continue to be. And if all else remained, and he were annihilated, the universe would turn to a mighty stranger – I should not seem a part of it. My love for Linton [her fiancé] is like the foliage in the woods; time will change it, I'm well aware, as winter changes the trees. My love for Heathcliff resembles the eternal rocks beneath – a source of little visible delight, but necessary. Nelly, I *am* Heathcliff! He's always, always in my mind – not as a pleasure, any more than I am always a pleasure to myself, but as my own being. So don't talk of our separation again.[48]

Then it happened to me. At every moment I wanted to know what D was doing. I needed to be able to imagine him doing it. I repeated our conversations in my head, things he'd said, ways he'd looked. I couldn't think properly, I couldn't take normal interest in my activities, I desperately needed to listen to music. It was as if all the furniture of myself was being shifted around, even the position of the doors was being changed. Nothing had prepared me for this and now no one explained what was going on or why. It was not the behaviour my parents and lecturers expected of me. I was absent-minded, clumsy, unsociable. It was like a sickness, my self was not my self, its essence depended on another.

Very soon the talk was of oneness. 'You are a more interesting me,' was his most memorable line (shades of Cathy's 'he's more myself than I am') and I felt that by living the miracle of oneness with him, I was a far bigger me. I was Self and Other all in one. A whole in one.

This relationship fulfilled the promise of *Wuthering Heights*. My Heathcliff was my own being and there was no separation and never could be. His spouse was a real-life version of Cathy's and his marriage was not in conflict with (because it had nothing to do with) the love he and I shared, which was beyond morality. It was Jung's idea that there's a force within the psyche not of our own making, which has to be acknowledged if we are to express our essence as individuals. Luther, unbeknown to me at the time, had felt that too, and solved the problem by disavowing his vow and marrying the nun, but here was a greater problem. My lover had a wife and growing children. Any or all of us could get hurt. His relationship with me was abusive in the sense of a person in a position of power exerting his will over an inexperienced girl, but in a way Brontë's use of literary power was far *more* abusive. It must have encouraged thousands of impressionable young people to believe in this kind of regressive romantic love which could not lead to a mature basis for marriage and could easily blight the development of a mature love for somebody else.

I began to feel dimly that Cathy-Heathcliff love could bring on too much intensity, too much us-against-the-world, too much desperation for non-separation. Or as Richard Ford's *Independence Day* protagonist, Frank Bascombe, puts it, 'the gnashing, cold but also cosy fear that after a while there'll be no *me* left, only *me chemically amalgamated with another.*' After a marriage breakdown Bascombe gets into another relationship, a kind where there would never be any question of losing the self.

> ...the proposition with Sally is that there's *just* me. Forever. I alone would go on being responsible for everything that had me in it; no cushiony 'chemistry' or heady synchronicity to fall back on, no *other*, only me and my acts, her and hers, somehow together – which of course is much more fearsome.[49]

At the Royal wedding of Prince William and Catherine Middleton in 2011, Archbishop Williams told the couple, in front of their families, friends, assembled dignitaries and the world, that faithful and committed relationships in marriage offer a way for the self to find fulfillment with another.

> The more we give of self, the richer we become in soul. The more we go beyond ourselves in love, the more we become our true selves and our spiritual beauty is more fully revealed. In marriage we are seeking to bring one another into fuller life.

Me a married woman

Not long after that tumultuous relationship I met G, the man I would marry. Everything about him was the antithesis of my Heathcliff. G was fair and slim, he mistrusted intensity, he saw the glass half full, I knew without question he would never go to other women. It was clear he would lead a 'godly, righteous and sober life'. He would be a loving, reliable, generous and wise husband. As for love: at that moment, I loved the absence of risk, the transparent honesty, the innocence of youth, the absence of competing affections and ties, the conquering of loneliness once and for all. Oh, but it feels presumptuous to put into words what on earth I was doing and why.

For me, one of the major impediments to a happy marriage was a supportive social structure. With our move to New Zealand, we were ripped away from family ties and people we had known all our lives. At first we made friends easily and we were swept up in the excitement of forging ourselves as teachers, joining with other forward-thinking twenty-somethings in fighting for new enlightenment in teaching methods. G's sense of humour made him popular and his pupils enjoyed maths as never before. But within a couple of years all had changed. We had moved to the bottom of the South Island and were teaching at a Catholic school where our companions were priests, brothers, nuns. Despite God's contraception I became pregnant and soon I was home alone with nameless fears and a growing foetus. I wanted children and looked forward to seeing my baby, but I felt deeply threatened. The old question arose: Who am I? As I imagined taking care of the baby, a being with open-ended needs and the potential to rob me of all control over my destiny (what if he/she were badly mentally retarded, physically handicapped?), all sense of myself seemed to evaporate. Here I was at the end of the world, next stop Antarctica, without family or friends, in a country that still felt foreign.

These were the underground worries. Above ground, I was joyous and filled with happy anticipation. G and I drew closer together, delighting in giving one another mutual support, proud that together we had created new life.

The doctor agreed G would be present at the birth but the matron objected strongly. After the birth, the baby was taken away and kept in another room. If G happened to visit at a time when she wasn't with me, he wasn't allowed to see her. The most he could do was peek through the glass of her little ward and glimpse her body from the cheek up. I would try to describe to him what she was like from cheek down. On Sunday when he came to visit he was turned away because he came alone and that was the rule on Sundays, parents and other children. I saw him accosted at the glass ward door by the matron, who was very firm. After she sent him away I was ordered to lie on my belly to get my fundus down. By the time I came home from hospital I felt an estrangement between me and my husband, between me and the rest of the world. As for the child, it lost weight, which was normal but I didn't know that and had no one to ask until the Plunket nurse visited. The nuns were not allowed to visit because 'socialising' diminished their service to God. I had no other friends.

Of course I survived, life went on. I learned to take care of my daughter Tama and later on my son Dorian. G continued to be a loving, considerate husband, and often we had fun and laughs and life seemed good. But somehow at the heart of it all was a loneliness that never disappeared. An abyss that lurked behind every joke and beneath every laugh. A nameless, ineradicable emptiness.

Judith and David

Not long after I moved to Auckland in the 1990s, I met Judith, a writer, and David, a software engineer and university lecturer. I came to admire their marriage, which had lasted forty years and combined a high degree of mutual belonging with a highly individuated sense of self. They had developed a knack for letting each other become the true selves that Archbishop Williams speaks of. Over a glass of wine one afternoon we chewed the fat on how it all worked. I asked them how they saw their identities just before they met and what they responded to in each other on first meeting.

David: Mine was very tied up with being a mountaineer. I was wandering around haphazardly in life. I'd been climbing and playing the cello in the mountains and I came to

Wellington to earn some money and take more cello lessons before I went back to more climbing. One day while I was living in Owhiro Bay, a friend said, Let's go to this party, so we went to the party and I met this girl who lived in Island Bay and this girl was Judith. I'm not sure what attracted me to her.

Judith: Cigarettes and tits.

David: Well, the initial thing was, as Bill and I arrived at this party, either he or I said, 'Let's see how many cigarettes we can bludge off these people for a smoke.' So we were at this party, and I was watching these flashing lights that went in time to music, which was a new thing then, and this girl started talking to me. She had been talking to someone else who had walked away and she thought she was still talking to this other guy.

Judith: I turned round and realised it wasn't the same person, but the new one seemed quite interested, so I just continued chatting.

David: And on top of that, she'd arrived with *her* party trick, which was a tin of Sobranie cigarettes, for a conversation piece.

Judith: Because I was a bit shy – I thought if I could offer people a special cigarette – they were Russian, multicoloured, each cigarette was a different colour. David came along.

David: I came to take and she came to give. That's the basis of our relationship!

Judith: And because I had cigarettes, David kept coming back to me.

David: No, that wasn't the only reason. The first time we touched, probably, was when we were eating garlic bread. She had some on her hands so I said, 'Wipe them on my jeans.' And she did.

Judith: He was a wipe-over from the start!

Jenny: Judith, could you tell us how you saw yourself at that time?

Judith: I had not long returned from travelling. I had been away for four and a half years, a lot of it in Africa, and I felt very free. I was interested in primitive tribes and different cultures and the world in general. Back in New Zealand, I started working in broadcasting but I was finding it extraordinarily difficult to settle down. People were quite conservative and all I wanted to do was save enough money to get out again. I had heard of primitive tribes in the Philippines who hadn't had much contact with civilisation, so I was thinking I might go there. Then I went to this party and somehow there was something about David that I related to. One thing I really liked about him was that he played the cello and he said he would play for me. There was talk of our going up to the top of this big hill behind my house in Beach Street and he was going to play the cello for me up there. He never actually did but I liked the romantic notion of it, I thought of him as a mountain man. His hair was frizzled by the sun, Jimi Hendrix style, and he'd scrape around town in his climbing boots and his best jersey was fraying at the elbows.

Jenny: Did you like all that?

Judith: Well, I was thinking it would be really good if he could get a new jersey and I was thinking it would be really, *really* good if he didn't wear his climbing boots all over town, but there was something in him that I strongly responded to. I can remember the day after the party, sitting in the kitchen in Island Bay and saying to my brother Johnny, who was my flatmate and had also been at the party, 'I really like that guy, you know, the cello guy.' Then the next day I was at another party when the phone rang and it was Johnny to tell me, 'That guy is here!' So Johnny came and fetched me because he knew David was special.

Jenny: David, can you tell us what you responded to in Judith?

David: She was adventurous. I like people who live outside the normal life. Like, I just wanted to live in the mountains and play music and be free in nature, that was going to be my whole life. And she had travelled in Africa.

Judith: We were both looking for something true and I felt there was something true within David. He wasn't hiding behind a mask, there was an honesty and realness about him. Intelligence, love of music, love of the mountains – and he always wanted to learn things.

The question of marriage came up and how they could go on being free while earning a living and bringing up children.

David: We both wanted a simple life. All we had in the world was a pack each. I just lived in tents and huts, wherever the next job was.

Jenny: Was your plan to keep your simple life and develop it together when you got married?

David: It wasn't a big plan.

Judith: I got pregnant.

David: There wasn't the aspiration to go and accumulate. Like even when we came to Auckland, all we had was an old van and two children.

Judith: There *are* pressures in society to accumulate but they didn't bother us. It was enjoyable to buy something nice when we could afford it, but the sense of aesthetic surroundings was what mattered and that was really a question of making a *home*, surrounding ourselves with lovely things, *real* things – and David built things. We didn't want to be caught up in consumerism, but I don't even think we were *fighting* against that. There was a wonderful fit between us and we loved each other.

Jenny: So Judith was pregnant – and then what?

Judith: At first David was always planning to go back to the mountains and I was planning to travel again. Then when we became pregnant, I just thought, 'Oh well, I truly love this baby.' There's no way that I would have considered abortion, even though in those days, 1973, the stigma of being an unmarried mother was tremendous. I didn't want to tie David down but the next thing David was saying that he wanted to be alongside me, so that's what happened.

David: My plan was to start up a guiding company in Wanaka called Mountain Recreation. A friend of mine who was my mountaineering guru was going to do it with me but then he fell off a cliff. Suddenly my friend was killed and we were having a baby. Everything was changed. We got married. We met in July, got married in December.

Jenny: So what did that mean in terms of job, income, supporting family etc.?

David: I was working for a software company that I had worked for since 1969. There was a lot of work around. Before we got married I got a job at Victoria University in Wellington. I was determined not to work five days a week. I started off at three. I wanted to be free, I wanted to be at home and around. I did a few little mountaineering trips with Philip Temple, over the Copeland, and then Judith and I went down to Mt Cook where we got snowbound in a hut with our little three-month-old baby.

Judith: Fortunately I was breastfeeding because otherwise…

David: We hopped off the bus, walked into this hut just by the road on the way to Mt Cook and when we woke up in the morning we couldn't see a thing. Snow all around the windows, there was no power or anything. And the roads in and out were blocked.

Jenny: And you took to these adventures happily, Judith?

Judith: I found the mountains quite frightening, awe-inspiring, very beautiful. But yes.

David: She was a traveller. We were travellers.

Judith: I was just curious about the world.

David: A lot of people today want to challenge themselves and do this or that, but it wasn't like that for either of us.

Judith: After we moved to Auckland, we eventually bought a house and then David was offered an opportunity to go to Seattle for a couple of years. He was saying, 'We can't go because we've just bought this house.' I said, 'We're not going to let the house tie us down, just because we own it.' So we rented it out and off we went.

David: I was prejudiced against America, Americans-in-Vietnam and stuff, which was just nonsense really, because actually it was wonderful. There were plenty of nice Americans and we had a lovely life there.

Judith: When David's contract finished, the company was going to pay for us to go back to New Zealand, but rather than just fly over the world we went through India, Nepal and Thailand. We were trekking for three weeks in Nepal, from one tiny mountain village to another.

David: With these two little children of nine and seven! It was incredibly irresponsible, but they were used to being in the mountains, they loved it.

Judith: Sometimes we'd be walking all day without any access to food. Sometimes it was eleven hours walking. Once we found a freshly laid egg in our room, in one of the little huts. We cooked it on our primus.

David: Judy's less anxious when she's travelling overseas. To this day it's exactly like that. Once we're out of this country she's free to become someone else. It's lovely being with her because she is suddenly this French girl or this Indian one. She tries to talk whatever language is going, whereas I feel more scared over there.

Judith: Like travelling through India for example. I noticed David tended to pull into our accommodation and read books about where we were, whereas I liked going and poking my nose along little alleyways.

David: Have you read that lovely story in *Visiting Ghosts* ['Soul Survivor'], about Judy going into Varanassi by the Ganges where people go to die? It's a holy place with burning ghats and so there are bodies burning there all the time.

Judith: I would get up before dawn, go down to the Ganges and talk to people and walk along the river and observe the scene. There was one particular funeral I went to where people explained to me what was happening and that's the one in the story.

Several years after they went to Seattle – and many adventures later – they returned to settled life again. David took a job at Auckland University and Judith combined her writing with looking after the children. Her short stories won awards, but peace of mind eluded her.

Judith: I think all my neuroses were seeded in New Zealand and when I returned, it was back to the place that fed my anxiety. All the expectations of how to act in New Zealand. I always felt I didn't fit in.

David: Your mother never approved of your free nature. She wanted you to wear twinsets and pearls – but that said, her mother also had that kind of spirit. She was very free, you can see that in her painting, she actually had this free craziness, but she was held in by societal conformity. So she didn't like Judy's hair, it was the wrong length, she didn't have enough makeup on or she wore the wrong clothes, there was always something wrong.

Judith: David encouraged me to be me. He accepted me as I was. I'd found someone who loved me for who I was.

David: That's why I liked you. Because of that, because you were
    like that.

Judith: I didn't feel like I had to pretend.

David: Also we had lots of friends here who accepted us, who
    were like us.

Judith: All our friends were a little different-ish. I suddenly
    realised one day that of our close friends, each had had
    something happen to them in their childhood that had
    possibly made them less embedded in their lives. For
    instance, David's father died when he was eleven. Each of
    us had something that made us watchful or made us aware
    that life wasn't just a smooth ride, that in a little family unit,
    mummy and daddy and children, things could happen out
    of the blue and therefore if one thing can happen, then
    anything can happen. I suddenly realised that we all had
    childhood events that had flung us out from the centrifuge.

From the beginning of the marriage, Judith found she needed
regular time alone. At times this meant being alone in the house, but
sometimes it meant living somewhere else for a while. Such times
were often her most productive writing periods.

Judith: There's a renewal thing that happens when I'm alone, like
    the flaking off of dead skin. Even when I first met David, at
    some period each year I needed to have time away from him
    just to have that sense of myself again and to miss him and
    to have the joy of going back to him again. It was essential
    for my well-being. It wasn't something that emerged as the
    marriage went on, as our togetherness lumbered on. Even
    in that first in-love state, I made it clear that I really loved
    having that apartness while knowing that he was there. If I
    had the apartness knowing that he *wasn't* there or if I had
    the apartness worried that he didn't love me or that we
    might not get together again, I would hate being alone, but
    a feeling of being alone, knowing that I am loved, is really
    important.

    If David weren't part of my life I'd have to reconstruct
    myself again. He's my nurturer and my solace. He under-
    stands me and we just sort of walk alongside each other and
    I'd have to reconstruct that. Alone, without him, I would be

lonely. His spiritual depth, his acceptance, his deep capacity for love – those things are really, really important and nourish me very deeply. I'd feel as if part of me was missing, my life companion would be gone and I'd be stranded.

When I was a child and felt misunderstood, my longing was that I would find someone who would understand me and love me. I realise now that the most important thing is not to be misunderstood. I can accept that people don't always understand me but I can't accept that people *misunderstand* me, because then they are presenting me as different from what I am. I don't have any sense of David misunderstanding me.

Jenny: And what's it like for you, David? Do you have any need for being apart?

David: Through circumstances it happens. But I can live in a more detached way. I can pull myself back from things that are happening without having to deal with them. Judith is much more immersed in looking after everybody and that sort of stuff. I mean, I have never felt not free. I didn't have both parents you see, I only had my mother, so I spent a lot of time on relatives' farms and it was natural to feel free. I have never felt the need to bugger off somewhere, because I can just go into the garden.

Jenny: If you have an experience without the other one, do you ever feel as if you haven't really had the experience until you've told them?

Judith: No, but I do like to share it with him. Sometimes, if it's a really interesting experience, I want to write about it first and then I'll tell him about it.

David: I certainly wouldn't write notes. I just come home and talk. When she's away I feel lonely. The thing I don't like is when I come home and see nothing has changed. It's exactly as I left it in the morning. There's not that randomness happening. Like when you have children there is a lot of random stuff going on, but when I'm here on my own, everything is just as I left it. And it's, 'Oh God, here I am again.'

Judith: We could hire someone to come and shift things around, move the cushions...

Judith and David's children grew up. Their son Clem went to

London, where he lived for many years, while their daughter ran a landscaping business for several years from their basement. After Xanthe left, Judith and David were alone together again.

Judith: There was a wee moment when it was just us – and then Mum came to stay with us because she was ill.

David: We have only lived together as just us for a very small proportion of our lives, because we had a baby very quickly and both our kids lived here until they were twenty-six. Then Judy's mum came to stay with us until she had to go into a rest home. Then we renovated the house and it was full of people again.

Judith: For about a year, from 7:30 in the morning we had these great bouffs lumbering around the place, banging and crashing, yelling across the valley. And now we have weekly responsibilities with the grandchildren.

Jenny: So when you have time alone how does that change things?

Judith and David: It's lovely. Hurrah!

Judith: It's always been a tug, you know, the two of us are always tugging to be together.

David: That's how it is.

Judith: It is lovely having them all around but when we find ourselves alone it's like, 'Hello, hello, here we are,' in a nice comfortable way. It also means that you don't have to do things...

David: Judy is the centre of gravity for our whole family actually. The whole family.

Judith: Only because I'm the cook. But David complains that I'm less adventurous at the moment.

David: I'm more keen to go travelling away and you've been less keen in recent times, but that's all right.

Judith: I've had the book, that's the other world I've been travelling in. That's been my adventure recently. [This became Judith's second novel, *The Elusive Language of Ducks*.]

As with many families, marriage and the advent of children created an extended family. Each adult became an in-law as well as a biological family member. The depth of the family bonds would depend on how much time they all spent together.

Judith: After the children were born, the two grandmothers would turn up on their birthdays. We didn't have a large house so they shared a room and they'd be chatting away. They were very different people but they had similar values. At Christmas and the children's birthdays the house was full. By the time our mothers were ailing and failing it was just an accepted thing that we would take care of them. David's mother didn't come and live with us here, but she needed a very big cancer operation and she came to Auckland because of family, because David and his sister live here. It was very much a matter of accepting that as part of the marriage you have the extended family and you look after them if they're not well. As Mum began to decline, she would stay with us for longer and longer periods until she came to live with us for a couple of years.

Jenny: With the in-law relationships, is there a kind of holding back at some level?

Judith: Perhaps a little barrier between you because you are not biologically kin. David's mother would put her own children first, so there was always a certain separation, but ultimately, if our in-laws needed looking after, we would.

When Lewy body dementia [associated with Parkinson's] started affecting Mum's rationality, there was a point when she thought something was going astray with her money. She felt that perhaps we were being a bit intrusive over her moving to Auckland, because when she came to live with us she needed state-subsidised home help here, and we had to cancel the help she'd had in Hawke's Bay. She felt I had no right to do that, but in actual fact it's the system. And we really needed that help because I couldn't manage the showering etc. on my own. In the end, David had a bit of an outburst, he just said, 'It is not like that at all and Judy is doing her best,' but he didn't do it very often.

As the extended family became more significant in their lives, there was less time for friends and gradually there developed a separation between family and other people.

Judith: The friends are very dear too but the family does have priority, a different sort of significance, let's say. You can be closer to or understand your friends more, but your family ultimately has priority. David and I have this very firm place alongside each other, but it's part of the whole package really. Even if there are little tensions amongst the family, you have to accept it.

My friends are very, very important, but if I try to identify love I'd say – well, for example, I have the love for my husband and the love for my brothers and the love for my mother and the love for my duck. The love for each could be categorised according to different characteristics. Ideally there should be a different word for each. If I put all those things together I'd say my love for my friends is just as significant but I guess it's a matter of some innate thing that says the family has priority. I don't know why, when I come to think of it.

With family, you accept them the way they are. David's mother accepted me as David's wife and David's chosen one, but it took her a long time to accept me for who I was. With your friends, you choose each other for particular reasons. It's exciting when there is that lovely meshing of ideas or understanding. Even if they don't react in the same way as you, they appreciate the way you react to the world and so your times with them are probably even more rewarding. Some members of the family we might not have anything to do with if they weren't family, just because they are very different.

And the cat belongs. He's been with us since the kids were teenagers. He's seen the kids with this boyfriend, with that girlfriend, at their parties, all the family get-togethers at Christmas and then the children leave and then there's the other little creatures that come. He has seen all these things and he just sits there and lets it all flow by. When I'm doing a flurry of tidying up, he probably thinks, 'Oh – more visitors.' He just sits there and he's part of us, it's me and David and the cat. He has seen the duck come and go, and so, even though he is just funny old Hank, he's part of our circus.

Once upon a time, way back *then*, your family would have lived in the same village or a little village down the road and you would have jumped on your horse or trundled down the path and you wouldn't have even thought about family because it would have just *been*. Now, of course, with globalisation and the spreading out of everybody, the family is our opportunity to make a little village of belonging.

Both Judith and David have gold cards now and the time is long past when they had the strength for eleven hours walking. After forty years of marriage, they have to face the likelihood of dying at different times.

Judith: Sometimes we say, 'What if something happened to you before it happened to me? Oh gosh, what will I do without you?' There's this strange awareness that, oops, anything could happen at any time.

David: There's this vulnerability to losing the other one.

Judith: Absolutely and we sort of talk about it in a light-hearted or a sorrowful way, because David's father died – like that, poof! and my father died like that, poof! and, okay our mothers died more sensibly but we know anything can happen. We might have just watched a movie or we suddenly have a thought, 'I don't know what I'd do without you, my life wouldn't be quite, my life would have to be, Oh without you it would be, Um...' And then there's this, 'Look out there. Darkness, what is it?' It's there, and there's this awareness that we're on this planet for an incredibly short time, when you think of the solar system, the Earth, life on Earth, suddenly we're just little dots. Totally expendable.

David: You think of your grandchildren, you think well, you don't know how long you're going to know them for. You never thought that about your children.

Judith: I did, right from the beginning.

David: But with the grandchildren you think, 'It is great to have known you until you're at school. It would be nice to know you until you're... And then it would be nice to know what you're going to do with your life and who you're going to marry.'

Judith: And then suddenly you want to know the whole blooming lot. You don't want just the first chapter. You want to know the whole book. And you want to *play* in quite a few chapters of their life.

David: I find that very strange.

Judith: It's peculiar and we realise that in a very real way we are in the sunset of our years.

David: When the government starts giving you money they are basically saying, 'You're of an age where we don't expect you to look after yourself. You've done your bit and off you go. Here's something to keep you alive so we don't have to drag you out of the gutter.'

Jenny: You grow up separately, you go through birth and child-hood separately, then you get together, you make a life together, but as you get older and you're facing death it's like you're facing separation again, it's like having to be *prepared* to separate.

David: It's like the Buddhist thing. Everything that is joined is separated.

Judith: I thought that right from our very beginning. I wrote this poem, a cheesy sort of poem, but it was about being together and looking at a seagull and saying that when I looked at one seagull in the sky I thought of this deep loneliness. It was because I was with David, looking at him and looking forward to our lives together. Even then, the pain of the separation was lurking.

Companion of one's fate

One day when we were on holiday, I saw from the bedroom window that there was a spectacular sunset. I called G to come and see it too. He came down the hall and into the bedroom and I said, 'Look at the sunset!' He agreed it was 'very nice' and, putting his arms around my waist from behind, started pulling me towards the bed. I was expect-ing to drink in the beauty of the sky to the last moment, but for G a single moment was enough. To him 'bedroom' meant something else, something overriding, against which the fleeting apparition of intense colours had no traction. I resisted his efforts but the moment was over because we had not been able to share it, and in that moment I realised the gulf between us. I stood, facing the window, trying to recapture what I had felt so short a time before but now, instead, I felt an ocean of loneliness.

My marriage ended after seventeen years. For thirty years I have lived alone – barring short periods with flatmates and English-language students – openly flouting my society's preference for unions of two selves as the prime basis of belonging. In marriage, the theory goes, two people can be authentic with one another, reassured that each is not alone. Lacking this, I had to find other ways of staying afloat. Not that my risk of drowning is greater than anyone else's, but ruptured shoulder tendons, combined with wrist and hand damage, have plagued me for years with bouts of disability which prevent me from writing. Not long ago, I felt so ground down by pain and fear that any prospect of ending it, including death, beckoned as sweetly as the devil to Faust.

I, like everyone else, need a companion of my fate. I only recently identified this after reading a quote from Balzac's novel, *The Inventor's Suffering*:

> ...man has a horror of aloneness. And of all kinds of aloneness, moral aloneness is the most terrible.... The first thought of man, be he a leper or a prisoner, a sinner or an invalid, is: to have a companion of his fate. In order to satisfy this drive which is life itself, he applies all his strength, all his power, the energy of his whole life.[50]

Did I have a companion of my fate? If not, how was I managing to survive? Perhaps it was possible to have more than one. Perhaps I could have several, tailor-made for different purposes. Perhaps they could go back in time and across space. Perhaps they could even be characters in books. Perhaps I had all of history to choose from.

The companion I have found for my pain and frustration is Beethoven. In 1801 his ears hummed and buzzed all day long and he was having increasing difficulty with hearing. An unpleasant bark treatment applied to his arms failed to improve his ears. He escaped to the village of Heiligenstadt, where he wrote a letter of desperation that became known as his Testament.

> Ever since my childhood my heart and soul have been imbued with a tender feeling of goodwill. But just think, for the last few years I have been inflicted with an incurable complaint. Endowed with a passionate and lively temperament, I was soon obliged to seclude myself and live in solitude. I could not bring myself to say to people, 'Speak up! Shout! I am

deaf'. My misfortune pains me doubly, inasmuch as it leads to my being misjudged. I must live like an outcast. How humiliated I have felt! If somebody heard a shepherd sing, I heard nothing. Such experiences almost made me despair and I was on the point of putting an end to my life. The only thing that held me back was my art, for indeed it seemed to me impossible to leave this world before I had produced all of the works that I had felt the urge to compose...

I was comforted that Beethoven went on to write the Ninth Symphony, as well as many other works that bring joy and meaning to people's lives. If Beethoven could find life worth living in spite of his affliction, then of course my life was worth living too. And Beethoven would always be there beside me when I needed him. So would others – people I'll never meet who offer wisdom gained from experience, or those I have known so intimately that their identity will be part of me forever. And then there are living friends and family, one of whom may be able to offer the exact solace I need on a particular day.

Of course, it matters who you choose. You could say Cathy in *Wuthering Heights* was a poor choice. Likewise a violent gang, a religious cult or a terrorist cell. As with marriage, the trick with a companion of your fate is to choose well. In my defence I think that my reaching out for womb-oneness through passionate love was not in vain. It laid the ground work for learning how to find a companion of my fate wherever and whenever I needed one, whether in present or past, here or there, through literature, music or art. I discovered that if I tried I could find an element of oneness with every creature everywhere. Even with trees. Even with stones.

When the writing is threatened or curtailed I am vulnerable, because the writing is what makes me happy to live alone. But so long as I have a companion of my fate I can call on in times of need, I am able to hold on. One companion is not enough. It has to be a playlist. For pain in the shoulders, it's Beethoven.

The need to write is why I can't live easily with another. Or perhaps the reason lies deeper – in an inability to be fully myself when another is always with me. Perhaps it is all about being fully myself and writing is a mechanism that facilitates it, whereas constant companionship pulls me all over the place and I cease to be able to think.

In a concentration camp during the Second World War, Viktor Frankl needed more than a rock to sustain him. In his inspiring book

Man's Search for Meaning, he describes his discovery that one way of making survival possible was by thinking of his wife:

> I heard her answering me, saw her smile, her frank and encouraging look. Real or not, her look was then more luminous than the sun which was beginning to rise.
>
> A thought transfixed me... that love is the ultimate and the highest goal to which man can aspire... I understood how a man who has nothing left in this world may still know bliss, be it only for a brief moment, in the contemplation of his beloved.
>
> I didn't know even if my wife was still alive but I knew: love goes very far beyond the physical person of the beloved. It finds its deepest meaning in his spiritual being, his inner self. Whether or not he is actually present, whether or not he is still alive at all, ceases somehow to be of importance.

Another time the prisoners were made to dig a trench. Frankl relates how he stood for hours hacking at the icy ground. The guard passed by, insulting him, and once again he communed with his beloved:

> More and more I felt that she was present, that she was with me; I had the feeling that I was able to touch her, able to stretch out my hand and grasp hers. The feeling was very strong: she was *there*.[51]

Self upon self

A recent trend is for women unable to find Mr Right to marry themselves and commit to being their own best friend. 'Sologamists get to feel like a princess, surrounded by friends and family, and enact every non-legally-binding part of a wedding ceremony, including the photos and promises. They get the memories without the man, and the celebration with no fear of future acrimony.'[52] After seven years single, artist Tracy Emin married a rock in her garden. The rock would never let her down and was something she said she could identify with.

Self-marriage seems like the ultimate statement of individuality. In a curious way though, it demonstrates the bedrock nature of the need to belong with something more than oneself. Women who marry a rock or reserve a space at their wedding for a non-existent groom are performing a feat of imagination – in their minds they have found another with whom they can commit to sharing their innermost thoughts and deepest moments.

Family in change

Since the sixteenth century marriage has diversified beyond anything Luther could have foreseen. In 2013 when the Marriage Amendment Bill had its Third Reading, Green Party member Kevin Hague interpreted the passing of the Bill into New Zealand law as a message from the country to its gay and lesbian communities: 'Our society is big enough for you too. You belong – unequivocally and without having to compromise who you are.' This point was reiterated by speaker after speaker. Gay people needed to know they belonged and society should affirm it. The Bill passed by a majority of seventy to forty-four, there were heartfelt hugs all round and the debate ended with a respectful, dignified rendering of New Zealand's arguably most popular song, Pokarekare Ana. One day, gay people, just like straight people, may be pressured by their parents to 'find somebody nice, dear, get married and have kids'.

The family is evolving in other ways, too. Not necessarily for the good but certainly in adaptation to our changing world and in tandem with belonging. As families spread out across the globe, modern technology prompts constant connectivity. Members can see and speak to each other across the seas and follow the minutiae of one another's lives, even text their last words while dying under a heap of rubble. Modern family belonging also extends tentacles through vast stretches of time. As James Meek has pointed out in a review examining Jonathan Franzen's fiction,

> A generation born in the 1930s can easily have living grandchildren who might survive to see the 22nd century. That's 170 years; and the grown-up children in *The Corrections* find themselves smack in the middle of this temporal expanse, approaching middle age themselves, looking in one direction at old parents whose infirmity might last decades, and looking in the other at children of their own whose minorities will last just as long, while they themselves feel bitterly that they haven't yet lived that obscure best bit of adulthood, the part where love and money and achievement are supposed to bring them a carefree happiness.[53]

And the current economic system, with its eroding of the welfare state and the prevalence of unaffordable housing, is forcing many families to take up the challenge of helping their members out while rich families exploit the system to become super-rich dynasties. Parents take on greater and greater responsibility for facilitating their children to win in a competitive world. Children have less and less time just to be children.

Nowadays our extended families rarely belong to one geographically-based community. Weddings and funerals assemble people who have never met and most likely never will again. For a few hours, they try to piece together by hearsay the lives of the newly married or newly dead before spreading out across the globe again. Ain't natural.

SIX

COMMUNITY

A finger in the fondue

Nowadays the word community is used to include all kinds of group interaction, whether on the internet or in the physical world. In this sense, there are any number of communities one can belong to based on identification of a common interest, but when I think of community, the kind I longed for in my early married life, it's the face-to-face kind based on living in the same locality.

My longing was for a community of people who would lend each other garden tools and sugar, watch one another's children grow from babies to toddlers to teens to adults, talk over the fence or on the pavement, figure out together what they think about a new local building plan and, above all, accept each other as part of their lives. The kind of thing I read about in books by George Eliot and Jane Austen or in my university studies of traditional societies.

An anthropology course introduced me to the concept of utopias, man-made societies that could be imaginatively grasped in their entirety, unlike messy constructions that evolved over centuries. I read Thomas More's Renaissance *Utopia* and B.F. Skinner's twentieth-century *Walden Two,* but these attempts to imagine a community where people lived in harmony struck me as stifling and fake. I wanted real-life people in real-life communities – like the Amish and Hutterite communities of the United States and Canada, who set up utopian sanctuaries in the New World after suffering severe persecution in the Old. Inevitably, utopia wasn't utopia. To stay intact as a community amid the hedonism and competitiveness of their surrounding society, it was necessary to exercise control over every aspect of their members' lives. Group support was guaranteed only so long as members obeyed the rules. Any who wanted to be different or to think for themselves would be shunned or exiled, even by their own families. There was a deep sense of belonging but at the price of individual freedom. This was not the *kind* of real-life community I wanted.

At first G and I were enchanted with our new lives. Living in a small town of 7000 inhabitants was a novelty after the crowded suburbs and cities we had known in England. Parking was always available, as was farm produce. It was delightful to collect half a sheep or a quarter of a cow from a local farm and deposit it in our bought-for-purpose deep freeze. Everything was on a human scale. One evening at the cinema the projectionist for an audience of five offered to skip the adverts. We chortled.

Along with our new teacher friends we adopted the latest fads. Fondue dinner parties, a communal eating experience for non-hippies, were in high vogue. Fresh to consumerism as well as to marriage we considered it fitting to acquire a stainless steel fondue set and throw a dinner party. We prepared sticky concoctions of cheese and wine, chocolate and whipped cream. We laid out neat cubes of bread and fruit on brightly coloured plates. A candle placed at the base of the fondue heated the gooey matter to melting point, upon which our guests spiked their chosen 'dippable' and lowered it into the bowl, where the skewers jousted against each other, regardless of danger. And danger there was. At any moment someone could get burned or the sizzling goo adhering to dippable could trail its glory across polished table or spotless tablecloth. Hippy-like, we eschewed such bourgeois concerns. Through shared activity we bonded.

In my first experience of small-town life I had hoped for easy assimilation and acceptance, but we were newly arrived and our street housed a ragtag collection of people with a minimalist approach to geniality. G and I knew hardly anyone apart from teachers and those we liked most were transients, here this year, gone after a couple. The fondue bond was not strong enough for the long haul. When our friends started having children, the dinner parties stopped. While others looked to families, for us, far from home, nothing took their place.

When I swapped teaching for child rearing, I found myself increasingly isolated. At the local playcentre, I was told that my needs did not count in comparison with those of my children, who were 'the important ones'. It was not okay to leave them at the centre; that was 'dumping them on the doorstep'. A need for time alone counted for nothing. In this way I learned at first hand the inverse relationship between belonging and individuality.

Tribal pursuits

Long ago my brothers and I, cross-legged in a circle in Surrey, thumped our cut-down broom handles on the floor to the rhythm of foreign words. We learned to chant as we thumped. Our mother, homesick for New Zealand, told us that in a faraway place there lived a different kind of people who sang these songs for real. I sensed the power of tribe and longed for it. Years later in New Zealand, whenever I watched Māori singing their traditional songs tears sprang to my eyes. Caught without a handkerchief I have often had to hope no one noticed them rolling down my cheeks.

Tribal belonging was not on offer to me, but I figured I could get some understanding through reading. Around this time Dr Michael King wrote a biography of Princess Te Puea, who had been instrumental in binding her people together. Under her leadership, they transformed a swampy site covered in blackberry and scrub into a splendid marae and model village community. For years they raised dollars by giving concerts to tribes all over the North Island. To save on transport costs, performers often walked thirty miles from one venue to the next. Their shoes had to be replaced with cardboard; their disintegrating shirts, mended at the front, were held in place by a jacket and tie. The concerts revived Māori interest in the haka, which had been falling into disuse, and showed Te Puea the extent of common interest between tribes. She decided to help them become more united and better able to preserve Māori ways of doing things amid the onslaught of Pākehā culture. Through the help of the East Coast leader and politician Sir Apirana Ngata, generous government funding was made available and her tribe was able to complete the project. It became possible to host cross-tribe events on a massive scale and Tūrangawaewae Marae became the physical base of the Māori kingship.

Eight years after I arrived in New Zealand, my opportunity came. At the final class of an evening course on Māori traditions, we were welcomed by Māori elders who encouraged us to share their indigenous culture. 'This is your heritage too,' said Dr Pita Sharples, 'and you should not be afraid to claim it.' I had never thought of this and the idea went through me like an electric current. I could not leave the class that night without doing something bold. The demeanour of one of the elders encouraged me to approach her over a cup of tea. During our conversation, she invited me to attend the fourteenth anniversary of Te Arikinui Dame Te Atairangikaahu's coronation. I had no idea who I was taking tea with but she turned out to be a highly respected, sometimes controversial kuia (female elder) and her name was Mīria Simpson. She made it her mission to induct me.

Over lunch a week later she explained in detail how the event would proceed and what I would have to do. First I must approach one of the groups queuing up outside the marae and ask if I could join it. She explained that each member of 'my group', including me, would be personally greeted with a hongi or a kiss by each member of the welcoming party. Then, she said, I would find *her*. There would be thousands of people there, nearly all Māori. I was terrified, but Mīria wasn't going to let me off the hook now. 'If you went to a coronation in London, wouldn't it excite you to see all those people? Would you feel isolated because you didn't know them?' All right, yes it would and no I wouldn't.

Mīria identified strongly with her father's Scottish heritage. She told me about her first visit to the United Kingdom.

> I chose to arrive by boat so that I would see first of all the white cliffs of Dover. The channel crossing was rough and there was mist all round but I followed the direction of other people's gaze and then I could make out the white folds of rock. Above that I saw the grass swaying like Māori kuia with their welcoming ferns. Here I was, come all the way to the UK to claim my Pākehā side, and here were my Māori people, welcoming me.

Her people welcoming her on the white cliffs of Dover! Now she was talking about Queen Elizabeth:

> When I was in London and Queen Elizabeth was coming to New Zealand House, I and my Māori friends wanted to organise a welcome. Unfortunately, a Māori culture group attached to New Zealand House objected to our sudden appearance.
>
> They resented us because up until then we had taken no interest in their activities. But my friends and I didn't need an organisation in London; we had each other and felt strong in our Māori roots. The New Zealand House group were mostly non-Māori. On foreign soil they had discovered a need for New Zealand identity and developed a sense of ownership about Māori cultural events in London.

The leader of the club placed Mīria and her friends at the back of the group and forbade them to launch the welcome chant upon the Queen's appearance. Not for nothing was Mīria later nicknamed 'Taniwha No. 1'. She disobeyed. 'I knew that the Queen – she of all people – would know and understand the meaning and what was required of her.'

This reminded me of something I had read in Michael King's book. As a grand-daughter of King Tāwhiao, Princess Te Puea had been encouraged to dominate other children and as a young girl she ordered an older boy to pick up a stick for her. When he refused, she lashed him about the legs until he bled. Te Puea's mother called all her children to her.

> Listen to me. You are no better than those you have been beating. You are all equal in rank. It is only because of their agreement that you have been elevated in status so that you can be called people of consequence. So it is for you to honour these people, whether you consider them greater or lesser than you. If they are cold, give them clothing. When they are sick, look after them. It is only through the people as a whole that you will be called somebody of note. But if you have to blow your own trumpet because of this, you are worthless.[54]

Mīria trusted that the Queen of England, too, had been reared in rangatira ways.

As for me, I followed Mīria's instructions to the letter. I arrived at Tūrangawaewae just after nine in the morning, and succeeded in attaching myself to a group. Together we were motioned by wardens to go through the gates. The waiting hosts began their karanga or welcome chant, which was answered by kuia in my group. This continued until we rounded the corner onto the marae, where I found myself before Māhinārangi, the meeting house built by Te Puea and her people. In front of it was a bust of Te Puea, wearing her hallmark scarf. On the left-hand side of the meeting house, the tangata whenua or host party were waving ferns. My group was motioned to sit down on the right-hand side, with women and children at the back.

Then began the exchange of speeches, first by one of their speakers, then by one of ours. One of our kaumātua laid down an envelope containing koha (contribution). The other side picked it up. Members of my group came forward to sing a song. We all went up to greet the tangata whenua. The women offered their cheeks, the men pressed my nose in hongi or just shook hands. Some offered a friendly greeting which I fondly imagined went something like, 'Greetings Pākehā, it's really good to see you here!'

I spent the rest of the morning with Mīria, watching the public welcoming of other parties onto the marae. Again and again a speaker enumerated the long line of begetting that preceded them – as though their individual self were of minor importance and what mattered was to establish their belonging. When I asked Mīria why the delighted chuckles in response to a particular speaker, she said it was a reference to someone who had died, a description of his physical appearance: 'He was well known to be ugly.' As each speaker evoked the coming of the canoes and the fishing of the North Island out of the sea I saw the drama unfold before me, and as each speaker identified his tribe, his river and his mountain, the physical environment began to feel very present. The weather was inclement but rain stopped nothing. Dancers in traditional clothing called piupiu lay down on the concrete as though it were soft dry grass. I had to look up at the sky to be sure it really was raining.

Later in the afternoon, Mīria took me to Pare Waikato, the sleeping house where we were to stay overnight. Dozens of mattresses had been laid side by side along the length of the building. Two inner rows were laid back to back. The windows sported bright floral curtains, and, beneath the many mirrors, vases of flowers perched on little shelves. Every sleeper was provided with a sheet and a pillow in a hand-embroidered pillowcase. Numerous wastepaper baskets dotted the room, which was clean and fragrant.

But this was more than just a place to sleep. This was another public speaking space on the marae. Later in the evening, we lay on our mattresses and listened to people talking about the Black Power gangs and whether or not they should be welcomed onto the marae. Everyone spoke in Māori and all I could catch was the occasional English word, 'Black Power', 'patch' and 'that's right'. I asked Mīria why people spoke sitting down. 'That's one of the things the elders tell you as you are growing up: you sit down when you speak,' she said. Sometimes everyone in Pare Waikato was listening to one person; at other times the discussion involved a small group, but anyone could join in. There was much chuckling and nodding of heads. I commented to Mīria that most of the discussion was open to everyone.

We like to keep things general. You don't bring up topics which don't concern everyone, you don't talk about matters that concern only your tribe. You might sometimes whisper, but men hate being whispered at. I frown on it too. I like the public nature of the house.

Mīria lent me a body singlet and a long black petticoat to sleep in. With both men and women sleeping in the house I wasn't sure how to go about getting undressed. Not wanting to appear prudish, I began stripping off, but Mīria intervened. 'Turn your back to these men, put the petticoat on before you take your trousers off. Be modest.' She pointed to some girls just down from us and told me to observe how neatly they were doing it. The relief of rules! Mira opened up her bag like a blanket and spread it over us both. I slept fitfully, anxious not to rob Mīria of her share of sleeping bag, but as I listened to the peaceful breathing of those around me it was as though we were all in one vast bed together.

Far too soon I was woken by a light blazing into my face and voices. 'Good morning, kuia' and 'Wakey! Wakey!' People started talking and laughing again. It was five o'clock. I had woken at the pā.

During karakia, the morning service, I caught the word Ezekiel. The people joined in singing a hymn. Mīria and I talked quietly to each other. Suddenly Mīria realised that everyone else was up and Pare Waikato was emptying out. The mattresses were piled high, the wastepaper baskets were full.

'Shame on us!' she cried, and we raced to catch up. Everything, including the wish to avoid opprobrium, spoke of belonging. I understood, even without understanding the language of karanga, mihi, kōrero or karakia, that these people belonged.

As I emerged from Pare Waikato in Mīria's petticoat, I saw the roof of Māhinārangi picked out in little lights, the river beside, the mountain beyond, people moving in the dim morning light. Me moving too, on my way to the ablution block. The sun, struggling to find a patch of blue through which to shine in the early morning upon his people. Te Puea, with her decisive, friendly smile.

If you google 'Tūrangawaewae' you will find that little has changed. Queen Te Atairangikaahu is dead now, succeeded by King Tuheitia. Metaphor and symbolism are still present, still working their magic to bind people together. Here is Mamae Takerei in full flood:

Who symbolises autonomous identity on our marae? It is

Māhinārangi, descendant of Porourangi. What more needs to be said? She represents the epitome of female paramount. Turongo and Māhinārangi connect all the tribes of the Māori people.

So, reach for the basket hanging in the house and extract the white, red and black threads and weave together those connections that link us to King Tuheitia under the authority of his ancestors. The day he was crowned king, the names of Pōtatau, Tāwhiao, Mahuta, Te Rata, Korokī, Dame Te Atairangikaahu and Tuheitia were recited. Tūrangawaewae is the elegant lady who cares for the people, feeds and loves them with grace and faith. Forever and a day.

If I must sum up my weekend at the marae I can do no better than to recall Mīria in Pare Waikato as we listened to the hours-long discussions; Mīria beside me on the mattress with radiant face, saying, 'This is life to me.'

Meanwhile in suburbia

When, after several years, I drove through the small town where I once passed ten years, it was as if my life there had never been. The teachers had moved on, friends had moved away, shops had disappeared, the garden into which I had poured unstinting love and labour was a tidy geometry of square lawns and oblong beds filled with Ferrari-red salvia. Even the family I had known had dissolved – my husband was no longer my husband and our children had abandoned childhood.

I have lived in cities for decades now and have stopped yearning to embed myself in one community life. Instead I cherish individual strands of community experience. Strands designed, like Lego, for maximum flexibility with minimum commitment.

In my own street, which is dissected by a busy road, I am on 'nodding acquaintance' with most of my neighbours and we congregate once a year at one of our houses on a 'bring something to eat and drink' basis. Chatting over a glass of wine we generate a convivial spirit and there is always a strong desire at the end of each gathering to repeat it 'before too long'. In between we exchange greetings on passing one another in the street. We take an interest in each other's gardens and sometimes bring home cuttings. Pauline and John across the road exchange books and ideas with me, while the next-door neighbours on both sides are friendly and ever-collaborative around fencing and tree-pruning issues. Even if these neighbours might be hidden from view when I am in my garden, the very fact of knowing they are friendly makes me feel more at home on my own property.

At election time, I get a sense of community by attending local meetings. I sense community when I queue up to vote at the local primary school. Or when I attend a lecture across the road at the native bush reserve. Sometimes I help one of my neighbours checking rat traps and replacing the dehydrated rabbit bait.

And then there is shopping – an experience meaningful though fleeting, fleeting but endlessly repeatable. I only have to go to my local garden centre to be greeted by name by Cindy, who will do her best to help me work out what plant I need for a dry, shady patch under a tree. Down the road at Mitre 10 I am entitled to someone's full attention for all the time it takes to describe what tool I want and for them to find it for me. Together we discuss price, weight, quality, durability, fitness for purpose. Both of us will be genuinely interested in the conversation and if we each give of ourselves a little bit we'll have a sense of well-being at the end of it. We'll share a joke or discuss an item in the news. I suppose it's unsurprising that the majority of my community encounters are based around capitalism.

Here's a day in the life of myself. Yesterday. At 9am I phone Charles the printer about the non-delivery of my mother's memoir. He promises to chase up the courier. It becomes a shared task for the day, he chasing up the courier, me reporting its continued non-appearance at my mother's panting door. I call on Reuben at Form Furniture and we discuss a little cabinet he is going to make, something small but beautiful to hold my entertainment equipment. He says I have to choose between real wood or mdf, varnish or oil and as I consider, the sexiness of timber and the sensuality of oil hover like fragrances in the air. After lunch I phone Geoff from Home&Dry about replacing an ecological light bulb that has died far in advance of its advertised life. Geoff drew up an action plan about a year ago to help me make my home 'warmer, drier, healthier, greener and cheaper to run', so there's a sense of renewed acquaintance. He promises to call in with a replacement the following day. Then I talk to Jim, my computer pro-fessional, about whether I should follow Microsoft's urging and buy a new operating system. Jim takes no prisoners: 'Do absolutely nothing.' We discuss Microsoft's insatiable appetite for profit and somehow the conversation gets onto sugar and how it is now public enemy number one, at least according to the media.

In all these exchanges, I focus with another person on a shared project. Once the project is achieved I won't see him or her again until I dream up another one, but I can have encounters of this kind every single day. They are always meaningful, they make me feel I matter. And though Cindy will leave the garden centre to take care of her ailing mother, I'll see her at the supermarket checkout and even at the hairdressers, and we'll chat. She'll ask how my garden is, and I'll ask after her mother. Such brief encounters heal the weary soul. Shops are our meeting houses for communities bound together by capitalist society.

Tama

In the tiny Grand Duchy of Luxembourg my daughter Tama is 'learning a foreign community' – a process similar in many ways to learning a foreign language. It has made her consciously aware of what is involved in becoming part of a community.

Tama and her husband Daniel spent the first four years of their married life in Christchurch before returning to Daniel's native France, but in 2009, work opportunities took them and their two children to Luxembourg. After they had been there for three years, I asked Tama if she felt at ease in her local community.

'Yes, but I'd feel *more* at ease if I could speak Luxembourgish. There are three languages: French, German, Luxembourgish. I know French, I'm getting German and then I'll learn Luxembourgish to some extent – even if it's just phrasebook stuff, being able to say hello or ask for a loaf of bread. When we were buying the house, we dealt with the lawyers in French but they talked to each other in Luxembourgish. The plans for the house are in German and the contract is in French – so there are all these different languages going on. If you can speak German and understand the architect's plans, that's already helping even if you can't speak Luxembourgish. Our organic vegetables come from Germany, they are delivered by a German and the people who came to fix the windows are from Germany. Having different languages is useful in the supermarkets. I had a big culture-shock moment when we first came. I stood there for ages because I didn't know what things were and I couldn't find what I wanted. We go to Auchan, where everything is in French. Then we go to Delhaize, that's a Belgian supermarket, because they have hummus and some things we'd have in New Zealand. Then we go to Cactus, which is a Luxembourgish supermarket with another range of products again, and there are German supermarkets as well.

Everybody chooses where they go according to their taste. A lot of people take a bit of each.

'People in Luxembourg switch all the time from one language to another to another to another, depending on the circumstances and the situation. Much of the media is in German, the administration is in French, they just switch. So the more you can switch and the more you've got all those languages, the more comfortable you would feel. I expect to learn the languages wherever I live. I don't like it when I can't. Everything is much more trouble if every time you go to a shop you have to psych yourself up to think how you're going to ask for this and that.'

At the beginning, Tama found she had to learn many new rules about behaviour.

'It's more formal. Like if you invite people round for dinner you can't invite them round for a plate of pasta. And I think people make more effort with their clothes. You have to learn the ways of doing things, how it works in cafes and restaurants for instance. At first you don't know what to do, you sit there thinking, do I sit down or do I go to the counter? You feel much more comfortable when you know.

'You have to learn to operate according to the seasons. So at the end of October you need to change your car tyres for the winter. If you leave it too late you have problems. I used to wait until it got cold before I started looking for winter coats for the kids, but they're all gone by then. You have to know when you should be doing each thing and do it at its proper time.'

As Tama had lived for several years in France before coming to work as a translator in Luxembourg, she was able to compare the experience of making friends in the two countries.

'I never really felt I cracked it with French people. They are more reserved. At parties, they won't ask you many questions and then you're not supposed to ask anyone what they do for a living – but I haven't worked out what else you can ask them. You're supposed to come up with witty things to say. I find it artificial.

'At the school gate, they seem to need to *see* you a number of times before they want to talk to you, it might be ten, it might be twenty. Then you become part of the furniture and you can talk to them and they'll talk to you. In New Zealand, you would just go up to someone and talk to them. I didn't get a very good response doing that in France. At the beginning, you tend to think it's personal. If you wait until you look familiar then it's different.

'I'm reading a novel at the moment by someone who lived in Lux-embourg. There's a character who describes the different nationalities at an international school, including 'the eternally smiling Austra-lians' and 'the aggressively friendly Kiwis'. I suppose we just go up and ask people questions and talk to them, but for other people that's not very normal.

'Because I work for the EU, I mostly mix with English-speaking people, so it's easier than it was in France. But even here I'm always censoring my language and changing words to make it fit English people, whereas at home I can just think how I want. I modify my accent here so that people understand – whereas at home I just let go.'

Jenny: Have you had any problems with isolation over this period?

Tama: At the beginning in each new place I'd feel isolated because I didn't know anybody. After about six months you know people, but you realise you don't know them very well, so you feel isolated again. Then you carry on a bit more and after a couple of years you have got a few people you know quite well – but not enough of them. After three or four years it starts to fall into place and you have enough people you know well enough.

Jenny: So how many times have you had to go through this?

Tama: Four. Strasbourg, Christchurch, Montpellier, Luxembourg. So when we came here we wanted to stay unless it was dreadful. We were not looking for it to be bad, we were looking for it to be good. Unless Daniel had dreadful problems finding a job or we really hated it for some other reason, we didn't want to move again.

Jenny: It must take a big toll on you, going through that period.

Tama: Yes. We would get to that point and enjoy it for a year or so, then we'd leave it all behind. In each of those places we left behind good friends. Then you have to start all over again with working out who is suited to you. You think someone might be a friend but then they obviously don't want to be your friend, and there are others who want to be your friend but you don't want to be theirs. All the small talk you have to make to get to decide! It's horrible. We got saturated really. We're both friendly, outgoing people so we did it each time, but we got to the end of our tolerance.

We just wanted to settle somewhere and have friends and build up more friends and relax with the friends and not have to be making more. We have moved around so much, we just want to be settled somewhere and here is fine.

Jenny: Do you have a feeling of greater understanding between you and other Kiwis in Luxembourg because of shared culture?

Tama: With some Kiwi people. Not others. Some I react against and some I feel at home with. Like with my friend Julia, I feel we are closer friends because of our shared culture and a shared way of looking at things here, than if she had come from England or Ireland. There is a deeper level to it. We understand where we have come from, as well as the place where we are now and so we look at it in a similar way.

The question of education for the children involved difficult issues. After much soul-searching Tama and Daniel decided not to send them to the local school.

'It was tricky because a local school would have been the easiest way to meet local people and integrate. The boys go to a European school for the children of EU staff, so there are children from many different countries but hardly any from Luxembourg.

'Nicolas was already six and he would have been going into a school where the children had been speaking in Luxembourgish from age four and were then switching to German. It would have meant having two languages at home, English and French, that were no use at school, having to pick up Luxembourgish, learning German through Luxembourgish and not being able to communicate with the other children in the playground. It just seemed too difficult.

'People have said to me, "Oh, but children are resilient. He would have learned." Well he would have learned, but I think he probably would have got depression for a year. We've talked about it and he says he is so glad we didn't do that. He found it hard enough to cope, leaving all his friends and coming to a big school in a new city and having to get to know new children. That was very stressful for him even in English and I think a local school would have been too much.

'But there are other factors too. The Luxembourgish system is very traditional. There's a lot of rote learning and a bit of humiliation of children. Teachers get upset if you write with the wrong-coloured pen.

Some things should be underlined in red and others in blue, and if you do the wrong thing it's *all* wrong, and I've heard of people wanting to move to the European school because they don't like this discipline. I didn't like that approach in France and this was an escape route, as the teachers come from the UK and have a UK approach.

'The cost has been integration in some ways, but 50% of the population of the city are foreigners and even in the country 40% are foreigners. There is much less here to integrate *into* than in France, and in the end I decided it's okay to integrate myself into the foreign aspect of it. As long as I'm involved in things like the school, that's enough. My local integration may simply involve speaking a bit of the language and feeling comfortable in the shops and so on. I may never have any Luxembourgish friends, but that's okay – though if I do meet some that would be fantastic. But even if you only mix with foreigners you are still mixing with half the population.'

Tama and Daniel found Luxembourgers more reserved than people back in New Zealand and that slowed down the process of integration.

'We have had our neighbours round for coffee but we've never been inside their house. The wife is very nice, she brings us cakes and fruit, so I think she likes us but we've never been into the house. Matisse plays over the fence with a grandchild who comes to visit every now and then. For two years they played over the fence, throwing balls over, and just this year the neighbours invited him over the fence and he played in the garden, but he still never went into the house. So it's not like it's easy.

'Daniel joined the volleyball club at the beginning but he never felt he really belonged. They would speak to him in French but because they speak to each other in Luxembourgish he felt out of it, and they weren't that welcoming really. If you could speak Luxembourgish it would probably be different, because they would feel you'd made an effort and then you would be part of the conversation. I don't think it's true that people are unfriendly, I just think they have different ways of being.'

In an effort to feel more at home, Tama wanted to go walking, as she had in New Zealand, and learn to relate to the landscape.

'In France, I didn't do much walking. It was difficult because the children were young, and I didn't really know where to go, plus it was often too hot. When we moved to Luxembourg the children were still young and it was often too cold and wet, but after about a couple of years I made an effort to be out more in nature. We bought a book of forest walks to do with the children so that I could get to know the Luxembourg landscape and start to appropriate it as my own. That made a big difference to feeling at home. I felt like I knew where to go. This book showed me places where I could see beautiful things without being surrounded by people. It's helped me not to pine for my landscape in New Zealand, but to find beautiful things here and take that on. We've done it as a family.

'Another thing that helped was buying our plot of land. Suddenly we owned this piece of Luxembourg, a very small piece but a piece nonetheless. I think once the house is built and we are living in it, that will feel different again, but even just having land we can visit and know is ours – that makes a connection.'

Janet

Janet* grew up in a community that reads like something out of Alan Duff's *Once Were Warriors*. In the 1950s, people kept quiet about what they saw going on in other families – or even within their own – and it was many years before Janet was able to live without being subjected to violence. Now she is nearing retirement age after a productive working life which included bringing up her son to become a balanced, kind and highly respected person.

As a child, Janet was frequently beaten by her father, her siblings far less often. Intervention by other family members was out of the question. She understood that in some fundamental way she did not belong in her family. She felt 'black to their white' and, as if to underline the difference, her skin colour was darker than theirs.

'When I was nine, I marched up to my auntie's house. I needed to find out who the hell I was and where I actually belonged. "I'm here to find out who my real father is." "Don't be silly, Janet, you know who your father is, your father is your father." "Well he's not mine."

Janet started biting her nails, sucking her thumb and wetting the bed. Then her great-grandmother, the mainstay of her life, died and weekends away from home abruptly ceased.

'It became even more slippery for me after that. He had this huge stick for the copper – there were times when I couldn't go to school because of the bruising. As for belonging, I didn't want to belong there anyway. There was a nice lady up the road who was in a wheelchair, so I ran up there one night but he chased me and never stopped

---

*   Names and other identifiers in this section have been changed.

beating me, even in her lounge. It was a small town. Children were seen and not heard and anybody that had a gob on them like I did was in trouble. I didn't realise that then, I thought it was something in me that they so hated.'

Her parents tried everything to make Janet stop sucking her thumb. They tied her arm behind her back at night and put aloe on the thumb, but nothing made any difference. The bedwetting continued too.

'And of course that was grist to their mill. I was being even *more* naughty and I was ousted even further from the family group. They used to go for a Sunday drive sometimes. I wasn't invited and that was okay with me. Then one particular Sunday when I was fourteen, I *was* invited. They took me to Tokanui Mental Hospital and left me there.

'Now, to be fair, I questioned everything. I'd say, "Well I don't see why I have to do that." So I was put in the mental ward. They used to take us younger girls to stand outside the rooms where they did the shock treatment. I was so frightened, I wet myself. I wasn't hanging about for my turn, so off I went. I walked from Te Awamutu to Hamilton along the railway lines.'

After a few days, Janet managed to get to Auckland, where she found a job at a bed-and-breakfast, but the police were looking for her and it wasn't long before she was recognised and sent to another mental hospital.

'Now that was Belsen. Oh God, we had people who urinated into a thermos flask and served the contents to other patients as afternoon tea. We had a German woman tied to a chair and she used to stand up, chair and all, heiling Hitler every thirty minutes. You had your defences up the entire time because there were so many things that could happen to you there. I was fifteen by then and I got through it by singing the Beatles' latest hit 'Love Me Do', all day long. Then I went back to court and the magistrate said that according to the tests they'd done, there was nothing wrong with me and he could see no reason to keep me incarcerated so he sent me back to my parents!

'I wasn't going to hang around there so I took off to the next town. Eventually I got some work and a bit of money then I buggered off to Auckland again. I slept on the streets and after a bit I joined up with two others. There was a particular restaurant that had white, starched tablecloths and I reckon the owner knew we were hungry because there was always some pretty good food left close to the bin.

'We were only young kids so we went where we were accepted and inevitably we fell in with the wrong people, so it went downhill pretty quick. The cops called you Idle and Disorderly if you didn't have two pounds and tuppence. Well we didn't have two pounds and tuppence, we didn't have tuppence, so the police could pick us up if they wanted. I went to court on several occasions, for stealing and so on. I was sleeping in a telephone box one day and somebody peed on me. I could have strangled the little bugger. I had no mates. I was a loner and I still am.

'In prison my friendships with the other inmates were pretty tenuous. You had to make sure that mentally you were one step ahead of them, but they were just as crafty as you. I got tougher in there. My health was a bit rocky because I had pyuria [pus in the urine] and gum disease. Result of poor diet. All that had to be treated, but I finished School C in borstal and, somehow, I passed. I was very determined.

'Survival. That was it, nothing beyond today. I was twenty when I got out for the last time, but I knew that this time I was never going back. The superintendent said to me, "When will we see you again?" I said, "You won't see me again." And they never did.

'I started off as a mail clerk in a Woolworths bulk store in Wellington. I loved it. Then they gave me a job in accounts and that's where I got the grounding for the work I did later. It was money and I had a flat on my own. I didn't have much left over at the end of the week but I had a bath, I had a bed and a radio. I could lock my door and it was *my* door and I was quite happy. Stealing was probably easier but – I don't think anybody steals because they like to. I stole because I was hungry and I didn't have anybody I could go to. I came from such a *closed* community.

'One day when my prison days were over my granddad took me to the cricket. We were sitting down, eating corned beef sandwiches, and I said, "Do you know that I've been in prison, Granddad?" And he said, "Was that when I used to get those brown envelopes? No, I didn't know, nobody told me, Janet."

'When I wrote to Granddad, I didn't say where I was. There was just no bonding at all. We were just individuals flopping along beside each other, no cogent thought, no nothing.'

Back in free society Janet began to construct a workable life. She returned to the Waikato and, armed with a reference from Woolworths, found a job. After a few months, she had saved enough to buy a car. Then she met someone she liked. It was time to settle down, she felt, but that also meant becoming part of an extended family and Janet's early childhood had conditioned her to fear large gatherings.

'Steve was one of eight children, his mother was one of eleven and his father was one of fifteen. I thought, Oh, my god, how am I going to cope? But then I put on my coping face and got on with it. I still won't get on a crowded bus. I don't go into movie theatres full of people.'

The couple was unsuited for the long haul but for a while they were happy. After the divorce, Janet returned to Wellington, where Steve's aunty and uncle offered her a home. She remained close to them until they died many years later.

'I've been shown some really true kindnesses in my life. One night when I was living in Auckland, I was wandering down Grey Lynn, looking fairly dishevelled I suppose. The houses were close to the footpath and there was a lady sweeping her porch. As I wandered past she said hello. Immediately I felt suspicious, but, long story short, I went into her house and she ran me a bath. The bathroom had tongue in groove walls, isn't that amazing? I had this bath, I washed my clothes, she gave me a cup of tea and some toast. I never knew her name nor did she know mine. It was those little balls of humanness that made me think, Well maybe. But it took a long time, it took a lot of years for me to get there.

'I was probably in my late twenties when I thought, You can either go on with what you have been living in and believing in, or you can strike out the other way and see what life on the right-hand side has got to offer. I was about thirty-two before I got a handle on it all. By then I'd been married and divorced and married again. My second husband was pretty bad with money but I decided, Well, we're going to buy a house, and I went through it in steps. I was a compulsive planner. I wouldn't deviate from my plan no matter what. I'm not so bad now because I'm more open to the odd failure. I know I can't be what everybody thinks I ought to be and most of the time I can't be what *I* think I ought to be.

'You can't keep wandering around in the quicksand, you just can't, you've got to have some purchase on life. I had violent tendencies, especially when I was in prison, and that needed to go. When I was going for a job, I used to have a panic attack thinking: Now, if they say you haven't got the job, don't swear, don't say anything bad, and it was such a strain. It was the unlearning of all the bad stuff.'

Life steadily improved. When Janet was forty-one she and her second husband had a baby. As Caleb grew, he brought her deep happiness. And a few years later, she finally found her father – through the efforts of her older brother, who, looking for his own dad, found hers instead.

'So then it starts to gel and you're not wobbling around in jelly. You think, I actually belong to somebody. And my father was marvellous, he wrote me the most beautiful letters. I told him to call in next time he was cruising by. One day he stood at the door, a very tall man, and he said, "It's been a long time since I've seen you." I said, "I have never seen you," and he said, "Yes you have, you were about two days old." He had gone to the nursing home and that was when Mum told him she had married somebody else. Because he was Māori they weren't allowed to marry. I can still see her walking down the block on a Sunday night, arms linked with that other bastard, because that's respectability, the two white people. But that's okay. I don't favour either my dark past or my white past, my blood is red like everybody else's.

'I don't have to know everything there is to know. I just have to know that somewhere in the past I belonged – and I did. Apart from with my oldest brother, who is illegitimate, I don't have anything much to do with my other siblings. When my stepfather died, I wasn't invited to the wake. I felt very sad that my stepfather and I never got on. He was an army man, so when I knew everything was cracking on at the funeral, I set up my computer and I played the Last Post.

'I no longer populate my life with people who cause me grief. I'm probably the closest I've ever come to belonging to somewhere now. I'm secure here in this house and I've got a job that I've had for ten years. I know I'm going to have to retire and that is going to be hard because not only does it mean I'm old, it means the end of my working life. But there will be things to replace it with.

'I've still got friends from when I was married to Steve, people who knew us both. No matter what I was or appeared to be, to them I was worth knowing and they've held on to the friendship. One of them said to me recently, "You were such a tough bugger. You used to lean up against that wall, and everyone wanted to reach out to you, but we all knew, just don't go there." And I said, "I'm sorry about that." She said, "Oh, that's all right, we're still around, aren't we? Still friends." For the first time, I have peace of mind. I suppose that's it, I have peace of mind.'

A few years ago, Janet met my brother Timothy through work and they became close friends. He introduced her to books.

'Tim is my best mate. You can always rely on him to come up with something you don't want to hear! Always, and he does it in such a lovely way, with words you have never heard of and I run for Wikipedia. I've never finished tilting at windmills [*Don Quixote*] and I never will. I *love* it but once I finish it he moves away from being my friend really...

'And I absolutely adore your mother. We went and saw *Ladies in Lavender* together at the Rialto and I thought she'd died, because she just never moved, she didn't blink or anything, she was so engrossed in it. You learn a lot from those sorts of people in your life... I remember when I came to Auckland and stayed with you overnight. Tim still remembers when I said, "Why would she let me in, she doesn't even know who I am." And Tim said, "Well I told her."

End of life

My mother's community is designed to extricate people from the terrors of diminishing human capacity and the loneliness and boredom that often come with it. For years she had coped impressively with a complex and demanding life, but as time went on and she saw my father was gradually dying, she lost her motivation to handle all the demands of life in suburbia. Even the garden seemed like an endless round of strenuous jobs requiring attention. In a retirement village, all such worries would be taken care of. Suddenly, that was where she wanted to be.

Ageing forces change because we ourselves change. Bones and teeth soften, vessels and soft tissues harden. In olden times we hardly noticed such changes because as a rule we didn't grow very old and death came suddenly, but that's all over. Now we grow older and older and when we can no longer 'do for ourselves', carers of various kinds come to 'do' for us. As our legs cease to move us and breath comes shorter, it's easier for our carers to do all the jobs themselves than to lend a helping hand.

In earlier times when folks grew old, they were often taken in by family. And what could be nicer than being surrounded by loving children and grandchildren? But we don't want lace caps any more, we don't want rocking chairs. We've got individual identities that define who we are and how we belong. And our children, stressed about getting to work or ferrying their own offspring to football and jazz ballet, find it difficult to accommodate an old person's relentless demand for individuality and control. It's easier to sit us in a corner while they rustle up some dinner, but heck, we want to help! Yes, to help – we don't want the corner, that creeping assault on the link between who we were, who we are, and who we want to be. Without this, we cannot lead an authentic life and do not belong anywhere.

But, oh dear, bits of our bodies and minds are changing. We cannot do what we used to do. We cannot go where we used to go. We are helluva slow compared with how we were and it's only going to get worse. Soon Voltaire's question will be our broken record: 'What am I? Where am I? Where am I going? Where did I come from?'

Retirement villages can be brilliant at taking away our worries. My mother lives in one run by warm-hearted and enlightened carers. Health-wise, there are nurses regularly at the village centre, residents are given an alarm pendant to call for help in emergency, and can ask for transport to get to the doctor. Maintenance-wise, someone will come and change a light bulb or mend whatever gets broken. Gardeners will assist with beautifying the space outside your unit or do it for you if you prefer. You can get help with hanging out and bringing in the washing and with housework. On the sociability front, dozens of activities cater for every kind of personality type. Residents run these themselves and are free to create more. Food-wise, a convivial, non-profit restaurant delivers dinner on request (plates collected next day) and a communal lounge attached to the restaurant is available, not only for residents' meetings and activities, but for family clans to celebrate anniversaries, birthdays, whatever. In other words, everything is kept in good nick, you are surrounded by good cheer, and you don't need to worry about a thing.

But human beings need more than a worry-free zone. For my parents (initially it seemed possible that my father would be able to live there too), one of the important things offered by the two-bedroom unit at the lower end of the village was that it looked out upon hills. To reach it they drove down a meandering road bordered by colourful gardens. No straight lines. No uniformity. These things reminded them of earlier homes they had loved.

Ostensibly a retirement village offers older people a new community, somewhere they can belong all over again, even though they have just arrived. But because belonging is mediated by identity, every individual has to make choices. How much a part of the community do you want to be? Do you want to join in group activities or take an active role in the management side of things? If you don't, then what will your belonging consist of? It's going to come down to what makes you feel you can be yourself in the presence of others.

For John and Betty James, who live halfway down the hill from the village centre, it was a no-brainer to become involved in village life. In their younger years they had managed half an acre of land in the bush.

John was a farmer, had been a firefighter and helped with Riding for the Disabled; Betty ran exercise classes. Now Betty tutors tai chi and aquarobics classes and belongs to the Monday walking group. She is a keen user of the library. John plays bowls three times a week, snooker every day. Sometimes one activity almost runs into another and they have to hurry to be in time. 'There is never a dull moment here,' says John. 'We're busy every day.'

My mother was never a joiner but when she came to the village, she tried out a few activities. One was mahjong, through which she felt a connection back to her own mother, who played with a set of tiles made from bone. She joined the book club too, but both these activities asked for a level of commitment she found a bit too intense. For physical exercise she tried pétanque and the walking group as well as aquarobics, but these proved too stressful for failing limbs.

The truth was, it was her home activities that meant most to my mother in terms of belonging and identity. During her long married life she had often travelled with my father on field trips to treat eye diseases and collect data that later enabled him to develop ground-breaking medicines. While the Shah of Iran was in power, they used to take a team of doctors, including Iranians, into remote villages and work intensively for three weeks twice a year. They did similar work in Sudan and Nigeria. Eventually they created a centre in London for preventive ophthalmology. It offered training and career advancement to people from developing countries, with a view to their returning and helping their own people. After my father's death, my mother began recording these experiences, in the hope that later generations of the family would find them of interest. From over 2000 slides, she compiled albums of annotated photographs. She produced illustrated booklets telling the stories of their travels and endeavours. Thus she shaped her life in retrospect. In her nineties she went on to write a full-blown memoir with side stories on the lives of her parents and their forbears. The memoir in particular brought a new fear – the fear of dying before she completed it. Apart from that she was happy: 'The day is never long enough.'

Despite not taking part in village activities, my mother has a sense of belonging in the community.

'Everybody is so kind and always there for each other in a rather special way that you don't often find in the wider community. The people here have known of another era. We've all got that kind of back-ground which the young don't understand, it's completely different.

We have retained what we liked of it, so that gives us a bond. We have problems but you never hear anybody talk about them. You go up and down the village and you'd think everybody was all right, but if you get to know a bit more about them, you realise they're not. That doesn't matter if they can cope and they are helped to cope.

'I'm a bit of a village hermit. I don't mean to be and they understand that. I have no feeling that I am being organised. It's up to me to make the most of what they offer or go my own way, it doesn't matter. Nobody is criticising me. The staff recognise we are all human beings with different needs and they give us opportunities to help us find what gives us pleasure, but there's no pressure to join in more than we want to. I've got all the freedom in the world here.

'It's a funny thing but Dad and I, so long as we were together, we didn't care where we were. We'd quite as happily have stayed in Iran forever because we loved it there. We loved the people and their sense of humour. We were working as a team, which is always exhilarating. I feel as if I'm a citizen of the world really. I don't want to be tied down to any particular country. Even now that Dad's not actually here, I feel as if he's still here with me. I'm not on my own. They are always wanting me to join the singles club but I can't do it. I don't feel as if I'm single. I mean, they have a lovely time, they have a meal together every few weeks and the kitchen is always doing something special for them, but somehow I don't want to. I'm very comfortable just being with Dad here. I'm not looking for another life. I have my photograph of him on the dresser and I keep a few fresh flowers beside it. Alstroemerias are very good, they last for ages.'

As my father's mind and body deteriorated it became clear he would never join my mother in the retirement village. One day I was shown into his nursing home lounge where residents were sitting in a big circle. I couldn't see him. Many heads were slumped deep into chests. No one was speaking, no one was reading, no one was even looking. I scanned the faces of those I could see but there was no humanity there and it was as though there never had been. My own existence fell into question. I wanted to run away. Then I recognised my mother's friend, Ave. 'Ave! I'm the daughter of your friend Pauline Jones.' Her face became itself again. She smiled and greeted me and pointed across the circle. 'There's your father.' I went across to him and his face too became human.

As people move into extreme frailty, it's harder and harder for them to retain a sense of their own identity. Life offers them less and less reason to remember how to be human, but people such as Dr Bill Thomas, whom Atul Gawande writes about in his book *Being Mortal*, have found ways to enable even these to express their warm and caring side. Thomas persuaded his employers at the Chase Memorial Nursing Home in upstate New York to allow a menagerie of cats, dogs and a hundred birds to join the residents, along with live plants in every room. The initial result was pandemonium but gradually benefits began to emerge. 'People who we had believed weren't able to speak started speaking. People who had been completely withdrawn and non-ambulatory started coming to the nurses' station and saying, 'I'll take the dog for a walk.' Individual parakeets were adopted and named by residents, who gave the staff daily reports on their birds: 'sings all day', 'doesn't eat', 'seems perkier'.[55]

One day, when my father had reached a stage of almost complete silence, my mother and I managed to take him out for a picnic. Dad indicated he would like some port, so we stopped at the wine shop where he had spent many happy hours. Perhaps because he was seeing shops and roads after so long or perhaps because he was *outside* the grog shop, unable to go in, he suddenly said, 'Oh, I'm not in this world anymore.' We were trying our best to keep him in it but mentally he had already left and daily the divide grew wider. We tried to breach it with smiles and hugs but he and we knew he did not belong and never would again. We drove into the retirement village, past residents' allotments to a wilder part of the property where there was some bush, the kind in which he had once tramped and botanised. Suddenly he came to life: 'Oh, this is New Zealand!'

He was cold as usual, so we stayed in the car and handed him his food. Every so often a hand appeared between the front seats and we knew he was ready for more. Then his empty glass, a silent request for more port. He was enjoying himself. When we got him back to the nursing home, a staffer came to assist him out of the car, but he waved her away with the words, 'I know the anatomy of this car.' He was doctor and scientist to his core and his love of anatomy had accompanied him throughout his life.

That night he managed to contact us by phone. He told us how much he had enjoyed the day and being with us. When he was ready he ended the conversation: 'Now I'm off to slumber land.' Two weeks later he died.

SEVEN

BIOLOGICAL BONDING

Messing with the brain

There is increasing debate in the medical profession about a hormone that influences how we behave in groups. Oxytocin is anarchic, having nothing to do with reason. Its only requirement of the mind is willingness to act in concert with others.

At the face-off for their World Cup matches, the All Blacks stare down the opposition with a modern version of the ancient Māori haka. Its power is drawn from many elements: the stamping of the feet, the elongation of the tongue, the whites of the rolling eyes, the tattoos, the hands slapping against the body, the loud aggressive shouting and, above all, the synchronised rhythm. As oxytocin rages through their arteries, the performers become one multi-headed, many-armed creature. The dance triggers a state of consciousness in which there is neither pain nor fear. Within a single identity the dancers experience total trust in one another, together with shared invincibility against the enemy.

Oxytocin is not picky about which side it's on. Geoff Chapple experienced it on the Hamilton playing field during the 1981 Springbok Tour. Protests against involvement with whites-only South African rugby had been taking place throughout the country, dividing the country as it had never been divided before. Geoff described to me how the vastly outnumbered protesters on the Hamilton playing field became brave.

'We had invaded the field and as long as we were there we had stopped the game. The last time Waikato and the Springboks had played, the local team beat the Springboks and that was mythical, that was huge, so the expectations around this new clash were enormous. First there was going to be an attack from outside the ground and then we were going to pour over the fence from the inside of the ground. So when the others broke through from the outside, we ran on from the inside and we were there in the middle of the field saying, "Stop the tour!" and they couldn't play while we were there. The whole stadium was absolutely full of rugby players from Hamilton, jam packed with people wanting to see this game. So there's this little group, I mean you're talking probably 15,000 people surrounding about 200 protesters, whom they regard as being, I mean in the very mildest sense, "Get those fuckers out of here! Let us get on with our game."

'I was on the outside of this little group and so I could feel the human heat of it. We all linked arms, we were very solid, but we were in danger and we knew we were in danger, particularly as time went on and the rugby fans started beating on the tin fence. They might all rush onto the grounds and if the law was going to hold here, then basically the police had to do something about it and the police really didn't. They just stood between that crowd and us.

'This felt so strong to me, to be in that group, and I watched everyone just get brave. They were scared, a lot of people were scared, and yet there was no escape, and so you just had to bind back into the group. I had a sense of psychic energies, I know that sounds waffly but the hatred coming in, our defiance radiating out to the point where the lines almost trebled between those two where the police were, but I also had a sense that it went upwards like this, then down, our spiritual strength if you like *towered* upwards, I don't know how far, but it was just like a great big tree root.

'Yeah, I think that that's when you die for the cause. You don't cut and run. You couldn't anyway, but you don't want to, that's not what you want to do. And then we got a voice. And we realised that the voice was really strong. We had been shouting, "Go home, Springboks" and so on, which was weak but now our voice was, "The whole world's watching". There's always a sort of true chant. I don't know who said it first, but it was right. The cameras were there and they were broadcasting back to South Africa. So, "The whole world's watching! The whole world's watching!" And that made us stronger still, because we were carrying the flag.'

Oxytocin acts in different ways in different parts of the body. It's released during orgasm, labour and breastfeeding. In studies of group behaviour, when people were given nasally administered oxytocin they displayed higher levels of trust. When recounting a negative emotional event they were more willing to share at a deeper emotional level.[56] They found faces more trustworthy and were less afraid of being betrayed.[57] Even when excluded from conversation, they exhibited greater trust.[58]

Fortunately oxytocin does not make people trust those they already believe to be untrustworthy, but under its influence people find it easier to be dishonest for the sake of helping a group they belong to,[59] and will modify their own preferences to align with those of others. They will also defend others in the group and try to protect vulnerable members during conflict, though only by non-cooperation.[60]

Religious enthusiasts of the megachurch persuasion are onto the power of oxytocin. A University of Washington study has found that people worshipping in these churches experience an 'oxytocin cocktail' in the brain that can become chemically addictive. According to Katie Corcoran, a Ph.D. candidate who co-authored the study, 'The upbeat modern music, cameras that scan the audience and project smiling, dancing, singing or crying worshippers on large screens, and an extremely charismatic leader whose sermons touch individuals on an emotional level… serve to create these strong positive emotional experiences.'[61] The effect of oxytocin soon wears off and people have to go to church again to get another high. As one church member said, 'God's love becomes… such a drug that you can't wait to come and get your next hit… from God.' Thus oxytocin is turned into another readily available drug, another lifestyle choice – probably one day a bonding pill. Even the Dalai Lama, whose monks have taken part in experiments showing that meditation increases happiness by changing the brain, has said he would pop a pill to get the same effect.

Some researchers argue that oxytocin enhances all social emotions, including those of envy and schadenfreude.[62] While it can help you bond with individuals you see as similar to yourself, it may set you against those you see as different, because of race, for example, or religion. This in-group bias can extend to one's entire country and even to affection for its flag. Oxytocin cannot help with universal brotherhood – it's a hormone of the tribe. Fortunately, it cannot make us act against our personal beliefs.

The brain can further assist us to become one with a group. In 2005 a neuroscientist named Gregory Berns recruited thirty-two volunteers between the ages of nineteen and forty-one. He photographed their brains on an fMRI scanner while they tried to decide whether a three-dimensional object could be rotated to match a second one on a computer screen. When the volunteers played alone, the brain scans showed activities in areas of the brain associated with social and spatial perception as well as conscious decision making. They gave the wrong answer only 13.8% of the time. But when they were put in groups whose members gave unanimously wrong answers, they agreed with the group 41% of the time. The scans showed that, far from making conscious decisions to agree, the participants believed they had arrived independently at the same answer. It was as if the group had somehow managed to change the individual's perceptions. The amygdala of volunteers who picked the right answer despite everyone else giving the wrong one was kept busy dealing with such emotions as the fear of rejection. Berns called this 'the pain of independence'.[63] We could equally well call it the pain of not belonging and it points to why we find it so hard to dissent in a group.

Do we have an inbuilt bias against thinking for ourselves in a group? On a committee or a council, worse still a jury – can we be trusted? Is the cost of biological bias towards belonging paid for in loss of rationality?

Finally – synchronisation. Elephants and chimps beat drums when we require it, but never in time with each other, whereas humans do it instinctively and almost fresh from the womb. Singing together releases oxytocin, increasing feelings of trust and bonding, helping us overcome the pain of independence, enabling us to feel, even for a short time, that we belong. Catchy tunes and singalongs facilitate the release of oxytocin. Our bodies – hands, head, feet – start moving with the beat. Before we know it, we are acting in unison. Just listening to music can release the power of rhythm to shape our feelings and actions. In a process known as entrainment, our brains produce endorphins and the sounds we hear transform into sheer sensual pleasure. From sports events to concerts to royal extravaganza, familiar musical themes reinforce the human bonds of sorrow and celebration.

The famous annual Proms concerts in the UK use synchronisation to unite the audience, not only with one another but with audiences over the entire kingdom. 'Prommers' love being crowded together. On the final night, they wave their national flags, English, Irish, Scottish and Welsh. Helmets and hats are swathed in the Union Jack and men sport bowties in red, white and blue. At city parks around the kingdom, rain descends, but, though umbrellas are unfurled, spirits remain tinder dry. At last the concertgoers are invited to join in songs sung since the very first Prom in 1895, topping them off with the national anthem. On this night everyone belongs to the moment and the kingdom.

Synchronisation can be less benign. At the annual Arirang show in North Korea, up to 100,000 dancers and gymnasts in the world's largest stadium perform synchronised routines to praise the country's leaders and their communist ideology. A backdrop of 20,000 people holds up flipbooks of coloured card. On cue these coalesce into mosaics proclaiming how North Korea won the 'Victorious Fatherland Liberation War'. All done to music. Children as young as five take part in the festivals. The selection process takes up to four months and thousands of performers wait on standby in case someone fails to make the grade. This is community bought at any price, oxytocin harnessed to bring into being a beast that knows no individuality.

Rewiring for social media

The internet offers an alternative universe of virtual belonging. It's quite easy to get friends and once you have them you can summon their attention at any time. You can use Facebook to post a cute video of a dog and a rabbit cuddling up and be rewarded with 'comments' and 'likes'. Or you can post daily pictures of you with your new baby and receive comments about how beautiful he is and what a wonderful mum you are and how it's incredible you still look so young and gorgeous. You don't even have to remind people it's your birthday – social media will do this for you – and you will be surprised how many people send you birthday greetings. Then you can post a picture showing you with your birthday cake or tell your friends how your spouse gave you a diamond ring. They will respond by telling you how young you look, how well deserved the ring. Even if you don't get any comments, a dozen Likes will still make you feel popular.

But it may be that our brains respond to social media more than our hearts do. Every time we perform a task or experience a sensation, a set of neurons is activated. Those close to one another join together, and if we keep on repeating the task or the sensation, the linkings between the neurons grow stronger and more plentiful. As Hebb's rule puts it, 'Cells that fire together wire together'. In an evolutionary sense, this is beneficial because it enables us to adapt to changing conditions and learn new ways of doing things.

Now our neuroplasticity equipment is firing in service of our new love, the social media, enabling them to alter the way our brains work. Once we have developed new circuitry, as Norman Doidge observes in his 2007 book *The Brain that Changes Itself*, we long to keep it activated. So if we spend our time skipping from link to link to link on Facebook and Twitter, these are the circuits that will become strong and we'll want to keep doing it. Twitter fosters the addiction by continually prompting us to check how many people have interacted with our tweets. In Nicholas Carr's 2010 book *The Shallows*, he recorded that the more enthusiastic he became about MySpace, Facebook and Twitter, the more his brain seemed to be changing:

> It was then that I began worrying about my inability to pay attention to one thing for more than a couple of minutes. [My brain] was hungry. It was demanding to be fed the way the Net fed it – and the more it was fed, the hungrier it became. Even when I was away from my computer, I yearned to check email, click links, do some Googling. I wanted to be *connected*.[64]

A piece of 'flash fiction' by novelist Maggie Rainey-Smith illustrates the dilemma:

> *She Ticked Like*
> She ticked Like. Facebook was arbitrary in this way. You had either to make a comment, or tick Like. Now that she had 500 friends, and almost all of them were writers, she was trapped in a cycle of Liking. Many of her friends were publishing poems, short stories; novels even. She imagined knowing all these famous writers would enhance her own profile. But so far, she was worn out from Liking.
>
> She'd changed her profile twelve times. It was a matter of finding the right image. Friends posted photographs of shoes, cupcakes, sleeping cats, albino slugs; even grandchildren. She quite admired the profiles that remained blank. Just the white silhouette like a non-de-plume... the '*admire me for my art* and not how I look' sort of look. But she didn't have quite enough confidence in the impact of her own blank silhouette.
>
> She'd turned to Twitter for a while. People had some nice threads happening on Twitter. And she'd been punching above her weight there, talking to some really interesting people who had influence, the likes of D.H. Lawrence and Katherine Mansfield. Pinterest was her next interest. People said if you pinned interesting pictures this would make

other people interested in you. Your images became boards
and the naming of the boards could take a whole morning.
She tried not to think about the novel.

She was now engaged in a difficult digital dance. The
more she ticked Like, or re-pinned or re-tweeted, the more
people ticked Like, re-pinned or re-tweeted her. Authenticity
was something she valued. It was a tricky dance. She began
to lose the rhythm, she felt giddy, narcissistic and soon she
was face to face with her own reflection in the murky pool
of cyberspace. Finally, she logged out, before she drowned.[65]

It may be that social media works better for extroverts. A recent
study of 6428 New Zealanders aged eighteen and over suggests that
while extroverts send more messages and post more often about
themselves, introverts tend to be more passive, looking at what other
people are doing rather than doing it themselves. Those in the study
felt a more fragile sense of belonging with their social media friends
than the extroverts. Samantha Stronge, who conducted the study, suggested that introverts might be happier if they confined their Facebook
friends to their 'actual close friends'.[66]

My Facebook friends' posts tend to the excited or cheery. They're
proud of their spouse, children, friends, continuously appreciated
with likes and comments. If something bad happened to them they
report it with wit and laughter. The question arises, Can I show I'm
as loved, as balanced, as witty, as adept at finding the perfect animal
video, at showing my grandchild as cute as theirs? And anyway, do I
even have enough friends? Am I getting enough likes? Enough comments? Am I making enough comments on my friends to make them
congratulate me when I do something good like get a job or have a
birthday? This kind of belonging makes anxious narcissists of us all.

Since neuroplasticity is stronger in the young, it's not surprising
they are the ones with the strongest addiction to social media. All day
long the cell phone acts as an extension of themselves, a means of
being connected with peers and family. Among eighteen thirty-four-
year-olds, nearly half check Facebook minutes after waking up, and
28% do so before getting out of bed.[67] Their synapses demand connection 24/7. Superficial contact is a new norm for friendship and teens
are likely to share their most intimate thoughts with dozens of people
they don't really know. Their social standing is always at risk, always
having to be asserted. If they call a halt to their media involvement
they are liable to feel invisible.

Julia

Facebook does offer a type of community, however, that may avoid the dangers of narcissism, and that's the support group. Julia de Bres and her young son suffer from osteogenesis imperfecta, a rare disease of collagen deficiency in which the bones are extremely brittle and liable to fracture or break. Julia's Facebook support group helps her feel less alone.

'Although this remains a very rare disease, I now know hundreds and hundreds of people who have it, all over the world, mainly in America but lots in Australia and some in New Zealand. I feel these people really understand, without any kind of explanation needed, what it's like.

'One thing I put up last week that people seemed to really like, I put a post about how Paul and I had spent about twenty minutes in the middle of the night when Casper was crying, gently squeezing his body to work out if he was in pain anywhere before we realised that he had a snotty nose and basically he had a cold! Our first assumption was, Oh my God he's broken his leg! These are people I will probably never meet, but at moments when you're feeling vulnerable, when you've had to rush to the hospital say, people are at that moment replying to your post and saying, "I hope he's okay", at a time when your friends near home won't even know.

'Actually, I'll often not tell people in my real life. It's so exhausting sometimes to have to explain it all. I might have spent six hours in the Emergency Room on Sunday afternoon and I go to work the next day and if someone says, "How was your weekend?" I'll just say, "Good." People virtually elsewhere can sometimes be more present than those who are actually around. It's quite a powerful thing.

'I have ended up making actual Facebook friends with some of the people in the group, so they start to see what's happening in my life generally. A few of them I'm reasonably close to in a virtual kind of a way. When I thought Casper was hurt last time, I had a vision of some of them standing around us and giving me advice. It works and the others feel that too.

'They especially love to talk about things their doctors told them it was hopeless to expect their children to do, and which their kids actually did. People like to celebrate achievement despite the odds.

'But sometimes you will assume more common ground than there actually is. You don't really know these people. There are moments where you realise there's a big rift in how you think about things. Some of them I probably wouldn't get on with at all. They would have radically different political and religious views, for instance. I'm aware that some of what goes up is very much *constructed* and everyone fills in the gaps as they imagine in their minds. It doesn't take away from the fact that it's a really supportive environment.'

Neuroplasticity makes no moral judgement on the habits we develop and some choose social media for the practice of exclusion. Cyber bullies and 'trolls' aim to make their target feel unbearably isolated and unwanted. Ultimate success comes when a target commits suicide. Teenager Rosie Whitaker was a talented ballet dancer who developed anorexia and a compulsion to slash herself with a razor blade. She often visited websites where girls discussed their admiration for slim celebrities and reported attempts to take their own lives. In a blog, Rosie spoke of her struggles. Cyber bullies responded by telling her she was fat and urging her to commit suicide. A couple of months before her death, Rosie blogged, 'This girl just told me to go kill myself. I don't even know what to do. I'm sitting here crying my eyes out, praying that the people around me will be okay.' This went on for weeks until finally, a couple of hours after posting 'I'm so f******' sorry', Rosie lay down on some railway tracks where she was killed by the train to Ramsgate.

Even more focused in pursuit are the trolls. Nicola Brookes was in the habit of using Facebook for support after a severe bout of Crohn's disease in her mid-forties. But one night in 2012 she tried to defend someone on the Facebook page of a popular TV show. A boy was being abused: 'People were saying they hoped he'd get hit by a bus, or that they wanted to piss on him.' Under cover of anonymity, the trolls diverted their attention from the boy to create a new victim, dubbing Nicola child-abuser, prostitute, stalker and drug dealer. Then they cloned her Facebook account and sent paedophilic messages in her name to thousands of other internet users. They scoured the Net, unearthing details of Nicola's illness, which they exploited to humiliate her further. Support sites were a specially rich source of material. Any kind of vulnerability is music to the synapses of a troll and Nicola's situation offered just the kind they loved – a body ravaged by illness. It was as much fun as mothers of stillborn babies, Down's Syndrome kids, people grieving for loved ones. Nicola's trolls followed her wherever she went on the Net. When they found her seeking online support for a charity, they posted, 'Attention-seeking! Demented!'. Nicola was strong but not always strong enough: 'Sometimes, when I felt very alone, I broke down.' Even though she went to the police and secured the help of a legal team that forced Facebook to hand over information about the trolls, the abuse continued.

In Dinah's house, she and I talk across a table festooned with the trappings of tea and fruit cake. A white camellia floats on a blue saucer. We discuss books we have been reading and a painful spectacle we saw on TV of monks attacking a minority people in Myanmar, a country Dinah will be visiting soon. We are surrounded by sights and sounds and smells. Our conversation dings back and forth in 'real-time'. How much richer and more satisfying this is than visiting someone's Facebook page, trying to ignore adverts and email alerts, invitations to Skype, Tweet and generally go elsewhere. What a fully human thing this is, to visit a friend and share a cup of tea and good conversation. My synapses fire on all fronts as I enter the world of Dinah and she enters mine.

PART THREE

WORLD BIG WIDE

EIGHT

IN PUBLIC SPACE

Civility

At a certain point in history my English forbears found themselves in a quandary: how to live together in peace. In the fifteenth century they were being torn apart by civil war that seemed to have become the normal state of being. It was preventing them from doing things they'd rather do – like going in for commerce on a big scale. My Yorkshire forbears in particular were embroiled in the Wars of the Roses, their own house fighting with the house of next-door Lancaster. It had not always been so and it would not go on for ever.

One minute the unit of organisation is just the people in a tribe. The next minute it's all the people in a country. Within the tribe, the few hundred people get on quite well and have a sense of belonging, but they combine this with deep mistrust for those 'beyond the pale', where casual friendliness and mutually beneficial trade play second fiddle to offence-taking and unsentimental decapitation. When tribal organisation unifies into country, most people within the new unit don't know each other. It's a triumph that, while disdaining the customs of those they don't mix with and slamming unfamiliar dialects as impenetrable, they don't fight.

Of course, the transition is not a matter of minutes at all: it can meander over centuries, while people stagger through tribalism, feudalism and warring regional dynasties. During the Wars of the Roses private armies dominated the countryside and subjected the people to the terrors of lawlessness for thirty years, until the houses of York and Lancaster united through marriage and the reasons for fighting evaporated. My forbears then looked about for an idea of order, one that could underpin legitimate governance. Their first, tentative solution was courtesy. Instead of fighting with swords, warrior chieftains began to act alongside others in advising and serving royal power. Eventually they became incapable of acting independently in a military capacity even if they wanted to. Without quite intending, they had mutated into courtiers.

Civility began to trickle down through society. The middle classes quickly appreciated the advantages of replacing war with commerce and also saw the potential of civility as a pathway to peaceful leadership change. During the Renaissance, it brought refinement of the arts and sciences, along with improved technology. Above all, it brought manners. By the time the Kingdom of Great Britain was created in 1707, elections were routine and debate was no longer censored by the state. Despite great divisions of wealth, birth and class, the people understood that, regardless of spine-shattering roads and linguistic no-go areas, a shared destiny united them.

With a cast of millions, the time was long past when physical space like community hall, village green or market square could keep the kingdom together. It was necessary to move to a concept, something held in the social imagination, something Benedict Anderson, in his influential book on the origin and spread of nationalism, called an 'imagined community'. It was necessary to think not only public space but also public sphere.

Once upon a time, past and present were all one to my ancestors but by the eighteenth century this was no longer so and people no longer required long-deceased teachers and healers such as Jesus Christ or his mother to feature the same ethnicity and dress as their own. Technology enabled new ways of communicating and as people honed the arts of persuading and advising, it became possible to imagine other people living many miles off and to see oneself as part of a large-scale community continuously existing through time and geography.

In addition to individual people, society itself became a character in the work of early novelists. 'Meanwhile' was revealed to be pivotal as Balzac, Trollope, Eliot and Hardy brought unsuspecting characters into the same timeframe by depicting the society they all took part in. Newspapers worked in a similar way, as journalists juxtaposed unrelated events, bringing them within the compass of shared topicality. They would disappear, only to reappear weeks or months later, like characters in an unending Coro St in which their part had once again become relevant. Anderson illustrates the point:

If Mali disappears after two days of famine reported for

months on end, readers do not for a moment imagine that
Mali has disappeared or that famine has wiped out all its
citizens. The novelistic format of the newspaper assures
them that somewhere out there the 'character' Mali moves
along quietly, awaiting its next reappearance in the plot.[68]

Newspapers reassured people, thousands or even millions of them,
that his or her imagined world was actually rooted in everyday life. As
they sat down to breakfast with their morning paper, men and women
participated in a new kind of mass ceremony for which the buzzword
was circulation. Printing presses that never slept and Royal Mail
coaches rocketing around the country enabled them to consider, reinforce and refute one another's arguments *con brio*. These interactions
created a common space that didn't depend on physical proximity,
a space where people in their millions could experience 'a common
mind', something they could refer to as 'public opinion'. A sense of
continuity and meaning that had faltered with the collapse of religious
orientation to time and space was now restored. It offered a fine basis
for participatory democracy. A fine basis for belonging in the modern
world.

Springbok Tour

In 1981, New Zealanders' understanding of belonging in the public
sphere was tested as never before. Over the issue of racial equality one
part of the population decided to follow its cherished sport at all costs
while for another part anything except resistance was unthinkable.
The rest deplored the way the country, including its families, was
being torn apart.

Tension had been building for years. From the 1940s to the 1960s
South African rugby had pressured New Zealand to kowtow to its
apartheid system of separating black from white, and New Zealand
had complied by not including Māori players in some of its rugby
tours there. Even in 1960, when 150,000 New Zealanders signed a
petition demanding 'No Māoris, No Tour', the rugby union sent over
an all-white team. But it didn't send another one until South African authorities allowed the inclusion of Māori players in 1970. The
authorities did it the only way they knew how – by dubbing them
'honorary whites'.

For the next ten years there was dissension in the land whenever it
looked as though South Africa might play the All Blacks. In 1973, the

anti-apartheid organisation HART (Halt All Racist Tours) promised a campaign of civil disruption if the Springboks toured New Zealand. Government of the time stopped the tour, but its successor allowed the All Blacks to tour South Africa in 1976, prompting over twenty African nations to boycott the following Olympic Games. After that the Commonwealth voted to support an international sports boycott. None of this fazed or enlightened the New Zealand Rugby Union, which invited the Springboks over for a full tour and three test matches in 1981. Rugby fans applauded. Politics, they said, should be kept out of sport and they looked forward to the games.

Anti-apartheid activists tried for a government cancellation. When that failed they vowed to ensure the tour didn't happen. They aimed to halt it through civil persuasion and civil disobedience. It would mean marching in the streets. It would mean eyeballing those opposed to them. Clearly there was no common mind in the country but at this point commitment to civility was upheld by all. It was New Zealand's Public Space Spring.

My friend Eileen Cassidy was a fighter for justice all her life. Law-abiding, but a citizen of the world rather than just one country, she was prepared in 1981 to put law and order under pressure for the sake of fairness. Ten years after the tour she told sociologist and oral historian Alison Gray, 'If I ever lost my anger at injustice I would think there was no purpose in life. It has given me a focus outside myself.'[69] At about the same time she told me of her experience of demonstrating against the apartheid system in South Africa.

'There is something about facing an enemy when you know exactly why you are facing it, that can focus your entire mind and body with formidable intensity. At that time I was sixty-three and not as strong as I used to be, but when I was out on the streets linking arms with the others, I experienced such an onslaught of energy that I felt invincible.

'We failed to make it into the grounds for the second test in Wellington, despite our tickets. Pseudo tickets, I can safely say that now. So we had to come down Rintoul St, where police below us were assaulting protesters who were trying to stop the spectators getting through. My group, about forty of us, sat down, blocking access up the hill. We started chanting.

'When the police realised what was happening and began to approach, I knew a moment in time in which everything seemed to hold in my brain at once. On one side of me were the RSA rooms with "Parking for Returned Servicemen and Police Only" while on the other was the community hall. Beyond that, a sign offering accommodation and further up there were two-storey colonial houses, old and dilapidated most of them, that wound up the hill towards Athletic Park, where the game would start in the next half hour. Curtains were tied in a knot or linked back over the curtain rail or absent altogether and I thought, well that must make the rooms lighter.

'The police came level with us. I linked arms tightly with the person next to me. We all linked arms. It was our only weapon and there were nearly as many police as protesters. The sergeant shouted to his men, "Kick, kick, kick, kick" and the police advanced, lunging with their big boots, kicking into people's kidneys and stomachs.'

In his book *1981: The Tour*, Geoff Chapple also described the scene Eileen was caught up in:

> Move! Move! A police line knee-charged and rolled right over the top. The protest group held together by linking, but it began to bleed.
>
> The police tried again. The full gamut. Hair-pulling, ear-twisting, pressure holds, booting. A 27-year-old teacher sat arms-linked. A cop kicked his arm. The teacher grabbed the boot. Next time, the boot went into his head. He was kicked unconscious, bleeding from the mouth.[70]

Eileen's story continued: 'Unfortunately, I was on the outside and only had one arm to hang onto, so a policeman was able to pull me away. He kept saying, "Come on, Madam, come on, Madam now, come away" and although she hung on, Madam had to go in the end. There was a woman by the RSA rooms, pretty intoxicated, and she was shouting out quite a number of nasty words. This distracted the policeman enough that I was able to escape his grasp and dive under a big policeman's legs to join up again, but regrettably I didn't last very long.

'I was incensed at the policeman saying "kick". One of our group had a broken arm and others were suffering very badly, yet they were managing to stay peaceful. There had been so many discussions on committees and with marshals and at the big plenaries about the best way to demonstrate in the capital city. The feeling had been very strong that there mustn't be any throwing bottles, no physical activity in that way, or violence. It was just people outwitting the police, getting massive crowds – and groups of protesters going off in different directions, with the police scuttling around, not knowing quite what they were doing.

'It was then, when I saw in my own country something approaching viciousness from the police, that I realised the utter defencelessness of the Blacks in South Africa. If it was the last thing I did, I would stop that bloody tour. I took on the secretaryship of HART and worked in the office every day from nine to five.'

The protests were extremely well organised. Many were arrested, including Eileen herself. In the end only one game was actually cancelled after about 350 protesters managed to get on to the pitch, but the actions changed attitudes in New Zealand forever.

'Some mistakes were made, some hitches, and some people got very badly hurt, but it was inspiring in the way it showed what people could do if they felt sufficiently that something was very unjust and was going to lead to bad relations within the country itself. Some people weren't so much concerned with the injustices of Whites against Blacks but were upset by all the uproar and division. So, although only the second game was stopped, and due to immense police resources and a large outlay of money the tour did continue, we could be pretty sure it would never happen again until things got better for the Blacks.

'After the tour was over I didn't feel respect for the police force as a whole. I knew there were some police who were upset by it, but if they went on effecting a policy which resulted in great injustice, it didn't seem worthy of a great deal of respect. I didn't think the economic circumstances at the time were so bad that they had to do it for fear of losing their job.

'As for the upholding of law and order, that was a little myth which was strong in New Zealand society. I don't consider it is an orderly society if some members are liable to be bashed about. And the Blacks had taken a pretty bad bashing really, both physically and economically. If it is a bad law and you uphold it, you are getting into the realm of tyranny.

'Our protest showed people they couldn't get away with burying their heads in the sand and saying politics had nothing to do with sport. Also, it showed the millions of Blacks that they were not a forgotten sub-human race. In a far-off corner of the world, a large number of people felt strongly about the injustice being meted out to them. It was a message of hope to people everywhere who were suffering under tyrants and unfair systems.

'Sometimes I get a bit depressed about New Zealand, but that little show of fighting for justice gave me hope. It was a spontaneous uprising by people using their ingenuity. It showed what could be done if people were united and felt strongly.'

Divided we fall

While in one way, I belonged with the marchers, in another I did not because I could not join them in the street. I fervently hated Apartheid and had seen civility used as a shield for hypocrisy and cowardice, but the violence and hatred within the country upset me deeply. Many families divided over the issue and sometimes the rifts didn't heal.

> Although things had been far from perfect between my parents, the Springbok tour caused such tension and stress that we could not live together in the same house and function as a family unit. An example of the increase was when we, as a family, watched the evening news. Often one side would raise their voices in abuse and offensive name calling towards public figures. Later the abuse was turned in an indirect way on individual family members. This was done by blaming the chaos and disruption to rugby games on individual family members, their friends and associations. As the tour went on and the turmoil increased, the negative feelings intensified to such as degree that feelings of dislike, anger and incomprehension dominated our home.[71]

Rugby was a part of New Zealand culture I wasn't connected with. In the first couple of years I went with G to watch matches at other people's places but I neither understood the rules nor cared who won. Kiwi love of rugby excluded me so completely that I sometimes wondered if it had been a mistake to adopt the country. Every Kiwi was expected to love the All Blacks and watch the matches and care about the score and know the names of the players. Feeling as I did, knowing so little, what right did I have in 1981 to dictate whether or not my fellow New Zealanders could play or watch their favourite game?

I now realise that marching and demonstrating are about persuading – it's a conversation in the public sphere – but in 1981 I could not imagine that the street belonged to me or that I belonged to the street, so marching was not in my repertoire. Voices in my head grew clamorous. Arguments I couldn't voice out loud chased each other through my brain. It wasn't the Grand Inquisitor anymore; it was just two confused sides of me. Apartheid was cruel and unjust, but was it fair to deprive fellow Kiwis of their own rights by opposing it? If we stopped the tour, would the South African team embrace equality and would my fellow Kiwis then understand that you can't separate politics from sport? The marches could be seen as bearing witness to fellow-feeling with the oppressed Blacks, yes, but we weren't saying, 'We bear witness', we were saying 'Stop the Tour'. It made the pro-tour Kiwis appreciate the seriousness of the issue, it made them think about whether they wanted an all-White team to play with us while Blacks were being attacked and killed on a daily basis. But how divisive it was – the jeweller, remember the jeweller, how they broke his windows because he took part in a march? They say it's the closest we've ever come to civil war, My dear, it's not just chance that it didn't come to civil war, people on both sides exercised restraint. I guess they could have killed the jeweller. And I tell you what, after those fifty-six days of turmoil, which set family against family, husband against wife, anyone pro-tour against anyone anti-tour, there was no more touring between Springboks and All Blacks until the Apartheid regime was dismantled. So there was a kind of consensus about the importance of the public sphere as a place where people could argue peacefully. Everyone knew that if those tours went on in the name of the people, there would be civil war. We went to the brink, but only to the brink.

A child of the marae

Ritual and metaphor come naturally to those steeped in the oral tradition and one person who has used them creatively to fight prejudice and ignorance is Tame Iti. Not very long ago his ancestors were exclusively tribal and his iwi happened to be one of a few who refused to sign the Treaty of Waitangi. The Tūhoe tribe, living deep in the forested hill country of Te Urewera, has stood resolute against the incoming tide of Pākehā domination. Its people have never given up challenging the Crown and New Zealanders about the wrongs of the past – 'fixing history', as Tāmati Kruger, chief Tūhoe negotiator, calls it. The language is sometimes military: fight, battle, bombardment, revolution, but, Kruger says, 'in the Tūhoe historical context, revolution is the battle for your mind and heart... it is about de-colonising yourself... it's about getting our compass right and of knowing where your centre is... and where to act from'.[72]

In the battles waged by Tame Iti, he often used firearms for symbolic poignancy. Sometimes he generated anger, sometimes confusion – it was all part of the battle for hearts and minds, part of the effort to get people to feel history.

Tame Iti was a child of the marae, the public space where the hapū or sub-tribe becomes visible. He was surrounded by grandparents and great-grandparents, knew everyone in his 600-strong community, was always being reminded that 'Ruatoki is our universe, our world'.[73] When he left school and was offered a trade training course in Christchurch, it was the first he had heard of the third largest city in the country. Hardly a preparation for living in the modern world, one might have thought.

Except that the modern world itself is hardly a preparation for living in the modern world. It has eviscerated many of our most precious assets, such as community, and in the process treats us less and less as responsible citizens.

Iti's first protest erupted during punishment for speaking Māori at school. He began, docilely enough, writing out 100 times, 'I will not speak Māori'.[74] Then he put down his pencil. At the age of eight, Iti learned from his father that his forefathers had been shot for refusing to move off their own land. As he grew older he became angry. You could steal shoes or lollies but what could it mean to steal land? When landlords in Auckland refused to rent out to him and he heard himself called a nigger, his anger compelled him to action.

He travelled, he read, he identified his heroes. He learned to imagine himself in the shoes of Chinese under Communism, First Nations people in the US and Blacks in South Africa. He sheeted home his difficulty in renting a flat to universal issues: racial discrimination, historical injustice, environmental degradation. As his analysis of these wrongs evolved, he concluded that because his iwi had not signed the treaty, its people were entitled to sovereign independence in their own land.

Iti knew he would achieve little on his own. 'I find the best way is to work within an organisation... You don't need hundreds or thousands of people; all you need is a small number of hard-core thinkers.'[75] He joined activist group Ngā Tamatoa and began to lead them down the path of theatrical symbolism. As strangers in our own land, he told them, we should organise an embassy on Parliament grounds. Outside a hastily erected tent, Iti introduced himself to the crowd, who, he says, probably thought him a nutter. 'G'day, my name is Tame Iti...

I am here today to introduce myself as the new Māori ambassador.'[76] Police arrested him, which was part of his plan.

Believing it was time for people to smell the smoke and hear the noise, as his Tūhoe people had done 150 years earlier, he fired at the New Zealand flag during a Waitangi Tribunal hearing at a marae. Pressing the point of Tūhoe independence he set up a Tūhoe Embassy (a caravan this time) in a small town within his ancestral region. From there he issued eviction notices to Pākehā farmers who had settled beyond the Confiscation Line, which dated back to 1865. 'When we regain our sovereignty, they're welcome to stay. They can come to our marae and talk to us and we will shelter and feed them. But... they will be living under Tūhoe rules.'[77]

And then there was the ladder protest. During discussions about Crown compensation for historic land losses, Iti mounted a stepladder and handed the bewildered Minister of Justice a blanket – 'A blanket for our stolen land'.[78] The symbolism was powerful – payment by Pākehā for land in the nineteenth century was commonly measured in blankets and nails.

Some of Iti's kaumātua (elders) spoke sharply to him about his style of protest, but broadly they agreed with his politics and ideals. There came a day though when Tame Iti and sixteen others were arrested in police raids for allegedly participating in military-style training camps. The country was alarmed to read in its newspapers that it harboured a terrorist cell. This was never proven and Iti vigorously denied it – 'Why would I want to create chaos in my own community?'[79] – but there were four guns and 230 rounds of ammunition on the premises. Iti was sent to jail for two and a half years on firearms charges under the Arms and Terrorism Suppression acts. After early release for good behaviour, he made it clear he bore no animosity towards the sentencing judge. 'A couple of days and I got over that. I had to because I was doing two years in jail! So, I really had to reassess my thinking – mentally, spiritually, psychologically.'[80]

He threw his TV set out of his cell and got on with painting and reflecting. He mentored other prisoners in te reo and tikanga (Māori language and custom). On release Iti returned to his job as a social worker. At his home, he helped battered or scared wives. He faced their husbands, became part of a neighbourhood watch group and got on with painting and cooking. His participation in public life became less provocative. Since his release from jail he is, he says, 'a little older and wiser'.

There is much greater understanding now of the injustices Māori suffered under colonial rule and of the enduring consequences of those injustices. As part of its restitution efforts, the Crown now routinely includes a formal apology for past wrongs. In the case of the Urewera raids, the police commissioner visited homes of the raided and expressed remorse for the unlawful and traumatising way police had handled them. Iti urged his people to accept the apology. 'It allowed people to have their tears,' he said, 'held for the last seven years.' It was 'not wise or healthy' to hang on to those feelings of resentment and anger. 'We are happy to let it go.'[81] He sent his mokopuna (grandchildren) to meet the police commissioner in the driveway, where they bestowed on him and his colleagues a leaf from the tree of Tāne, 'the guardian of peace'. The theatre was classic Iti, but the message was new. The children represented the future, he said, and their generation was turning a new page.

In 1981, the year that so many Pākehā were putting themselves on the line for racial equality in South Africa, such things as Crown or police apologies to Māori were unthinkable, but after thirty years of turbulent conversation Māori and Pākehā have come to a new common mind. Most Pākehā now acknowledge the wrongs of the past and support a much more cooperative relationship. There is also broad support for the Crown making restitutional payments to Māori.

With part of its settlement money Tūhoe has built a centre for its scattered people. Designed to embody iwi values of living at one with nature, it is the first 'living building' in the Southern Hemisphere. That means it must produce at least as much energy as it consumes, use only rainwater falling on the site and be entirely carbon neutral. Its bricks, mortar and timber came from Tūhoe land and all components are free of harmful chemicals. Seventy percent of labour on the site was carried out by Tūhoe people, creating in the process a core of trained local personnel who know how to build healthy homes on a budget. Collaboration between experts and local people deepened personal relationships between the people of Tūhoe and its surrounding regions.

Incorporating a library, café and space for meetings, Te Uru Taumatua acts as a community hub that is also headquarters for the tribe. Tūhoe chief executive Kirsti Luke says the building 'reminds us about what's important; about people and our place within the bigger scheme of things'.[82]

In seeking to change the world Iti has changed himself. He no longer engages in provocative protest, but advocates 'sitting at the table'. He says race relations in New Zealand have reached a time of 'recognition and respect – we all have a place we can kind of work together.'[83]

For the 2014 general election Iti became a list candidate for the Māori Party because he believed their conduct had built trust with mainstream New Zealand. During his campaign, Iti and some mates undertook a three-day 280km road relay from Ruatoki to Auckland, incorporating much face-to-face kōrero. The point of the ride was 'as much for fitness as for democracy'; nonetheless it was vintage Iti. Four of the riders sported facial moko with tiwhana (tattoo lines fanning out above their eyebrows). They called themselves the Tiwhana Guys.

For over twenty years now, Iti has worn a full facial moko. His face reminds us of his rich identity: his ancestral belonging to iwi, hapū and whānau and at the same time his belonging as an individual – for who would expect to see a modern man sporting a full facial tattoo and what's more, teaming it with a suit and bowler hat or a sumptuous purple shirt and black waistcoat? At first his moko was seen as aggressive, like gang regalia, but, as a result of conversations in the public sphere, Iti can reasonably claim, 'The moko now doesn't look threatening, it becomes a way of life.'[84]

In 2015 a film about Tame Iti, *The Price of Peace*, was screened at the New Zealand International Film Festival. Tame Iti and the producer, Kim Webby, were present for a Q&A after the film's screening in Wellington. Bill Gosling, the festival director, also present, said that if all New Zealanders saw the film the country would be a happier place. A final comment to Iti from the floor, 'The whole nation owes you gratitude', was rapturously seconded by the audience.

These days Tame Iti paints a lot of pictures. He takes comfort in the thought that in the future, 'I die knowing I was involved somewhere in the making of history and where we are today.'[85]

Look, it's an intellectual!

Symbols are powerful because they speak to us at a level beyond rationality, but there is another aspect of public space that is equally important: the forum. This ancient word describes the space where matters of vital importance to society can be discussed, and people's opinions, though rarely achieving consensus, can be intelligently formed. In this space we both advance and, sadly, retreat. Though we have progressed from tribalism to civility as our basis of social organisation, our tribal genes sometimes overwhelm our civil constraints.

When Eleanor Catton, winner of the Man Booker prize in 2014, travelled overseas to talk about her book *The Luminaries*, she criticised her country's government. Neoliberal and shallow, she declared, dominated by profit-obsessed politicians who do not care about culture. 'I'm very angry with my government' reverberated throughout the land, but her criticism was not received as an expression of how much Catton loved her country and wanted the best for its people. Not at all. A radio talkback host accused her of being a national traitor, ungrateful to boot, and many listeners agreed. His argument appeared to be that because she had received a New Zealand Order of Merit, pocketed government financial help 'to write things' and was in paid employment at a publicly funded university, she had forfeited the right to publicly criticise her country's current policies or leadership. Novelist Chris Else saw beneath the vitriol a deeper sentiment: Catton was refusing to behave as a champion for her tribe.

> The champion fights on behalf of the tribe and the tribe identifies itself with its champion. If the champion wins, the whole tribe shares in the victory and triumphs through it. If the champion loses, the tribe falls apart and retreats in disorder.
>
> Sports people understand this role; they explicitly represent their tribe, be it country or province or ethnic group. Writers, artists and musicians are often taken by surprise. What they don't appreciate is that you don't choose to be a champion, the tribe chooses you whether you like it or not and, having chosen you, it then expects you to behave as a champion should.[86]

Catton was a champion because she had achieved international success, but she was not behaving as a champion should – she had been 'over in India bagging New Zealand', she shouldn't have spoken her mind at a global literary festival, she should think about going back to Canada (where she was born). Else again: 'Eleanor Catton was a traitor and ungrateful because she denied what the tribe considered its rightful share in her achievement; she thereby threatened its sense of identity.'

Ah yes, that most precious thing, the sense of identity – that which the tribe must protect at all costs in order to remain strong. Reject the person who threatens! Close ranks against her, cast her from the tribe!

The government, said the talkback host, is 'an embodiment of us all'.

If we could be less tribal, and perceive our identity in a way that incorporated allegiance to the public space and democracy, we might keep Catton with us. We might find that she and others like her, commonly known as intellectuals, have a contribution to make to the public forum. And there's something else – since the voice of an external God has lost much of its authority, it's now up to us to find a moral source within. This task gets harder in a world that bombards us with new issues where right and wrong are not obvious but consequences can cause suffering to millions. Intellectuals can help us develop a nuanced moral stance on such complexities, can help us pinpoint a humane balance between social and individual interests. Year by year the pace of change accelerates and, as Catton says, the last thing we need is a whole country of embarrassed writers slinking around.

Another intellectual, Nicky Hager, has made an invaluable contribution to the public forum by focusing on an issue, researching it meticulously and then publishing a well-written book on the subject. In 2015, *Dirty Politics* exposed dishonest practices being presented as objective journalism. It revealed the morally dubious relationship of some bloggers with high-level politicians. Hager's points attracted international attention and respect, but in New Zealand much media and public reaction united in widespread denigration. The then prime minister, John Key, dismissed the entire issue as one of personality: 'Oh, everyone knows Nicky Hager. Conspiracy theorist. No one believes him.'

You might imagine public intellectuals would be treasured like All Blacks for their ability to make a contribution of outstanding practical value. But more often they are mocked for being out of touch with the real world. Instead, it is politicians who are asked for opinions – and how can *they* be honest when their words are misinterpreted, twisted and used against them and mistakes are not forgiven?

There is scant respect for thinking deeply or taking time to form an opinion. State-subsidised radio, which valiantly persists in catering to the needs of thinking citizens, is challenged by ever-reducing government funding. TV producers say 'talking heads' make poor TV, while advertisements disrupt programmes to the point where they lose coherent substance. In 2012, despite marches in the streets, TV's only public service channel was cut. No loss, cried those who hate thinking and deny the worth of those who love it. Demand and supply, cried the market-driven TV corporation, which once saw its role as partly educative. The possibility of a minority nourished with good-quality information and analysis making a contribution to the country's well-being far beyond the weight of its numbers is condemned as an elitist idea and dismissed. Nor is consideration given to the loyalty of whistle-blowers and commentators who would like to help their country. Instead the very concept of 'intellectual' is repudiated. The Catton-hating talkback host, once a top news presenter on National Radio, found common cause with a caller:

> Host: She's an intellectual. What's an intellectual? Some people might say it's just a pretentious wanker.
> Caller: Some say it's a person who hears the William Tell overture and doesn't think of the Lone Ranger.
> Host: Someone who watches erotica not porn.

Bloggers had a field day: 'A lot of backlash on Radio Talkback and around the Water-Cooler at work regarding that pompous Catton woman'; 'I cannot recall another New Zealand female to go so quickly from hero to zero'; 'Seems ordinary Kiwis don't like being Pontificated to by a Self-Professed "Intellectual"...'

This refusal to accept the intelligentsia as integral members of the public space allows half-truth and bullshit to reign supreme. It encourages herd behaviour and the suppression of difference. It makes it uncool to read anything demanding or to engage in serious discussion. It may be more destructive to humanity and its democratic institutions than indecent literature, which we punish; it is certainly more insidious.

And yet there is something in this rejection, after all. People who live by the mind are prone to what historian Paul Johnson calls the deadly sin of intellectuals: the impulse to impose their ideas on others. When their proposals fail they can exhibit a tawdry detachment from unforeseen harm. Marx promoted intellectuals as important agents of change who should provide advice and counsel to political leaders, and interpret the country's politics to the mass of the population. The resulting 'establishment intellectuals' upheld the status quo of an authoritarian regime.

When we are talking of Russia, the intellectuals we like are the 'dissidents', those who criticise the regime. When we speak of New Zealand, dissidents are unwelcome; establishment intellectuals much more palatable. Thus the noble function of the public intellectual is reduced to taking sides. The point is not that the ideas of intellectuals should be adopted by society; it is that intellectuals should use their trained, intensely curious and high-powered brains to present issues and problems clearly in the public sphere. There needs to be debate about their ideas; genuine criticism of any pretension or pontificating obscurity, but not mindless dismissal.

Recently a new phenomenon has emerged – an explosion in tertiary education and people wanting to be involved with cultural values. The Hay Festival of Literature and the Arts, attended by 200,000 people over eleven days each year, is a case in point. People gather in the small Welsh town of Hay-on-Wye, happily sloshing through mud in Wellington boots, to hear, meet and engage with some of the world's most profound writers and thinkers. Says director Peter Florence, 'The public are not just viewers but participants. This whole festival is about exchange and the power that language, when you share it, has as a gift to inspire other people. Once it was solely a literary festival, now it's a place where ideas collide, clash even, where minds meet and merge, where intellects engage.'

In addition to literary festivals that occur all over the world, ideas clubs, discussion groups, book clubs are also enjoying unprecedented popularity. Sociologists call this new phenomenon 'mass intelligentsia'. Perhaps the growing desire to use leisure time for intellectual activities will encourage countries to value their intellectuals more and to see them as an integral part of our twenty-first-century community. It's certainly encouraging Dinah and me. Though in our regular meetings to discuss books and ideas we are a band of few – just Dinah and me, in fact – we track down books that will help us deepen our understanding of what is happening in the world and places we have visited. We cherish our country's intellectuals and wish we had more of them.

Revisiting authenticity

Rousseau's confessional memoirs, in which he advocated what we now call 'owning our feelings', led people to think that this was the entirety of his vision. But Rousseau also believed that to become a fully realised self, we need alternative perspectives, such as civic morality, duty, pity and imagination. These alone could counter-balance society's tendency to put people under such competitive pressure that they took pleasure in one another's pain and weakness. 'Then only, when the voice of duty takes the place of physical impulses and right of appetite, does man, who so far had considered only himself, find that he is forced to act on different principles, and to consult his reason before listening to his inclinations.'[87] Regrettably, added Rousseau, people found ways of abusing civic morality and duty for their own ends.

This proved prophetic. Rousseau was seen as having set the 'noble savage' against civil society, which he hadn't, and his followers cherry-picked his ideas, setting above all else the notion that everyone was equal and emotions should have full sway. The French Revolution, which began with good intentions, opened the door to totalitarianism and it was one of Rousseau's admirers, Robespierre, who became closely associated with the Reign of Terror. The great Irish statesman Edmund Burke watched from England as the revolutionaries overthrew their monarchy and the Catholic Church. To Burke this signified the destruction of the main engines for manners, which he considered even more important than laws:

> Upon them, in a great measure, the laws depend. The law can touch us here and there, now and then. Manners are what vex or soothe, corrupt or purify, exalt or debase, barbarise or refine us, by a constant, steady, uniform, insensible operation, like that of the air we breathe in. They give their whole form and colour to our lives. According to their quality, they aid morals, they supply them, or they totally destroy them.[88]

The French revolutionaries brought in a brave new world by edict, but one of the first results was the military dictatorship imposed by Napoleon Bonaparte – which was hardly what the people had been fighting for and proved Burke's apprehension well-founded. 'What is liberty without wisdom and without virtue? It is the greatest of all possible evils; for it is folly, vice, and madness, without tuition or restraint.'[89]

A new definition of the intrinsic self, one that left out civic morality and duty, survived the French Revolution as well as the suicides of Goethe's *Young Werther* readers. Now, it's a cliché. On television, a newly crowned beauty queen was asked why she had won the prize. It was because, she said, she knew who she was. Pre-Rousseau, people would have taken 'who she was' to be her name, her parentage and her place in society. In the twenty-first century, she could say 'I know who I am' and no one would question her.

The language of authenticity reverberates around us, creating the self in splendid isolation, but it can dump us right down a cul-de-sac, where we lose our inner source of morality. Then we chase external validation in fame or wealth until ultimately we feel lost, as Saul Bellow's protagonist in *The Victim*, Leventhal, discovers when he notices how everyone around him is trying to be themselves.

> Everybody wanted to be what he was to the limit. When you looked around, that was what you saw most distinctly. In great achievements as well as in crimes and vices.
>
> You couldn't expect people to be right, but only try to do what they must. Therefore hideous things were done, cannibalistic things. Good things as well of course. But even there, nothing really good was safe.
>
> We were all the time taking care of ourselves, laying up, storing up, watching out on this side and on that side, and at the same time running, running desperately, running as if in an egg race with the egg in a spoon. And sometimes we were fed up with the egg, sick of it, and at such a time would rather sign on with the devil and what they called the powers of darkness than run with the spoon, watching the egg, fearing for the egg.[90]

Manners, as Lucinda Holdforth writes in *Why Manners Matter*, help us resolve our double identities as social animals and proud individuals. 'They actively enlarge the social space. They expand the radius of human cooperation and potential. Witnessing a gracious gesture can unexpectedly fill us with joy.'[91] My mother, Pauline, witnessed one that took her years to appreciate:

> I was having an argument with my mother, perhaps I was playing up, and there were a few unkind words. Then there was a knock on the door. Mother said, 'Hello!' to the visitor as if nothing had happened and I thought, How can you when you've just been so nasty to me! Well I learnt a lesson that way – that you shouldn't let moods interfere with greeting other people who don't know what you've done or been through ten minutes before.

At first it felt to young Pauline as if her mother was playing a false game. What a hypocrite! Then, as limbs grew long and hormones guided her towards marriage, she reconsidered the behaviour and found it less a crime against authenticity than a celebration of common humanity. She had learned that if she behaved politely and cheerily with people, a sense of fellow humanity became part of her identity – a true part, not an add-on. She had built herself a precept that would sustain and guide her throughout the rest of her life.

The self that we belong with is not a thing separate from society. The public space is where much of the crucial interaction with society occurs and now that we have become a global village, the public space, too, evolves on a global scale. In January 2015, 230 years after Rousseau and the French Revolution, members of an Islamist terrorist group killed twelve people at the *Charlie Hebdo* offices in Paris. A few days later, two million people met in Paris for a rally of national unity, and 3.7 million people joined demonstrations across France to express solidarity. The slogan of choice was 'Je suis Charlie'. Even in countries where French was not spoken, the placards read the same. Impassioned debate across the world.

But how much actual debate was there? For those who marched, the issue was black and white: the massacre was an attack on freedom of expression; journalists must have the right to express opinions with impunity. But embedded in the massacre were societal issues: was it right to mock people who were relatively powerless and constantly being humiliated? Then why had a journalist at the same paper been fired for denigrating Jews? How could anti-Semitic be wrong while anti-Islamist was right? Did the firing express a sense of guilt for having 'sent Jews to the gas chambers'? Some people began to realise the complexity of the issue and argued that it was up to each individually to find a moral position, to decide what values should be uppermost in this particular case, but for others there were only two positions – freedom of expression in all situations or else sanctity of religious figures the only value. Such imperviousness to debate made a mockery of public space, and the distant goal of native and Arab French citizens sharing a common sense of belonging receded like a diminishing glacier.

NINE

HOMO ECONOMICUS

John Calvin turns in his grave

As a young mother and co-owner of a house, I was out of the workforce and demoted to housewife, but every Friday in the mailbox I received messages from society telling me which goods would be cheaper that week. To be a good housewife I must read all the brochures, seek the best good at the cheapest price and make a note of where to go for what. After a while I realised that my furnishing of the house and garden would make a statement that could bring a certain status. I wrote a short story about a character who became obsessed with owning a gravy boat. The only way to be a successful roast-provider was to serve the gravy in a stainless steel gravy boat with a dedicated gravy spoon. Jane, Barbara or whatever I called her only hesitated to buy one because she knew this would open her to another obsession and what was the point in chasing obsessions?

Had I known this was the modern version of proving you were one of the chosen, I would have felt less alone. I would have known I was part of a grand tradition even though I was experiencing its dark side. John Calvin would have understood, although he would have turned in his grave. He hadn't intended his followers to stake the meaning of their lives on personal acquisition.

It's over 200 years since Denis Diderot spotted a downside to changing his dressing gown. His beautiful new scarlet one delighted him until he noticed the rest of his possessions looked tawdry. He replaced an old straw chair with an armchair in Moroccan leather then ditched his old desk for an expensive new writing table, but there was no end to the demands he now sensed around him. Diderot was dismayed: 'I was absolute master of my old dressing gown,' he wrote, 'but I have become a slave to my new one.' Today's plethora of choice makes this kind of slavery so predictable that social scientists call it the Diderot Effect and consumerism rarely fails to produce it. As my eight-year-old daughter wailed when our family acquired a video player back in the 80s: 'Oh dear, what can I want now?'

What Juliet Schor calls the Upward Creep of Desire affects every aspect of our lives until our bodies, our minds, even our children are valued as commodities. Bodies used to be treasured temples of God, but now we are inclined to treat them as one more candidate for perfection because, when everything is on offer, there is no *excuse* for imperfection. People whose plastic surgery resulted in travesty take remorseful part in the TV series *Embarrassing Bodies*. 'Enough!' cries one with mutilated buttocks. 'Whatever you are, it is enough.' Meanwhile, demand for surgical improvement keeps rising.

Brené Brown, a research professor at the University of Houston's Graduate College of Social Work, concludes after years of study that pretending to others that we are perfect deprives us of love and belonging. 'In order for connection to happen, we have to allow ourselves to be seen, really seen.' Consumer slavery demands we measure ourselves by the opinions of others and here's where Facebook comes in, offering hundreds of 'friends' who are thrilled about our birthday, ageless beauty, pets, new baby. Until they are not.

Children used to be seen as precious gifts, but are now pressure cooked to achieve. Forced to measure themselves constantly against their peers, many, even when they make it to the top of the competitive tree, find no peace of mind because it's time to aim for the next hoop. The further they go the harder they have to work to keep up with peers as clever as they. At Harvard University, as many as 80% of students become depressed, and officials at American universities have nicknames for their undergraduates: 'teacups' have been so overprotected they are breakable, 'crispies' so pressured they have burnt out.[92]

Fame and wealth have become goals in themselves. In a recent study, 40% of British children between ages five to ten had no other ambition.[93] Thousands of young girls want to be as famous as Paris Hilton and have the minutiae of their lives reported daily. For folk with no claim on fame, reality shows offer the goods in exchange for psychological manipulation and there is no shortage of volunteers for sacrifice. On shows attracting up to 14 million viewers, fame-seekers eat live bugs, starve, get filthy and ragged, have tantrums, dissolve into tears and reveal their inner cruelty. Teenage viewers especially gain their own kind of fame by airing their criticisms and verdicts on social networks.

In medieval society, fame was hardly in our consciousness. Erich Fromm cites a craving for fame as one of the new energies of the Renaissance that helped forge modern capitalism.[94] As capitalism developed, it created more and more individuals who felt isolated and insecure in a hostile world and for whom fame held out promise of silencing one's self-doubt. Work harder. Work longer. Play the world stage. If not merely hundreds but thousands know your name, you'll be sure your life has meaning.

Minute by minute our minds are dominated by market values. Current affairs programmes are 'brought to you by' car or credit card company. Naming rights and corporate sponsorships degrade civic life by plastering company logos and slogans on our rugby fields and defacing our prestigious awards. Consumer slavery has downgraded citizenship, which used to be a vital component of democracy. Now elections are won and lost in terms of sales pitch and basic merchandising. Political commentators advise parties to, 'treat voters like consumers, give them what they want'. A losing party is likened to an old-style department store failing to stock the goods its customers actually want to buy: 'Shoppers are getting what they want from smaller, more flexible competitors enjoying a deregulated market.' The winning party politicians 'know what their market likes'. As consumers rather than citizens we can forget moral and social values, we don't need any vision of what kind of society we want and our sense of belonging is debased.

Another language casualty of marketisation is the reduction of 'people' to 'individuals'. Even charities fighting loneliness refer to 'lonely individuals'. *Guardian* columnist George Monbiot, who has written extensively on the subject, alleges, 'We can scarcely complete a sentence without getting personal. Personally speaking (to distinguish myself from a ventriloquist's dummy), I prefer personal friends to the impersonal variety and personal belongings to the kind that don't belong to me. Though that's just my personal preference, otherwise known as my preference.'[95]

The term *homo economicus* was first used in the nineteenth century to criticise John Stuart Mill's whimsical definition of the human being as 'a being who inevitably does that by which he may obtain the greatest amount of necessaries, conveniences, and luxuries, with the smallest quantity of labour and physical self-denial with which they can be obtained'. Mill, who was perfectly aware that this does not describe the whole of human nature, wanted to make the point that political economy only deals with that part of a person which desires wealth and adopts the most efficient method of obtaining it. Nowadays such 'rational behaviour' is frequently justified as the *only* rational behaviour. The language of material aspiration has droned incessantly into the ears of generations X and Y, with Z now hard on their heels. So why was I surprised by the life goals of my X-Generation son? For the first five years after leaving school he was going to buy 'stuff' (an entertainment system, a BMW). After that he would get married and buy a house. At the time of writing, my Z-Generation (ten-year-old) grandson was waiting once again for the price of a new computer game to reach a level he considered reasonable. Sometimes he cracks under the pressure: 'When I can't stand it any longer, I buy it.' As for me, I noticed some years ago that when I gave something of marketable value to the Salvation Army shop, I felt as if I had violated its essence. I was failing in my duty to perpetuate its value as an economic good. I was acting irrationally. I was not true *homo economicus.*

Milton Friedman finds God

This insistence on behaving as if we are no more than *homo economicus* has done us no favours. It has alienated millions of us across the world from our respective economies and often from each other. This is not what Adam Smith, the eighteenth-century 'father of economics', advocated. Smith claimed that behind individual actions an 'invisible hand' frequently benefited society even though the person had only intended narrow self-interest. That is remembered. Smith also described businessmen as people 'who have generally an interest to deceive and even oppress the public', and advised that their commercial proposals should be examined 'with the most suspicious attention'. That is forgotten. The first statement is used to champion rights of the individual. The second is an argument for checks and balances on the market. The first has acquired almost biblical authority. The second is rarely mentioned.

During the Great Depression, when huge numbers of people lost their jobs and families went hungry, governments influenced by the great British economist John Maynard Keynes made full employment a priority and laid the foundations for a 'welfare state' as a cushion against the harsher effects of capitalism. In due course Keynesianism, as it was called, lost favour and another economist, American this time, developed another theory. This one returned the notion of the individual to such prominence it became, in a sense, re-fashioned Puritanism. At first Milton Friedman was influenced by his mentor, Friedrich Hayek, who believed that as the market evolved through history, prices had emerged as a natural mechanism driving civilisation forward, 'an instrument of communication and guidance which embody more information than we directly have'.[96] Milton Friedman carried this further by arguing the right to 'freedom'. Claiming that no one minds other people's property as well as they mind their own, he argued that individuals should have full rights over their own property. A factory owner should be able to do what he liked within his factory, free of interference by trade unions. Taxation should be discontinued because it took property by force from individuals. The Friedman Holy Trinity was privatisation, deregulation and union busting. Individuals seeking advantage over each other for money alone, motivated by narrow self-interest, would magically, as 'a happy by-product', create a sustainable, healthy, balanced society. *Homo economicus* in all his glory.

In *Capitalism and Freedom* (1962), Friedman championed the free market as the purest possible form of 'participatory democracy' where 'each man can vote, as it were, for the colour of tie he wants'. Governments should not provide for the poor, sick, unemployed, aged or disabled and there was no need to take account of abusive parenting or prejudicial access to education or health services. Life was a simple quid pro quo. You did something, you experienced the consequence. The system was sometimes called consequentialist libertarianism.

Friedman saw no sense in President Kennedy's famous plea to America, 'Ask not what your country can do for you – ask what you can do for your country'. The idea of a country doing something for its people was paternalistic, while the notion of people doing something for their country was 'not worthy of the ideals of free men in a free society'. Friedman and his followers insisted their ideas were scientific, but like Communism and then Fascism, the Chicago School economists had absolute faith in its principles and if unchecked would make them absolute. It reinterpreted Adam Smith's 'invisible hand' – for individual self-interest to work its magic it must be *free of interference*. To permit any other world view was to muddy the economic signals and compromise the efficiency of the entire system. A complete monopoly on ideology was required. God was back.

Chicago School academics had no qualms about interfering with poor countries for the sake of the new religion. Their mission statement could be summed up in the words of Theodore W. Schultz, who in 1953 was chairman of the economics department at the University of Chicago: 'We want [the poor countries] to work out their economic salvation by relating themselves to us and by using our way of achieving their economic development.' It became standard practice for corporations to fund the training of economists in targeted countries, readying them to bring in extreme capitalist reforms when opportunity offered. Friedman publicly declared the tactic in 1982. 'Only a crisis – actual or perceived – produces real change. When that crisis occurs, the actions that are taken depend on the ideas that are lying around. That, I believe, is our basic function: to develop alternatives to existing policies, to keep them alive and available until the politically impossible becomes the politically inevitable.'[97]

It became routine for the crises to be accompanied by brutality, disappearances and torture, but the Chicago School economists insisted these were just something for the human rights people to sort out. The fact was that without brutal, undemocratic enforcement no one anywhere was going to accept an economic programme that in the short term was going to throw thousands out of work, dismantle health, education, social security and, long term, concentrate wealth in the hands of a very few. From Thatcher's Britain to Bolivia, Poland, China, South Africa, Russia and the Asian Tigers, subterfuge if not outright force was always necessary. The existing social fabric had to be torn apart, brought to its knees and left to recover as it might.

In 1987, Prime Minister Margaret Thatcher's famous statement, 'There is no such thing as society', showed that the pursuit of self-interest at the expense of others had reached a dangerous point. A healthy society encapsulating its citizens' values and aspirations is pivotal to a shared sense of belonging, but it can't survive unless people continue to have confidence in it.

In the case of Iraq, the US government's 2003 'Shock and Awe' policy had a devastating effect on Baghdad's citizens.[98] In addition to suffering at least fifty airstrikes aimed at knocking out the Iraqi leadership, the infrastructure was targeted. The bombing of phone exchanges made it impossible for families to contact one another, to check whether loved ones were alive or to reassure others. Then the lights went out. As *The Guardian* reported on 4 April, 'in an instant, an entire city of 5 million people was plunged into an awful, endless night.' After the bombing, the looting by civilians. The occupying troops seemed to have little understanding of what was happening.

The National Museum of Iraq lost 80% of its 170,000 priceless objects, while the National Library, repository of every book and doctoral thesis ever published in Iraq, was gutted. The people's memory of their culture and history was being destroyed.

Paul Bremer, director of the occupation authority, immediately opened the country's borders to unrestricted imports, while allowing foreign companies to own 100% of Iraqi assets. Foreign investors could take 100% of their profits out of the country. Subsidies to stave off mass starvation were abolished. The 200 state-owned companies, which produced the staples of the Iraqi diet and the raw materials of its industry, were privatised and persistent power cuts soon brought them to a standstill. Though there was plenty of public money available, the factories received no contracts, no generators, no help. The vast majority of new private contracts went to American companies and Iraqi workers had to look on as these companies imported their own workforce at up to ten times the price.

Friedman expected 'the happy by-product' of looking after freedom to be greater equality and confined the social responsibility of business to playing by the rules of free competition without deception or fraud. In Iraq, where all regulations were set aside and foreign corporations were given immunity from prosecution, deception and fraud became part of the business model. Greed liberated from all regulation unleashed an orgy of anti-social behaviour until profits decreased and the major US reconstruction contractors pulled out of the country. Reconstruction? Three years after the invasion, a US congressional inspection team set up to monitor reconstruction in Iraq published a damning report of failures by contractors, mainly from the US. While there was progress with schools and police stations, many Iraqis still had no access to clean water, and electricity supplies in Baghdad were below pre-invasion levels.[99]

As for the democracy part of the plan, Iraqis adopted free speech with a will. They started up hundreds of newspapers. They organised local elections around the country. But when the US government saw that Iraqis opposed a privatised economy, the elections were stopped and Paul Bremer filled the places on the Iraqi governing council by appointment. Iraqis were furious. 'Yes, yes, elections. No, no selections' ran the battle cry. Resistance organisations began to multiply. No sooner was one brought to its knees than another took its place and each was more brutal than the last. Young Muslims in countries around the world who felt isolated, disrespected, powerless and without direction, found in Jihadi brotherhood as much meaning and purpose as anyone could wish for.

A coup in New Zealand

I wish I could report that when pressure for major economic change came to New Zealand, this grand little country made sure to invite all its citizens to participate. It is true that by the 1980s, changes were desirable. The population was becoming less rural, many new manufacturers had become exporters and there was pressure to open up the economy to external markets. Prime Minister Robert Muldoon dug his heels in the sand and presided over ever larger dunes of financial deficit, but he couldn't hold things back for ever. Some New Zealand students had studied in the United States while American economics was becoming increasingly influential worldwide. Impressed by the glamour and elegantly simple framework of Chicago School economics, they decided that the neoliberal model would resolve the policy problems the country faced.

In pioneering days New Zealanders aspired to egalitarianism and loved to broadcast their successes: the first country to give women the vote! the first to settle industrial disputes by arbitration! the birthplace of the welfare state! the home of racial harmony! Such progress was hard-won, but the generation born after World War II lapped up the benefits without having known the hardships. Many found New Zealand boring. They were into Big: big shops, big quantities, big bargains. Full employment was their birthright; community just a structure underpinning battles for the individual: women's rights, Māori rights, civil rights. As battles wore on, attitudes to the collective mutated from all for one and one for all into 'it's all about me'.

The ruling conservative party's failure to manage change left the way open for the Labour Party. Once the party that championed workers' rights and introduced the welfare state, its leadership now adopted the messianic certainties of neoliberalism (a.k.a. economic rationalism); they were well supported by like-minded economists mainly, but not exclusively, based in Treasury. From 1984, when Labour won power, change came thick and fast. The new government ignored effects on social well-being and income growth distribution; it ignored differences of scale between its US-generated model and its tiny country of governance; and it ignored the open sesame to greed and fraud invited by the reforms. Prime Minister David Lange's new cabinet deregulated the labour market and sidestepped the unions by putting government workers on individual contracts. They ignored opinions from the universities, the public and dissenters in Treasury or their own party, while favouring those of CEOs for the country's largest businesses. Everything was done at speed. Finance Minister Roger Douglas' advice was, 'Define your objectives clearly, and move towards them in quantum leaps.' The objectives were all monetary. The reformers dismantled policies designed to ensure that people participated in and belonged to their community – policies evolved over the previous ninety years – and replaced them with the monetarist policies of Milton Friedman and neoliberalism. No shots were fired.

Afterwards, it was hard to understand how people had let it all happen. The excitement so heady and contagious. Such confident talk of the market regulating itself, the market being the thing that would, as if by magic, keep things on an even keel and make life better for everybody. It was so novel in the twentieth century, when we no longer had the comfort of knowing God was in heaven and hell awaited us unless we were good, to be told we could believe in an invisible hand.

The business world was one I had never belonged to but I could feel its hot breath on my cheek when I visited my uncle in 1985 and he praised the Labour Party. He was an accountant, he took a keen interest in the stock market, he was rich. Businessmen all over the country were praising the Labour Party. They could hardly believe their good fortune at the hands of an enemy. For me it was like winning a lottery. I had voted for Labour and now the most powerful in the land were coming to join me. It felt like magic, but it was true. There was no Left or Right any more. The whole country was pulling together. My friends discovered that they too could experience the excitement of investment. They joined groups to help them navigate.

There was a phrase much used by Cabinet, Treasury and business: 'no gain without pain', but it was becoming clear that, as academic commentator Jane Kelsey put it, this meant 'pain for the poor to achieve gain for the rich'.[100] There was pain aplenty as thousands of working people lost their jobs and unemployment rose from 3.6% of the labour force to 11.1% in six years. Towns based around a single industry found themselves populated by beneficiaries. Pacific Islanders brought in to help expand manufacturing industries were particularly badly hit; their unemployment rate rose to 29%, while that of Māori hit 25%. Between 1989 and 1992, the population estimated to be living in poverty increased by about 35%.

There was gain aplenty too. Business embraced the bonanza it was offered in public sector contracts, turning private consultancies into a growth industry. It raced to take over publicly-run enterprises, reaping private profit. Those who made fortunes in the speculative boom adopted lifestyles exponentially more luxurious, and those who had money to shop were treated to overseas retail chains, an exploding café culture, exciting new restaurants, swanky accommodation options, late-model car imports. New Zealand offered more choice, global connection, significantly less tedium.

The 'trickle down' theory predicted that eventually the poor would benefit. However, the real incomes of low-income households fell and income inequality as measured by the OECD grew more rapidly than in any other developed country. By 1993, one in six New Zealanders was considered to be living in poverty. Kelsey later decoded the dishonesty:

> The ethos of the market pervaded everyday life. Even the language was captured, dehumanising the people and communities it affected. It became acceptable to talk of 'shedding workers', as if they were so much dead skin. 'Incentives' meant cutting benefits to force people into low paying jobs. 'Broadening the tax base' meant shifting the tax burden from the rich to the poor. 'Freeing up the market' meant removing all impediments to profit making. 'Deinstitutionalisation' meant closing state institutions and shifting responsibility for the occupants to poor families and communities. 'An open economy' meant welcoming foreign purchases of the country's assets and resources. 'International competitiveness' meant competing with countries whose economies are based on prison and child labour, grinding poverty, and environmental degradation.[101]

It was confusing. A party that had championed the poor and the working class seemed to have turned on them, yet the language made everything seem normal, humane and, as we were constantly told, 'in the national good'. The caring, egalitarian, love-thy-neighbour kind of society that was part of our identity as Kiwis was disappearing before our eyes.

When the global share market crashed in 1987, the New Zealand share market, which had assumed life to be one never-ending party, suffered the worst collapse of any market anywhere. Many people lost their life savings, my friends lost their investments, the navigator groups dissolved in disarray. The government pressed on with privatisation, now targeting local government, hospitals, state houses, schools. Again the private sector benefited. Why bother chasing profits in private markets when there was easy money to be made from the government's social services? Eventually people became angry. In 1990, six years after the Labour Government started the reforms, it was decisively voted out. In came National, which offered more – and more – of the same. It seemed as though it would never end.

And it hasn't – yet. In the thirty years since New Zealand adopted what I call privilege economics, the number of people who are poor has doubled and the gap between rich and the rest has widened faster in New Zealand than in any other developed country. Unemployment has become structural, with much higher rates among Māori and Pacific Islanders. Our biggest city grows bigger and more expensive by Douglas' 'quantum leaps', causing families to crowd into damp, cold houses or even to sleep in cars, while small communities throughout the country are becoming known as 'zombie towns' and little is done about bringing jobs to those areas. As New Zealand has aligned itself with the National Party's global goal of a country good to do business in, it has become less and less able to nurture the confident participation of its citizens. What is needed is a government willing to put their belonging to society and economy at the very top of its agenda.

Being rich

How did our values of egalitarianism fall into disrepair? Research undertaken by social psychologist Paul Piff shows how a rigged system encourages a sense of entitlement for the lucky ones. Of 100 pairs of strangers, one in each pair is randomly assigned to be a rich player in a rejigged game of Monopoly. The 'rich' players get twice as much money as the 'poor' players. When they pass Go, they collect twice the salary. They are allowed to roll two dice instead of one. Hidden cameras record what happens.

Pretty soon one of the rich players starts to grow noisier. He slaps down his piece on the board. It makes an aggressive ping, ping, ping as he moves it around. Other rich players begin to munch greedily on snacks from the table, talk out loud and dominate their 'poor' partner with body language.

> As the game went on... the rich players actually started
> to become ruder toward the other person, less and less

sensitive to the plight of those poor, poor players, and more and more demonstrative of their material success, more likely to showcase how well they're doing. Rich Player: I have money for everything. Poor Player: How much is that? Rich Player: You owe me 24 dollars. You're going to lose all your money soon. I'll buy it. I have so much money. I have so much money, it takes me forever. Rich Player 2: I'm going to buy out this whole board. Rich Player 3: You're going to run out of money soon. I'm pretty much untouchable at this point.[102]

The poor players became quieter, lost their smiles and easy bonhomie, and ignored the snacks as if time were too precious to be spent eating. They concentrated with what looked like quiet desperation on the job in hand, trying to close the ever-widening gap between them and their opponent.

After fifteen minutes, the researchers asked the players to talk about their experiences during the game. The rich players focused on how they had managed to buy all their properties and how they had earned their success. They discounted factors such as the random flip of a coin that set them on the road of privilege. This enabled them to understand it in terms of their personal abilities.

Piff found in dozens of studies with thousands of participants across the United States that, 'as a person's levels of wealth increase, their feelings of compassion and empathy go down, and feelings of entitlement, of deservingness, and their ideology of self-interest increase'. He also found that the rich are less generous, more likely to lie, cheat and value greed as an asset. Those who felt rich took twice as much candy from a bowl they were told was reserved for children as those who felt poor. Another study looked at the relationship between the value of a car and the behaviour of its owner. Faced with a pedestrian crossing where a person was waiting to cross the road, all the cars in the cheapest category stopped, but close to 50% of those in the most expensive sector drove straight across.

In real-time society, rich citizens consider they have earned their wealth and privileges. In 1965, CEO pay at the largest 350 US companies was twenty times as high as the pay of the average worker; in 1989, it was fifty-eight times as high; and in 2012, it was 273 times as high.[103] It's very rare to hear a CEO admit that this differential is not entirely deserved or to advocate any kind of relationship between their own pay and that of the workers they employ. They resist any moves towards raising the minimum wage because of how it would affect profits. Sometimes the mental divide is so great that the rich refuse to cohabit with the non-rich at all. In Atlanta, USA, rich suburbs are setting up stand-alone cities. These new 'contract cities' outsource the functions of local government and eschew any involvement with the society around them. The idea is catching on.[104]

After Christchurch experienced New Zealand's most devastating earthquake for eighty years, it was up to the council to manage the effects. In earlier times its public servant, the town clerk, would have been in charge, but now it was a CEO. This one was New Zealand's highest paid local government executive, on a salary of over half a million dollars. On his watch the council lost accreditation as a building consent authority, so he was stood down for four months on full pay. He resigned at the end of the year with a payout of $800,000. Along the way, amid widespread misery and hardship, he was awarded a pay rise of $68,000. A firefighter who had had to amputate both legs of a trapped survivor with a hacksaw and pocket knife said that the CEO had just got, as a pay rise, in excess of what he himself earned in an entire year. When a reporter suggested to the CEO that his pay rise was perhaps not appropriate, he remonstrated that his salary could not be compared with that of the prime minister, the mayors of London or New York or even of President Obama because he didn't get houses, he didn't get limousines, he didn't get superannuation and he didn't get travel. As he told TV3's Campbell Live: 'All I've ever said to my council is, you tell me what the market is and I'm happy to be on that market rate, whatever it is. I have a very simple philosophy – whatever the market is, pay within the range.'

Homo economicus prides himself on his simple philosophy which reduces everything to economic considerations and calls those alone rational. CEOs in particular seem so diminished as individuals that the monetary reward is the only one they value. Some is good, more is better, more and more and more is better still. As moral values are discounted in favour of economic ones we are encouraged to indulge our ever-present propensity for greed, which isolates the rich no less than the poor. Greed held no terrors for Friedman, who regarded it as something to exploit: 'Is there some society you know that doesn't run on greed?'

This narrowed understanding of self-interest has led many to try their hand at economic crime. This now costs New Zealand up to

$9.4 billion a year – more than twice the combined annual budgets of police, the Department of Corrections, and the courts – and in a country long admired for its lack of corruption. Tax fraud at an estimated $2 billion a year costs us far more than the estimated $80 million cost of benefit fraud.[105]

A sense of entitlement has become so ingrained that for the purpose of power and profit the rights of the individual are being increasingly claimed for the corporation. In the US case of Citizens United vs Federal Election Commission (2010), a majority of judges ruled that corporate political spending is protected under the First Amendment. Because, like individuals, corporations have constitutionally-protected free speech, they are entitled to spend unlimited amounts in order to influence elections. The scope of the Fourteenth Amendment has also been subverted. Intended to protect freed slaves, its protections have gradually been extended to corporations to include a legal notion of 'corporate personhood'. For all Acts of Congress the words 'person' and 'whoever' include corporations as well as individuals – unless the context indicates otherwise. The presumption grows that they are one and the same, 'innocent until proven guilty'. Entitled until not.

Being poor

Despite the headlong rush to excess, there are still those who believe that everyone in the economy should be treated with dignity and respect. In Brazil, the Bolsa Familia programme is founded on the belief that the poor understand best their own needs and how to make meagre resources go farthest. It gives money to families without stipulating how it must be spent, while, in exchange, participants undertake responsibilities, *contrapartidas*, to ensure their children attend school, are immunised and have regular medical check-ups. Pregnant women are required to get prenatal care and to breastfeed their infants. Instead of feeling stigmatised by dependency, most of the beneficiaries are proud to be enrolled, and to be able to feed and clothe their children properly without having to beg. No longer excluded from the economy, they participate by purchasing bread and milk, also TVs, fridges and washing machines. The scheme, which eliminates middlemen and has benefited Brazilians generally, is popular at all levels in the country[106] and thus survives successive changes of government.

Globally there is a yearning for a renewed sense of belonging. In 2011, the Occupy movement began with a camp in Zuccotti Park in

Manhattan. Participants stood in solidarity with movements in Madrid, Toronto, London, Athens, Sydney, Stuttgart, Tokyo, Milan, Amsterdam, Algiers and Tel Aviv, as well as many other American cities. As the year wore on, people in many more cities added their voice.

The Occupy movement made clear its disillusionment with an economy that had brought 99% of the wealth to 1% of the population. Slogans pinpointed the discontent: 'We are the 99%', 'It's socialism for the banks', 'Wall Street Privatise Profits Socialise Losses', 'I helped create the mortgage meltdown and all I got was this $700 billion bailout', 'Corporations are in control of our democratic process'. American flags flying throughout the camp suggested that by insisting on a national discussion, the protesters were serving their country.

The movement embraced a diversity of views: 'To get our voice heard – that's all we're trying to do.' Prominent public intellectuals such as Noam Chomsky and Barbara Kingsolver announced their solidarity. Rallies for a Global Day of Action took place on the same day in more than 1000 cities around the world. In Vancouver alone, around 4000 people participated. A few days later Egyptian pro-democracy activists lent their support, releasing a statement in solidarity with occupiers. Police brutality and arrests simply increased the determination and numbers. The sense of belonging was documented both on TV and in a book by some who had taken part.[107] As participants expressed it: 'We all connected and we felt like family. We wanted to take care of one another, look out for one another'; 'The gift of giving is the driving force of Occupy'; 'It's a rebirth of America's sense of community, a sense of, okay this is where we can come and talk'.

In Zuccotti Park occupiers drew up Principles of Solidarity to ensure participation, mutual respect and responsibility. As there was no amplification, a 'people's mic' was used. Speakers bellowed their words in short phrases, to be taken up and sent on by the nearer listening crowd. Soon hand signals became an integral part of operations. 'Twinkling' (wiggling the fingers with one or both hands raised) expressed approval and a repertoire of subtle distinctions (the 'temperature check') evolved.

A meditation space around a tree became the spiritual centre of the park and a symbol of interconnectedness. Very soon there were 'departments' such as Kitchen, Comfort, Sanitation, Sustainability, Medic Tent, Legal Working Group, even the People's Library. People around the world responded to occupiers' tweets by ordering up food from local outlets for protesters to pick up. A local café made its kitchen available in the afternoons, so that Occupy's cooks could prepare dinner for at least 1500 people on weekdays and 3000 on weekends. The sustainability committee distributed compost buckets and took the waste away on bicycles. Pedal power was used to provide electricity. People began coming to the park expressly to work in the library. By November, when the protesters were evicted, the library had 4000 books.

After police destroyed the encampment and evicted the occupiers, many mourned its passing, including Jake Rozak, a business administration graduate:

> I miss it. The sense of community, sense of love, sense of understanding and passion, it was all here. Everything was in this park. You could feel like an outsider two streets down, then you'd come back here and you'd be welcomed unconditionally, no matter what walk of life you were from, how old you were, what your race was, you were welcome and that's rare. A lot of people have never seen that.[108]

Although the Occupy movement endured in this form for one short year and in Zuccotti Park for only two months, it had profound effects on countries around the world. American national dialogue began to focus on income inequality, the shrinking middle class, fair taxation and a more democratic form of politics answerable to citizens rather than corporations. The government raised taxes on the wealthiest Americans. The governor of New York proposed public campaign financing as 1.7 million people signed petitions to overturn the Citizen United law. European leaders and the former CEO of Citibank advocated the separation of commercial banks from investment banks. The US government called for cuts in the military budget and increased spending on job-creating infrastructure projects. France, Spain and Greece elected governments promising to resist bank-supported austerity measures and preserve social programmes.

Feel, think, act

Individuals all over the world understand the threats posed by governments and corporations to individuals, communities and the planet. With 40 million members in 2015, Avaaz is the largest online civic movement in the world. Refusing any contribution from governments, its funds come from online donations from individuals. Its campaigns are well-researched and carefully targeted and the organisation is well-respected. Former UK prime minister Gordon Brown and former US vice president Al Gore speak highly of its effectiveness while the *Economist* says Avaaz is 'poised to deliver a deafening wakeup call to world leaders'. Through joint action, members experience a renewed sense of belonging in the modern world. In the words of Alexandra from Germany: 'It is wonderful to finally be able to unite with other people on this planet, to stand up, to be heard.'

Although there is ample evidence that the rich seek to maximise matters to their own advantage, regardless of the effects on the lives of others, Piff's research shows that their attitudes change according to circumstances:

> In fact, we've been finding in our own laboratory research that small psychological interventions, small changes to people's values, small nudges in certain directions, can restore levels of egalitarianism and empathy. For instance, reminding people of the benefits of cooperation, or the advantages of community, cause wealthier individuals to be just as egalitarian as poor people.
>
> In one study, we had people watch a brief video, just 46 seconds long, about childhood poverty... and then presented a stranger to them in the lab who was in distress. After watching this video, an hour later, rich people became just as generous of their own time to help out this other person, a stranger, as someone who was poor, suggesting that these differences are not innate or categorical...[109]

In real-time society, Bill Gates, one of the world's wealthiest individuals and a person who for many years was single-minded about building his Microsoft empire, now says, 'Humanity's greatest advances are not in its discoveries, but in how those discoveries are applied to reduce inequity.' Following a tradition of American philanthropy, these days he devotes his time to the Gates Foundation, working to improve healthcare and reduce extreme poverty worldwide. And through the Giving Pledge more than 100 of the US's wealthiest individuals have pledged over half of their fortunes to charity.

A notch higher on the enlightenment ladder, dozens of grassroots movements recognise the rigged nature of the economies they have succeeded in. Through organisations like We Are the One Percent, the

Resource Generation, or Wealth for Common Good, the most privileged members of the population acknowledge the injustice of privilege and leverage their privilege and economic resources to advocate changes in social values and policies, and also in people's behaviour.

A financial journalist friend of mine, Mary Holm, has for many years written regular newspaper columns, lectured and given seminars aimed at boosting people's confidence and knowledge about investing. She is so unequivocally against people setting out in life with money-making as their prime goal that her university course includes a session on money and happiness.

> I get the students to rate at least five people, one to five for wealth and one to five for happiness. We look at the correlations and it usually turns out that as they go up into the middle and higher wealth levels, the happiness is about the same.
>
> A lot of research shows the correlation between more wealth and more happiness is quite tenuous. I say to the students, I want you to learn to make good decisions with the money you do make and then you've got more time to enjoy the things that really matter in life – like friends and reading novels and getting out into nature and giving.

Holm's accountant is of a similar mind:

> He gets clients sometimes coming in and saying, 'I've worked out a way I can do this and this and pay very little or even no tax.' He says to them, 'When you leave here are you going to drive down a road? Who made that road? Who maintains it? Someone drives into you, you ring up the police – who pays the police? So you're going to live in the society and enjoy all these things and not contribute your share of it?'

Some lawyers and accountants would say it's not their job to write the law, that's for the politicians, and it's not their job to judge the morals of their clients. Says Mary, 'I don't see why they don't say to the client, "Do you feel okay about this? Do you think this is fair?" Because they are in society themselves and there's more to life than the laws, which, God only knows, are written by politicians and officials and they don't get it right always.'

We don't have to look far to find New Zealanders who are concerned about the effects of inequality. During the 1990s Kate Frykberg and her husband realised they had everything they needed materially, so they set up a charitable trust and looked about for ways to give that would create change. Like Piff, Frykberg considers empathy one of the most important qualities for behaving well with others. Her mantra for giving is 'Feel, think, act'. She explains, 'It's not necessarily easy to break out of your world and see what other people's realities might be.' The father of economics would agree. Adam Smith gave us one of the greatest reasons to read fiction:

> Though our brother is upon the rack, as long as we ourselves are at ease, our senses will never inform us of what he suffers. They never did and never can carry us beyond our own persons, and it is by the imagination only that we form any conception of what are his sensations... His agonies when they are thus brought home to ourselves, when we have thus adopted and made them our own, begin at last to affect us, and we then tremble and shudder at the thought of what he feels.[110]

Fortunately, our need to belong works naturally in the direction of more equality, dignity and respect for all. In his book *Out of the Wreckage*, George Monbiot writes of the spectacular degrees of altruism and cooperation exhibited by human beings. These are the 'central, crucial facts about humankind.'[111] His assertion is backed up by recent research in several different sciences.[112] He says that our good nature has been thwarted by several forces, with much of the blame going to the ideology of extreme competition and individualism. This has been so persuasive that we have come to believe this is how we naturally are: 'Our atomisation has allowed intolerant and violent forces to fill the political vacuum. We are trapped in a vicious circle of alienation and reaction... Through invoking our capacity for togetherness and belonging, we can rediscover the central facts of our humanity: our altruism and mutual aid.'[113]

TEN

INSIDE A NATION

Why we made it up

We now come to a kind of belonging which has the power to both exalt and degrade us. It can be benign, certainly it can be benign. It can make us help strangers, especially when earthquakes or volcanoes lay waste their lives, and it can make us feel part of a much larger, possibly eternal whole. But it can also rob us of respect for individual human worth. It can make us kill and maim, engage in massacres, commit unlimited cruelty against the weak and vulnerable. It can make us reduce our own towns and villages to rubble, throwing in for good measure the infrastructure that makes life comfortable. For this kind of belonging we will betray deeply held values and love, even our family.

Nation is not synonymous with state. A state is a bureaucratic thing with practical outcomes. It is concerned with controlling, administering and defending both the people in its territory and the territory itself. It has an organised economy, a legal system, a government that provides public services, education, transportation and other infrastructure, and of course policing. A nation concerns a people's feeling about those they share culture or history with. In his book about Russia, Geoffrey Hosking offers a useful definition: 'A nation, it seems to me, is a large, territorially extended and socially differentiated aggregate of people who share a sense of a common fate or of belonging together, which we call nationhood.'[114]

Nation-builders foster a sense of belonging through symbolism such as national flags and national sports teams, or by nurturing a sense of uniqueness in language and architecture. A nation can exist without even having a state, though those without one usually want one. Examples are Jews before the state of Israel was created, Kurds across multiple countries in the Middle East who fight stubbornly for 'Kurdistan', and Quebec, many of whose citizens would love their homeland to be a nation-state. So-called Islamic State is a statement of desire, disseminated by mass media.

Above all, a nation is something we make up. Like the public sphere and the market economy, it's an 'imagined community', that odd setup where members will mostly not know each other, yet carry an image of common communion in their minds. As part of an imagined community we can experience belonging to a very large entity, but it can only happen in conjunction with a fully functional public space. For we who have known nothing but the reality of living within an imagined community, it's hard to un-imagine it, yet it was not until the late eighteenth century that our modern idea of nation was even spoken of.

The time before

In the time before nations existed, religious faith and one's place in a hierarchical structure brought all the sense of a larger belonging that was necessary. As a parishioner, you were linked to a priest who was linked to a bishop who was linked to an archbishop and you relied upon the clergy for access to sacred scripture and an almighty god, while as a peasant, you were connected to a lord who was connected to a king. There was no possibility of direct access to a governing body. During dynastic times, English nobles felt little loyalty to the country that bankrolled them; much less than nobility across the regions of Europe.

The Habsburg family outclassed most other royal houses by extensive intermarriage. Originating in the 1020s in modern Switzerland, it spread its wings in modern Austria. Eventually its territories extended right across Europe, both within and outside the so-called Holy Roman Empire. A monarchy and an empire, it was never a nation: each conquered province was governed according to its own particular customs. The regiments garrisoned in their towns seemed like beings apart.

But nothing stays the same. As aftershocks from the Protestant Revolution rampaged through Europe, royal houses began to stumble. At first the challenge to papal authority worked in their favour and they were quick to take advantage, plundering monasteries and bolstering their own power. But Protestant convictions of equality before God encouraged German peasants to demand greater social equality, and the gift of direct access to God seemed to call for direct access to government. As people experienced the beginnings of individual identity, they began to see the interior life of individuals as a preferable basis for social organisation. This freed them from the constraints of the medieval mind and heralded the beginning of the scientific method; it also suggested that if God was not personally looking after them, fate could be a matter of chance. Mere chance!

Once upon a time people had confidence in paradise. At the end of their lives, assuming they had been faithful and good, they would go to heaven, where everything would be lovely. Paradise connected them with a bigger purpose, it endowed continuity. But by the end of the eighteenth century many people were no longer certain of a better future or that anyone beyond their family and friends cared about them.

Then there was a change of focus. In 1784, Johan Gottfried von Herder, building on Rousseau's notion of the naturalness of ethno-linguistic groupings, asserted that a people's language, race, culture, religion and customs as well as their natural economy were shaped by *geographic* realities. In other words, nothing to do with top-down legitimacy coming from a monarchical dynasty. It was the first hint of nationhood and indeed Herder's disciples became known as Romantic Nationalists. To protect the spiritual value of local customs and traditions, they promoted folklore and national languages. The brothers Grimm employed strict rulings as to what was or was not a truly German tale, for without a unified country the Germans yearned for a national way of thinking. The fad for folk epics, the retelling of legends and fairy tales, spread to other countries. In the Russian empire, national minorities tried to assert their own identities through national poetry, which often incorporated much earlier writing. In Britain, self-identified Anglo-Saxons seized upon *Beowulf* as their missing national epic. Composers like Verdi and Rossini enjoyed heroic popularity when they based operas like *Nabucco* and *William Tell* on their country's unifying myths. People were reaching for the sense of a national spirit, something that went so far back in time as to seem invincible and eternal, something that could make them all feel linked to one another, beyond their own individual identities.

Meanwhile, Europe was changing in ways that demanded practical adaptation. In addition to reading, writing and 'rithmetic, growing market economies required populations to understand basic facts about the society they lived in. States began providing systematic education and often one language was selected to be the official one.

With the loss of hierarchical structures and the command of God, it fell to state governments to protect people from inflicting violence on one another. State-funded police forces were a start, but much more was required if the people were willingly to pay taxes, obey freedom-curtailing but socially desirable laws, occasionally take up arms on behalf of the State and generally do what it wanted. That required not only homogeneity but a sense within people of belonging with their fellow countrymen. Out of this belonging would emerge our modern sense of nation.

The Romantics were eloquent in rhetoric, which was perfect for national consciousness. It inspired revolutions and helped countries such as Germany and Italy find political unity. Unfortunately, however, it also contained the germs of what would develop into full-blown ethnic cleansing, especially when Darwin's theory of natural selection became influential. The Romantics tended to regard those with a *racial* claim to territory as superior to those who merely participated in the culture, so much so that the great composer Richard Wagner attacked Jews for inadequate assimilation and claimed they were incapable of comprehending the mysteries of German music and language.

When Otto von Bismarck successfully unified all the German states except Austria, people adulated him because modernity felt somehow empty. Aspirations to liberal democracy, constitutionalism, representation and popular sovereignty gave way to a vision of nationalism based on Prussian and Protestant cultural dominance. A movement based on the German 'Volk' caught people's imagination. It reminded them of their roots and that it was Germany's destiny to rule over lesser peoples. By the end of the nineteenth century, ethnic self-determination and transformation of Europe into a Greater Germanic Empire was seen as very desirable.

Novelist Joseph Roth describes in *The Radetzky March* how, in the days before nationhood, the inhabitants of a small Slavonic town viewed the soldiers of the Royal Imperial Army in their midst, two of whom have just killed each other in a duel:

> To the shopkeepers and artisans of the little town these strange gentlemen became stranger still. The officers moved among them like incomprehensible worshippers of some remote, unappeasable god, whose gaily decked-out, gaudy victims they were. People shook their heads as they saw them pass, they even pitied them. They have all kinds of

privileges, the people said to themselves, they can swagger about with their swords and attract women; the emperor himself takes a personal interest in them and cares for them as if they were his sons. And yet, at any moment, if one insults the other, it has to be avenged in red blood.[115]

Count Chojnicki, who understands that the end of empire is drawing close, tries to explain things to his friend, Herr von Trotta, who cannot imagine life without the monarchy:

This age has no use for us. This age wants to form independent national states. People no longer believe in God. Their new religion is nationalism. Nations don't go to church, they go to independence meetings instead. Monarchy, our monarchy, is founded on piety, on the belief that God chose the Habsburgs to reign over a certain number of Christian peoples... The German Emperor could still reign even if God were to abandon him. Perhaps by the grace of his people. But the Austro-Hungarian Emperor must not be forsaken by God. And God has forsaken him.[116]

It is all very disturbing for von Trotta, whose grandfather had done all major decision-making on his son's behalf and whose father had been responsible for him in the same way, but whose son has decided (decided!) to leave the army. His chess buddy understands what is happening:

'It was different in those days,' answered Skowronnek. 'Not even the Emperor is responsible today for his monarchy. It almost looks as if God were refusing to be responsible for the world. It was easier in those days. It was all so certain. Every stone lay in its proper place. The streets of life were decently paved. The houses were all roofed. But now, Commissioner! Now the paving stones are all lying around haphazardly in dangerous little heaps all over the street, the roofs have holes in them, so that the rain pours into the houses, and everyone has to find out for himself which street he really wants to go down, and what kind of house he is trying to get into.'[117]

Karl Marx's ideas about exploitation of workers by their employers had been increasingly taken up by artists and intellectuals in the decades leading up to the First World War, but working-class solidarity across Europe was not strong enough by 1914 for people to oppose the war in large numbers. Most working-class parties sided with their own national governments rather than pursue a common interest in fighting national bourgeoisies, capitalism and imperialism. The bell tolled anyway for imperialism, finishing off the Austro-Hungarian empire, along with the other empires of Russia and the Ottomans. Even Germany, whose imperial ambitions only dated from Bismarck, lost her possessions.

In the modern world, empires were too unwieldy and its peoples too diverse to inculcate the degree of belonging that could win wars. Nations were more effective, because they could be large and at the same time inspire undying loyalty. The map of Europe was redrawn to form a range of smaller states in which new nations waited to be born. There was nothing easy about the birthing. The countries that remained intact struggled with impoverishment of various kinds. For Germany, the great loser, restoring the national spirit was imperative, but right across Europe there was a faltering in confidence. A chasm had opened. For new nations, the way forward was clear. Nation-building.

Stadium of four and a half million

In a new colony there is no nationhood. The newcomers bring what they can from the old world, pots and pans and beliefs and memories. On making landfall in unknown seas, they struggle to understand the strange new soil. They suffer failure and setback. If there are people there already, they perceive them according to their belief about what constitutes a human being and who is superior, us or them.

The newcomers hope to make a buck or a better life or to offer salvation to the natives – 'Our ways, our gods are better than yours'. They leave the old world in rebellion or because life there was too hard. The Puritan Fathers came to North America in dissent. For them Protestantism in Britain was corrupt and indigestible, little more than a new hierarchy of religious authority. Sooner or later their descendants would fight against the government of the old land, which still tried to constrain and exploit them. For my great-great-grandparents, who landed in New Zealand in 1842, it was different. They were poor people who had lived in the jungle of filth and disease, injustice and moral turpitude that was London then. They were young and hopeful, they set to work with a will, but they missed their motherland terribly, they longed for news of their loved ones and of the country that existed for them only in memory. They feared that their new land, with its lack of infrastructure, its lack of history, was inferior to their old. They had no option but to develop a love of their new place, but it was hard and always there was an underlying sense of inferiority. Sooner or later their descendants would do anything to show they belonged with each other in the new land and it was different, it was so different from belonging in the old country.

From the time of its introduction to New Zealand in 1870, rugby helped people overcome the isolation of their tiny, far-flung communities and man-against-nature physical labour. Men came together as a team. They learned that with the right spirit they could achieve amazing things. Bonding became a deeply held value. It involved giving the game every muscle and sinew they had, playing down pain and even permanent disability from injury, cheering each other on, inspiring each other to do better – for it wasn't just about having fun or playing their best, it was about winning. Rugby offered male New Zealanders a chance to hold their own even in relation to their motherland, it gave them a sense of living fulfilled lives. After the game, there was drinking and initiation rites featuring the fast route to inebriation. The men learned to run fearlessly together and the reward was a peerless belonging. I think it made them feel they existed, really existed, that this was their meaningful place even though they were at the end of the world and people overseas thought them of little account.

Māori, who had for much of the journey towards nationhood watched from the sidelines or been actively rebuffed, took to rugby as though it were made for them. They were descended from the great warrior Tū and this was a warrior sport. Rugby was their chance to become part of New Zealand culture, to show they were worthy of respect. The very first time New Zealand took rugby back to the motherland, it was Māori who took it. Many of the Māori players on that 1888 'Natives Tour' felt they were going 'home' to the centre of civilisation. They began to perform a haka on the field before a game began, calling up the spirit of Tū before going into battle. Tongues lolling, eyes bulging, voices marking the beat, it was old incantation in a new setting and for a new purpose. They were pioneers again, with a new tradition to be proud of.

Rugby was certainly a game for warriors and it wasn't long before the connection with war was used by political manipulators. Richard Seddon, the prime minister who became known as Minister for

Football, was an expert. He saw 'two perfect vehicles for asserting New Zealand's place in the scheme of Empire: rugby and war'.

He sent 6500 strapping young men, hard trained by the game, to Britain's war with the Boers in South Africa in 1889–1902. Her own volunteers were clearly inferior, many turned down for combat. The colonials had become, through rugby, the Territorials of the Empire, with a place they came from and a role to play. After the great rugby tour of 1905, when the term All Blacks was coined, Seddon greeted the returning heroes with something approaching state celebrations. It seemed as though the All Blacks represented the very essence of the country's identity.

Ten years later, men undertook the horrors of the Gallipoli campaign as though it were a game of rugby. In a 1996 television documentary, 'The Game of Our Lives', Finlay Macdonald explained how 'Whole teams and clubs signed up together, often serving in the same battalions, often dying together in the same wasteland of mud and barbed wire. They thought of themselves as members of different teams and spoke of war as rugby: "It's just like football. There is not a man who has disgraced the old Christchurch football club. They died as heroes, everyone."' Another wrote to the father of his mortally wounded friend: 'He played the game to the bitter end.'[118]

1924 offered further tickets to eternal glory. A New Zealand rugby union team toured Britain, Ireland and France. They played thirty-two games including four test matches. Through match after match Kiwis bit their nails to the quick as the line of wins remained unbroken. The colonials departed their motherland as winners at her own game. 'The Invincibles' had won all thirty-two games, with only 116 points against them out of 954. It was a dazzling contribution to nationhood. The myth grew that New Zealand and rugby were indivisible. Their rugby players were winners and so were they.

As the twentieth century wore on, people needed a date for the country's coming of age and they pinpointed 1915, the year when New Zealanders and Australians had sailed to Turkey in their thousands to fight for the motherland. The country had lost the battle and thousands of fine young men, but the rout marked their country's birth as a nation, or so they believed. Something about all that futile sacrifice drew the people – the scarred returning soldiers, the parents and sisters and wives – together. The soldiers had seen the British Army command style and knew they came from a different place after all. It provided an eternal reference point for 'when we became a nation'.

On my arrival in New Zealand in 1970 I was told about the Anzacs and all it meant, but the part of Kiwi nationality that I saw around me was the bonding by rugby. They did say at my interview in London, 'If you like the outdoor life you'll be fine', but I didn't quite realise what they meant: the taxi drivers who'd tell me how the latest big match was going; the people at bus stops and parties whose way of being friendly was to talk about 'the rugby'; the dinner invitations to watch 'the match' (what match?) and the mortal sin of talking when the forwards were running the ball. I appalled my colleagues in Corso with my ignorance when we were considering big names to front our TV annual appeal. 'Do you really mean to say you don't know who Chris Laidlaw is? He's only an ex-All Black!'

I'd been nineteen years overseas but perhaps I wouldn't have known anyway. Games bored me. Scores bored me. People tussling on the ground bored me. Rugby was male, competitive, bruising, and it was a herd activity. I didn't want to be part of a herd – but I did want to belong. The country's small population gave the majority a stranglehold on what it was to be Kiwi, and rugby created in me a sense of exclusion so strong it sometimes felt like a mistake to have come to live in New Zealand.

I have described how, while the 2011 Rugby World Cup was in full swing, I was taxi'd to Auckland airport with three rugby-loving males, and how the experience caused a shift in my psyche. But that was only the beginning. The rest of the transformation took several more weeks and much of it was owing to chance.

It happened that on my return from Tauranga I underwent a train-ing course for home tutoring with refugees and migrants. During a coffee break, a young woman asked me if I was interested in the rugby. I didn't say 'No', as I would have a week before. I said, 'It depends what you're going to ask me.' She showed me a schedule of games on the wall of the classroom. She wanted to understand who was playing who the coming weekend. So I looked at a schedule for the first time and tried to work it out. The teams were divided into four evenly balanced pools, ABCD. Beneath that it listed the countries that were playing and where they were going to play. I saw Mt Eden, where I used to live, and also Westpac Stadium, in Wellington, where I live now. I thought of my son and his family who were going to watch a game at the weekend.

The next day Christine grinningly told me she had worked out how to read the schedule. We went to the board and she explained how it worked. A first grade had to play a second grade because if firsts played firsts and second played seconds, everybody would be wanting to be a second. I didn't understand it completely even then but I liked being taken to the board and invited to examine it. Christine told me she and her five-year-old daughter had gone to a match. They bought tickets at the gates just before it started. Christine laughed as she told me how they had been entirely caught up in the game.

And so it came to pass that I sat down in front of the TV and pressed the button. I could hardly believe I was doing this but I set the channel to the All Blacks playing Argentina in a quarter-final and I watched the whole match. I kept looking behind me to see if anyone was watching – no, not really, but so many people would have been astounded if they'd known. I watched the game on the Māori channel because that didn't seem such a break with my identity as if I went commercial.

I lost my normal sense of time. With deadline set but outcome unknown and the happiness of the country hanging on it, every moment mattered. The next minute, the next hour could bring good or bad news. The excitement of being passive, waiting, watching, having this *done* to me. The dangers of injury, of tempers being lost, of disappointment erupting in rage. The luxury of primal emotion, tribalism, combined with unbelievable skill, teamwork, alertness, speed. Two of the All Blacks gave each other a complicated handshake as one went off and another came on. There was heaps of blood and it was like war, hand-to-hand combat with rules – but unlike war because everyone was allowed to watch. Injuries were expected and even when horrific we were shown. After All Black victory, the TV commentator said he couldn't wait till next week for the semi-finals and I thought, 'Oh my God – I'll have to go through this again next week.'

But I didn't wait for the semi-finals, I watched the quarter-final between Ireland and Wales, knowing that James, the kind Irishman I shared a taxi with a week ago, would be watching too. I didn't understand the rules but the skill of the men was beautiful to watch. I even listened to the commentators talk about the match afterwards. I learned that in the scrum everyone's weight counts. You should push as hard as you can even when you are very tired because your weight will still count. On Saturday I watched a semi-final. Wales versus France in Wellington. That night I dreamt about the All Blacks.

Diary entry: I called on the All Blacks. They wanted to dress me as one of them. First they stripped me to my underwear to examine my fitness. They looked in my mouth to see whether it would take a teeth guard, and tested each part of my body. As each part was examined, I remembered its weakness – my shoulders, my lungs, my heart, my teeth, my knees. I was sad to recognise all that weakness, but in no way did I feel humiliated standing in front of the All Blacks in my underwear. I was exhilarated to be among them – to be seen and paid attention by them. When I was dressed I would be strong and worthy of their respect.

Suddenly I got it. I understood Kiwis' feeling about the All Blacks. What it means to a country of tiny population – a stadium of four and a half million, as a British commentator put it – to have one thing where they are second to none. One irrefutable thing. Yes, I feel it. At the same time, there is my disbelieving self: it's just a game, it's just rugby, it's just men on the field running up and down. It's ego, yearning for status, the old desire to be better than one's fellow man – with all the attendant dangers. Yet there is also interconnectedness – all those countries' teams being in New Zealand, joined together in the game, the quest, the engagement. And all their home supporters, like 60,000 people watching at the Millennium Stadium in Cardiff as Wales played (and lost to) France.

After that match, I needed to learn about the rules so I phoned G before the second semi-final and took notes. He phoned the next day to ask how I got on with the match against Australia. Then he invited me to come and watch the final with him after 'a bite to eat'. Prodigal wife comes home and the rejoicing is great.

Diary entry: The tension is overwhelming and has taken me by surprise. Last night I couldn't sleep again. I don't think it's really because of tension over who will win. At least, *not for myself*, but perhaps because I have caught the *contagion* – the radio and TV folk speak of little else but the rugby and friends mention it regularly.

Diary entry, 3.15 am: This feels like an addiction – it's in control of me, troubling and disturbing me, and yet I look forward to watching the game on Sunday. It's the third night since I watched ABs vs Australia and I'm still waking, unable to get back to sleep, and though my thoughts aren't filled with rugby, my sensibility is still on that pitch with those bodies. The physicality runs through me like the memory of a great fuck. The tension of not knowing the outcome fuses with the fearless tackling and the pounding scrum. Crouch – touch – pause – engage! The chanting of the crowd, All-Black, All-Black, it's tribal and I feel tribal. I'd be Jack in *Lord of the Flies*.

Women friends seem to be having a similar experience. Ruth confessed, 'I watched the rugby. Did I say that?' Sarah: 'To my astonishment I've become a rugby fan.' The country is united. You can see it in the countless flags flying from people's houses. The billboards shriek for victory. Hollywood-style signage on the hills around the airport forms the sacred text 'All Blacks'. Even flowers in oval council beds push up as flags.

Oxytocin is soaring through our arteries, making us feel we belong, making us invincible against the other side. And yet, there's another value in the mix – the old value of community. In small towns throughout the country, where minor teams go to play their pool matches, people make them welcome. Schoolchildren choose a team to support in addition to the All Blacks and Kiwis wave its national flag during their match. It's hospitality, but the bottom line for New Zealand is that nothing but a win will do. James had even faltered in his support of Ireland: 'When you see how much it means to New Zealanders you feel you couldn't deny them a win.' That's why it had been 'the cruellest blow' when Dan Carter dropped out of the tournament after tearing his groin. The public mood was described as funereal. Brian Moore of the *Telegraph* wrote, 'It's a remarkable experience to be in a country where the entire mood is genuinely swayed by this kind of sports news. You can't grasp it and probably will not believe it unless you are actually in New Zealand.' A clinical psychologist, referring to New Zealand's last win twenty-four years ago, said, 'It's a wound that opened in 1991 and we've been putting sticking plaster on it ever since. Dan Carter's injury unleashed our fears and the spiral of negative thinking begins.' I can't be doing with all that but I have found a way of being a rugby fan and still being authentic. I bring to it my own style of enjoyment, which includes social analysis, critical thinking, my love of learning, my need to belong. I think I had to become very sure in my own identity before I could reach out to the rugby, because it's a kind of surrender. It's a tightrope walk, being a rugby fan and still oneself.

When I think of the underside of rugby in New Zealand – battered wives, men spoiling for a fight, blind drunkenness – it seems a pity that rugby is the thing we use so heavily for our sense of nationhood. Unfortunate that by doing so we emphasise a certain set of values that include violence, aggression, macho maleness, exclusion of women, mindless tribalism.

It makes us callous sometimes, insensitive to the effect on immigrants from certain countries. For my French son-in-law it started even before he reached the shores of his new country. In Rarotonga in 1999, he read the New Zealand newspapers. France had just beaten the All Blacks in a semi-final of the Rugby World Cup, in what has gone down in history as 'the greatest game of rugby ever played'. With mounting horror, Daniel read what the citizens he was about to join were saying about the citizens he had just left. During his total of four years in New Zealand, there was no let-up in the gloating whenever New Zealand won against France. Daniel has an easy-going sense of humour but it was too much. By the time he and Tama went back to France he could hardly bear the torment of watching the All Blacks play France, and Tama no longer cared about the All Blacks winning. An Australian friend who lived in New Zealand for several years had something resembling post-traumatic stress disorder by the time he left.

But rugby is what we have chosen, rugby is the material we have to work with, rugby is what has grown organically of our soil. It helps us transcend class, race, income, personal achievement – and so I feel I must embrace it, while trying not to lose sight of values I hold even more dear.

Just before the final, I began to feel conflicted. After all, my son-in-law and two of my grandsons would be cheering for France. But when the All Blacks stumbled I realised how much I wanted them to win. And just as important to me as their win was watching it with my former husband. It expunged any lingering negativity associated with a darkened lounge on a sunny Saturday afternoon. We shared a drink, a meal and then the rugby. I said I was sorry this hadn't happened while I was married to him. He said he was delighted I was enjoying it now. I saw the best of him again, relaxed, energetic, humorous, kind. The final of the 2011 Rugby World Cup was the single most watched television event in New Zealand history and I was part of it.

Due recognition

Anyone who is an All Black knows he is regarded as very wonderful. An All Black is likely to feel comfortable in New Zealand and to believe it's a great nation. If he stops being an All Black, he becomes an 'ex-All Black', another drawcard for honours. But for a democratic society what matters far more than honouring or being honoured is equal dignity. Let's say you are gay, (abnormal or ungodly), or Black (born to servitude or slavery) or female (designed for the needs of men and procreation). You feel within you a compulsion to same-sex relationships or economic independence or unfettered exploration, but your society is not having any. It mirrors you as perverted, lazy, stupid or inferior, and these attitudes enter your psyche, filling you with self-hatred. Just as important as avoiding ostracism, gaol or lynching is your task of shaking off these degrading perceptions.

In *The Victim*, Saul Bellow's main character Asa Leventhal keeps overhearing people making derogatory comments about Jews and is quick to imagine they don't like him. Although he has rejected his father's attitude to the world, it haunts him. Leventhal's father had suffered under Europe's centuries-old habit of herding Jews into money-lending and despising them until eventually he internalised the contempt and made money his only value. Leventhal junior wants to be different, but his father's imaginary enemies have become his too. When one of his few friends tells him he shouldn't abuse people if they refuse him a job, Leventhal feels he can't because that would mean pretending not to know he had been humiliated. In his confused way, Leventhal is trying to be authentic. Accepted only grudgingly in society, his choices of action are limited. If he acts subservient he feels oppressed and imprisoned, but assertiveness leads to more rejection. Instinctively he knows that to belong truly in his society, he *must* be authentic.

Identity today entails being true to one's particular way of being and we need our societies to encourage us to express it. As the sociologist Charles Taylor, who identified this 'politics of recognition', wrote: 'Due recognition is not just a courtesy we owe people. It is a vital human need.'[119]

It's also, in modern nations, a no-brainer. When people feel their true selves are imprisoned, they form solidarities. Unresponsive rulers and citizens reduce their nations to social disintegration and economic collapse. Their nationals either abandon the country or fall victim to violence and degradation as opportunists rush to fill the vacuum in the public space. When a nation doesn't accord each of its members due recognition, the result is chaos.

Tarek, Sara and Margaret

To Tarek and Sara,* it meant everything to live in a stable country. Under Saddam Hussein there was limited freedom but good infrastructure, world-class education and the sense of belonging to an ancient civilisation. By the time they married in 1991, Saddam's prosecution of the Iran-Iraq War had eroded this and, just before they married, his invasion of Kuwait enraged the outside world. A 'Coalition of the Willing', led by the United States and supported by thirty-three other countries halted the invasion and forced Iraqi troops to retreat. They left Saddam in place, saying they were not interested in governing Iraq. Nonetheless American sorties bombarded Baghdad, where Tarek and Sara were living. Sanctions imposed in 1990 were extended, resulting in high rates of malnutrition, lack of medical supplies, and diseases from lack of clean water.

Tarek and Sara found life in their homeland precarious and decided that for the sake of the family they wanted to become, they couldn't stay there. They moved to Jordan, hoping to return to Iraq when things settled down. But things didn't settle down and eventually they came on to New Zealand. They were able to find work in the central North Island, though not at the level they had commanded in Iraq. That was how I got to know Sara – she needed somewhere in Auckland to board while doing further training. She stayed with me for eighteen months, visiting extended family on the North Shore at weekends or going back to the town where Tarek and Sara's mother were looking after the children – Maha, born in Jordan, and Margaret, born in New Zealand.[†]

In New Zealand each member of the family engaged in a dialogue. For Tarek and Sara it was with the nation they had left and the nation they wanted to be part of. For 12-year-old Margaret, it concerned the nation she never knew and the one that was all she knew. Her grandmother, who came over because she had no choice, also had to navigate how far she would adapt her identity and belonging to different circumstances.

Our conversation for this book began with Tarek telling me how deeply attached he was to Mosul, the home of his forbears. He was ten when his family first took him there from Baghdad. Born to a Christian family, he was moved by the enormous abbeys.

'I think from that age I started to develop an interest in history.

---

*   Names and other identifiers in this section have been changed.

†   Maha was in Auckland at the time of this conversation.

There were big abbeys, one of the abbeys we used to go was built about 500 years after Christ. And it's on a mountain, it's beautiful. There's a very famous pathway up the hill to that abbey, we stayed there for three days – that was breathtaking for me. Then when I was more independent I used to go almost every year to Mosul to see my ancestors, to go to the libraries and the abbeys. Belonging. In Mosul I met my family from my father's side and my mother's side, my second cousin from my mother's side, father's side. They are very hospitable people and so you go from there to there and they know who you are. Family is very important in Iraq, so when you go there and knock on the door and tell them that you are Tarek, son of Nabila and Farid. Oh, my God, they treat you as Royals, period.'

In 1991, when Tarek married Sara, he wanted to take her to see the people and places he came from. This was after the Gulf War, and there was continuing friction between Kurdish insurgents and the government. Despite the danger, he drove Sara to the abbey along a road that was eerily empty. Later that year the couple left Iraq for Jordan. They couldn't speak freely about anything and there was always a shortage of something. They had endured eight years of war between Iraq and Iran. Friends of theirs had died in inner-city bombardments and other friends had died in the army.

Sara: Then the Americans came and just destroyed everything. I don't care what they tell us, that it's for freedom or whatever, if you're fighting for someone else's freedom you don't go in and crush every single infrastructure they have. On the seventeenth January they just came and with all their mighty power, bombarded all the communication towers, the water supply, electricity generators, they crippled everything. They broke all the bridges to Baghdad. We were just coming out of an eight-year war and then here we go again. We lived without electricity, without water supply, without any communication for six months.

Tarek: [Presents his laptop after googling] Do you see how the abbey is on the hill? At the top of the mountain? It's like a pilgrimage when you visit this abbey. You go on foot up this hill, it's very steep, so older people ride a mule and the mule knows its way. This is Iraq but of course what you see in the news is totally different. This is the inside of the abbey, so there is always room for guests. We used to go and spend two or three nights there. I tell you, if it is safe, I'll go tomorrow.

Jenny: Are you still in touch with lots of families there?

Tarek: Yes we still have family there, we are still in touch, but not very often because communication is difficult. We can send emails every now and then.

Jenny: Do you keep up with the news from Iraq?

Sara: We gave up in the end because it is so sad, so terrible. They usually portray Iraq as a primitive, useless place when actually it wasn't like that. They always pick the worst area to show on the TV and you think, I am sure there are much better areas worth showing. Not just on the war but anything. It's usually the worst possible places.

Tarek: Iraq is not the same as it was before. It is totally different. There are a lot of abbeys in this area, I will try to google another few of them. St Matthew who gave the name to the abbey didn't actually live there, he lived in a cave which you can visit. You can see the indentation on the floor where he knelt to pray. This is the church from the inside, you see all the rooms, this is the old part and then you go into the mountains and the caves are there.

I ask Margaret how she feels about Iraq.

Margaret: Do you mean do I consider myself Iraqi or do you mean am I brought up to be Iraqi?

Jenny: Both.

Margaret: Well! The first one is kind of difficult because I've lived here all my life so I've grown up around Kiwis and my friends are Kiwis, but then again, my parents brought me up with Arabic culture so I'm kind of half and half. I don't really have *one*. I have two sides, my Kiwi side and my Arabic side.

Tarek: Is it good?

Margaret: Well, I don't really know, it's just what I know.

Jenny: Do you ever think about it?

Margaret: Sometimes, because people can misjudge me because I'm Arabic and they sometimes think that I'm not a Christian, they think some things I do are weird and that my parents are incredibly strict.

Tarek: Margaret, would you like to go to Iraq?

Margaret: I would, I think it would be cool just to see where I actually came from.

Jenny: Do you have a feeling that part of you is Iraqi?

Margaret: Yes. I look different because I have darker, thicker hair and darker skin and sometimes I have an advantage over other people because a lot of Iraqi people are born quite smart so it makes me feel naturally smart. I'm Iraqi therefore I'm smart! All my aunties and uncles have got professions that you really need to work for.

Sara: Education is important in Iraq.

As immigrants, Tarek and Sara had to decide which aspects of their old culture they wanted to hold on to and which of the new they wanted to acquire. Comparisons were unavoidable, a fact that Margaret, working hard to forge her own complex identity, deplored.

Margaret: From what my parents say, the Iraq that they lived in before the war wasn't entirely happy but they loved it. I hear my mum complaining about New Zealand – about the strangest things! Like a couple of weeks ago she said, 'Since we moved to New Zealand we've had no love for colours, it's just black and white.'

Sara: Yes, when I first came to New Zealand I used to wear all my clothes, which are bright and nice and coloured, and wherever I go they look at me, 'Are you going out? You are overdressed', and it turned out they are not used to colours. It was all greys and blacks and now after sixteen years I hardly buy anything colourful.

Margaret: Well if they hated it so much they could have packed up and moved to Australia. They just need to get over it. There's really no point in complaining and then doing nothing about it.

Sara: The things that I'm bothered about are just trivial. Colours are nothing.

Tarek: I am very happy here. New Zealand is my home now, but you always have nostalgia for your country where your roots are and you can't help making comparisons. We lived our lovely childhood there, we lived our teenage years there and then I graduated. We got married in 1991, so all that building of my personality and happiness were there, then suddenly we moved somewhere else. We went from a happy irresponsible life to...

Sara: Happy everything to nothing.

Tarek: Yes, to nothing. For example, in Iraq if anything happened to me I wouldn't have to worry about my children because the extended family would take care of them. Here I have to think about the future, I have to work ten times harder, I have to build myself up, not only for me but for my children, because we are on our own. So the nostalgia is for Iraq, my memory is there, my friendship is there. That doesn't mean we're not happy here. New Zealand is my country but we still have nostalgia and comparison.

Sara: I will give you an example. A couple of years back, there was a FIFA soccer game between New Zealand and Bahrain, so here is an Arabic country, which we are quite close to as Iraqis, and New Zealand, where we live, playing together. And we were all cheering for New Zealand. At the same time my brother, who is a New Zealand citizen but lives in Bahrain, was cheering for New Zealand from the *inside*, because he can't show it on the outside. He told us he was praying that New Zealand would win. When the New Zealand frigate docks in Bahrain, he always goes and enjoys the atmosphere and the haka.

Tarek: We'd be in a dilemma if New Zealand and Iraq will play. I don't know who I'm going to support.

Sara: I will support New Zealand.

Tarek: I think I will support New Zealand. Do you know why? It is partly because the Iraq we know has changed.

Sara: Yes, it's not the same. I personally still have feeling when I see an old player who used to be in the [Iraq] team, we sit and listen to what he says, but when one of the new members of the team comes up, who cares? It doesn't mean anything.

Jenny: Are you New Zealand citizens?

Tarek: Of course! We are Kiwis now. Ages ago.

Sara: Margaret is born and bred Kiwi!

Jenny: So, have you brought the children up to be aware of their Iraqi heritage?

Tarek: To some extent I think yes, but you can't bring them to great depth with that. [He is looking at a bull with a human head and eagle wings on the internet.] Do you know this bull? It's a very famous statue. It's from the Neo-Assyrian Empire. They have one at the British Museum and when I took a tour, the guide asked me, 'Do you know about it?' I said, 'Actually I came from there.' She said, 'What!' I said, 'I came from there.' The Assyrian Empire is one of the oldest civilisations in the world.

Jenny: It's amazing to think of being related to it. How different New Zealand is. Such a short history.

Tarek: Yes. That is what we are missing. We are missing history. But it is different now. People say to me, 'Don't come to Iraq because the people you know, the city you know, the streets you know, it's all ruined now. If you go now you will feel depressed.' If we go back to my old house, I will say, 'This wall was red, now it's white.' I'm not complaining, but it's a comparison.

Margaret: But you guys say it in a critical way. Like, there's a difference between saying, 'They changed the wall colour' – of course, I'm going to say that too – but you're saying, 'Oh you guys have forgotten this, you guys don't know this!' It's like you guys brought us up and then it changes in two seconds because you have some other perception of New Zealand. One second they love it, the next second....

Sara: Which tells you we're not criticising in a bad way but there are things... She has some genes of the Kiwis, she doesn't like criticism!

Margaret: I just don't understand why you criticise something or somewhere that you live and then you contradict that.

Tarek: She is feeling a bit annoyed and defensive. She is a Kiwi.

Margaret: Yes, I was born here. It's like, even though they live here and even though I'm Kiwi, I feel as if they're making fun of half of what I know, half of what I've grown up around. Because I am the first generation of New Zealanders in our whole family. Even my sister wasn't born in New Zealand, so I'm the only one that actually understands what it's like!

Tarek: The other thing is, for example if we reverse it now, me, I am total Kiwi, I feel really strong if anybody talks bad about New Zealand. Like she said, I am more Kiwi than the Kiwis, I am.

Sara: He is very patriotic. He refuses to go on any plane apart
from Air New Zealand.

Tarek: Because I am a Kiwi now, period, this is my country.

Sara: I am with him on this, but everything is intense with him.
Like, for me, I do not necessarily go on Air New Zealand,
but for him it's a strong matter, like he needs to support
Air New Zealand, it's that kind of feeling. And every time
he travels and comes back he goes, 'I don't want any comments, any criticism, we are in the best part of the world'.

Tarek: What Margaret says is right, we compare and criticise, but
if you give me a choice, even if Iraq is good now, would I
go back to live there? No.

Jenny: Because you have made the transition to this country and
you want to get on with it.

Margaret: But being the first generation of Kiwis has advantages.

Sara: Like? *You* can be prime minister, not us!

Margaret: I have the best of both worlds because on one side I got
the Kiwi self and I'll be considered fully as a Kiwi, but on
the other hand the Iraqi stuff, sometimes it is really cool
because I get to see my family in Auckland heaps, and all
of my close friends who aren't in [this town] are Arabic
and we know a lot of people really, really well. Sometimes
I find it better to be with my Arabic friends because they
understand what it's like to be Arabic. My Kiwi friends
will ask me, 'Oh, why aren't you allowed to have a boyfriend? Why aren't you allowed to have Facebook? Why
aren't you allowed to have e-mail?' My Arabic friends
understand where I'm coming from because they grew up
around the same things. When I'm with them, it's like the
normal me. Whatever I like, they'll like and whatever I
know, they know.

Tarek: They have the best of both cultures, like you, so they can
understand better.

Margaret: With me and my friends we always talk about what
it's like to be Arabic and to live here and why it's so hard
sometimes. If we just lived in Amman or if we lived in
Dubai it would be much easier because we could just fit
in. I feel that sometimes you can tell I'm not actually from
a Kiwi background, like, I look different from most people
and they always think that because I'm Arabic I'm Muslim

and they don't really know what it's like to be Arabic. Unless you're Arabic you don't actually know what it's like. It's funky.

Sara: Maha suffered at school a bit because they were always telling her, you are Arab, you are Arab. For the first couple of years.

Tarek: She makes a joke of it.

Margaret: She will say, Yes, I am Arabic, I am full of petrol and I'm rich!

Tarek: They love her for that.

Margaret: And having the Iraqi side we also celebrate things altogether and it's much better. I grew up around massive groups...

Sara: We are sort of like Māori, we are always in gatherings, we always have that social networking and informal get-together.

Margaret: When we go to Auckland, everybody makes a big deal out of us. We'll stay with one family, then another family comes, visitors and another and another and another and we'll end up having like, five families in one house.

Sara: Yes, we put mattresses on the floor. But having said that, the Iraqis are not a close community like the Chinese or the Asian. Asian tends to stick together. Most of us, we don't mind mixing here, we mix with the Kiwis. We go out, we go in, no problem.

Margaret: When my friends are here, my parents will be very *sophisticated*, just laughing at the *political* jokes and all the *serious* things and they stay very quiet, but when we have these get-togethers in Auckland, you won't hear them stop laughing. They will be talking all night and they'll be having so much fun. They can change without batting an eyelid, they can sleep and wake up and be a completely different person. It's like two different kinds of culture.

Sara to Margaret: You choose the best of both and you will be the best. In Iraqi culture as a child she shouldn't be sitting with the adults and discussing stuff. Children have to get permission before they jump in and talk, but in New Zealand culture, they are allowed to do that without any restrictions or hesitation and that's an advantage for them.

Margaret: Think about it, if I just talked with people of my own age and I didn't talk to adults about things, then I would only talk about childish things. When I talk to my parents I grow up a little bit.

Sara: That's the advantage of New Zealand culture. And that's where my weaknesses come from. I'm always shy about discussing. If someone wants something from me, I will 100% say yes to please them.

Tarek: This is the way of respect we are brought up with, always put others in front of you. It is not weakness but here when you do it, it is like a weakness. Like when I was asked if I would chair a meeting and I said, 'I don't mind'. It was the way of my politeness, but here it sounds negative.

Sara: It's very difficult to change that deeply ingrained trait.

Sara's mother, who has sat silently throughout our conversation, says good night.

Tarek: If you ask Sara's mother she would have a different perspective. I think she will love the Iraqi way much better because here she does not merge with the community, she is quite isolated. She knows 5% about New Zealand, she doesn't go outside by herself, she doesn't speak the language, so her perspective will be totally different.

Sara: It is different from one generation to another, like when she comes to Auckland with us, you can see she enjoys being with his aunt because they are the same age group, they speak the same language. She has always been reliant on my dad, he used to speak five languages so she wouldn't bother. She would say, 'If I need English your dad can speak'.

Now it is time for Margaret to say good night.

Tarek: For me, a lot of the Arabic culture I hate. I see a bit of laid-back, a bit of doesn't-fit-this-era, a lot of it I don't like. That's why a lot of times I go to conflict with them, I am more for Western culture. But we do think a child should know limitation, it should not get everything. Peer pressure is hard, so in Kiwi-land, because we are very relaxed, you don't say to your child, 'This is wrong and you should not do it' and a lot of people, especially teenagers, now more and more go to the wrong way. A few years back, one of our friends, her daughter, first day when she turned sixteen she was drunk and ended up in hospital. Her mother said, 'I don't want to tell her she shouldn't do that, because she may hate me or she may leave home.' I said, 'This is total rubbish. If you show your child you love them and you give them a good life, then they don't want to lose that. And they have to know their boundaries and they have to know what is wrong or right, because if you don't say anything she thinks it's not wrong so she keeps on doing it.'

We leave the table and Tarek's internet and go and sit on the sofa, where Tarek brings up another difference between Iraqi and Kiwi culture.

Tarek: We are like Italians, we speak loud when we laugh and discuss things. For example, if Sara speaks with her brother on the phone, if she speaks in the lounge you can hear her from the bedroom, you can't watch TV in the bedroom because you can't hear above her speaking. So when we have different opinions, for example, she says, 'This is beige', and I say, 'No, I think it is yellow', we usually go to a high pitch.

Sara: Margaret and Maha get really upset: 'Don't fight, guys!' We're not fighting. When we first came here, we talked with our hands, and I see people are staring at our hands, but it didn't occur to me why. Then we came to a conclusion that we are moving our hands too much, so we did it to a lesser extent. For example, you are saying to somebody, 'Go!' – we automatically use our hands, but here you say 'Go!' without moving your hands. Like when Margaret talked about her parents, when she moves her hands like this, it means she is making fun...

Tarek: She is outspoken, she is very good.

Sara: I can see her being a lawyer. She can speak, she can tell us when we are wrong.

ELEVEN

INGROUP OUTGROUP

An alternative to inclusion

Sometimes nationhood, far from drawing large numbers of people together in an imagined community, tears people apart. This was never more apparent than in the twentieth century.

In the dying light of the Austro-Hungarian Empire, a young man walked down the imposing facades of Vienna's Ringstrasse and pondered. He had come hoping to further his career as an artist but things were not going well and in the meantime he wanted to look at the architecture. He liked working out how to improve existing buildings, make them grander.

> From morning until late at night I ran from one object of interest to another, but it was always the buildings that held my primary interest. For hours I could stand in front of the Opera, for hours I could gaze at the Parliament; the whole Ringstrasse seemed to me like an enchantment out of 'The Thousand-and-one Nights'.[120]

The young man loved buildings that made him feel part of something much larger than himself, for he himself was a nobody without work or influence. He wanted eternal values that transcended ordinary notions of time (though, of course, one wanted the trains to run on schedule). What he wanted above all was a sense of belonging to a great nation. He was not very impressed with the Habsburg Empire. Too many non-Germanic races in it. He liked the stories of great German leaders such as Bismarck and Frederick the Great and he adored the operas of his favourite composer, Richard Wagner, in which mighty beings flung themselves into glorious struggle against their enemies. After seeing *Rienzi*, he could not get the music out of his head. He spoke to his friend Kubizek of a great mission in which he would lead his people to freedom, rather like the plot in the opera he had just seen.

In Vienna he heard a lot of talk about Jews, especially Russian Jews, who were pouring into the city. There was talk of a Jewish world conspiracy and some people who had read *The Revolution in Russia* were saying that if the Russian Jews got equal civil rights then people would be sucked dry, and governments would be forced into moral and financial dependence upon them. A newspaper editorial said that invasion by Russian Jews had gone so far that all national property had fallen into Jewish hands. It was an existential problem for the nation. It was a question of 'to be or not to be'.[121]

The young man knew there were many Jews in Vienna but it was hard to tell them from his own kind. Even his beloved Ringstrasse, which spoke to him of eternal values, was substantially owned by Jews who had migrated to the city after the emperor granted them civic equality. They blended in too well, wearing the same clothes as other Viennese.

One day he caught sight of someone in a black caftan with black hair locks. Is this a Jew? he thought. The longer he stared at the foreign face, scrutinising feature for feature, the more his question became, Is this a German? He began reading pamphlets about Jews and awoke to the reach of Jewish activity in the press, art, literature and theatre. He saw 'pestilence, spiritual pestilence, worse than the black death of olden times'.[122]

The young man found employment as a building worker, but he did not get on with his workmates, who disagreed with his belief in building a great nation. Instead they talked about solidarity across nations. The empire was still in control and many countries were demanding nationhood, but his workmates didn't want that. They said nations were an invention of the capitalist classes and that institutions such as law, education, religion and morality were tools to exploit the working class, oppress the proletariat, breed slaves and slaveholders and stultify the minds of the people. The young man kept arguing until the men gave him an ultimatum: either leave the building or be thrown off the scaffolding. He asked himself, 'Are these people human? Are they worthy to belong to a great nation?'

He thought about individuality, personality and the importance of the individual. At first he had thought democracy was good but when he saw Parliament in action, he understood its fatal weakness – the lack of any responsibility in a single person. How could there be responsibility if, after an unparalleled catastrophe, the guilty government simply resigned? Could a floating majority of people ever be made responsible for anything? Wasn't the very idea of responsibility bound up with the individual? Modern Parliamentary rule threw up inferior rulers because bargaining and haggling for the favour of the majority suited the small mind.

And there was something else. It was inspiring for an individual to submit to a higher power, to annihilate the self before Nature, Fate, History, Eternal Values. When a nobody like himself submitted to these things he himself felt invincible – he *was* invincible.

The young man thought more and more about the Jews, and more and more about his workmates, who called themselves Social Democrats. That Jewish devil Marx substituted sheer deadweight of numbers for the eternal privilege of power and strength. The fellow denied the value of personality and the significance of nationality and race – the very basis of human existence and culture. It was self-evident that Nature decreed some races superior to others. Most superior of all was Germanic or Aryan man, the Master Race, which Jews refused to accept as natural ruler of the world. They even invented forms of government based on equality.

If this was civility the young man wanted none of it. He imagined what it would be like to live in a country where everyone was of his own kind. No Jews, no Communists, no Gypsies, no homosexuals, no cripples. His grand scheme would require unrelenting manipulation of the press regarding disposal of bodies, it would require superhuman powers of organisation and efficiency, and a lot of fighting, but the reward would be a German nation that extended over the whole of Europe, whose identity would be secure forever.

He would create a nation based on his own kind or die in the attempt. Fighting was nothing! Those who did not want to fight in this world of eternal struggle did not deserve to live. The young man had finally reached a clear conclusion: 'Hence today I believe that I am acting in accordance with the will of the Almighty Creator: by defending myself against the Jew, I am fighting for the work of the Lord.... this is a question of to be or not to be.'

The young man did not really believe in religion, but he had put his finger on the pulse of his time. As he set about dismantling the civility he had been born to and to build an ethnic nationhood, people flocked to follow his vision of the only kind of belonging he could see any sense in.

A longing for submission

In 1943, when the Second World War was in full flood, Stefan Zweig wrote of the first, 'The great wave broke over humanity so suddenly, with such violence, that as it foamed over the surface it brought up from the depths the dark, unconscious, primeval urges and instincts of the human animal – what Freud perceptively described as a rejection of civilisation.'[123] Hitler was right when he concluded, in a sweeping sort of way, that the majority of German people were not receptive to anything half-hearted or weak and felt threatened by individual freedom.

> The masses love the ruler rather than the supplicant, and inwardly they are far more satisfied by a doctrine which tolerates no rival than by the grant of liberal freedom; they often feel at a loss what to do with it, and even easily feel themselves deserted.[124]

Hitler knew his class – lower middle, and his time – post Habsburg Monarchy. The lower middle class in Germany had lost much of the sense of belonging it enjoyed under the empire. It's hard being an in-between. You aspire to rise higher while you fear falling lower. It makes you liable to love the strong and hate the weak, to envy many of your acquaintances, fear the stranger. The in-betweens still suffer, as artist Grayson Perry discovered with a group of middle-class women when preparing a TV documentary screened in 2012. Wailed a late-comer upon hearing that the subject was middle-class angst, 'Where do I start!'[125] During the days of empire, each had his or her definite place in a stable social and cultural system. In Germany, religious faith and traditional morality held firm for generation after generation and Father's word was law. But the loss of empire hit people hard. They had seen the Kaiser publicly ridiculed, officers had been attacked, even the family was under siege. Father was challenged by his children, who under the new conditions felt themselves smarter than their parents. The decline of the middle class gathered speed, inflamed by inflation and the Great Depression. What with Communism and Socialism and the social status of the working class rising, there was hardly anyone to look down on any more.

The lower middle class preferred the drama of national symbols to rational economic and social analysis. And what better candidate than the Treaty of Versailles, which had robbed Germany of all its colonies and much of its territory across Europe? Nobody cared to be treated as inferior, but to be treated as *nationally* inferior at least made the thing seem more significant. Meanwhile, the working class, which had experienced some gains from the revolution, had by the beginning of 1930 grown disillusioned with any kind of political activity. Even the liberal and Catholic bourgeoisie, hostile to Nazism from its beginning, found its will to resist collapsed quickly. Hitler convinced more and more citizens that Germany was Hitler and Hitler was Germany, leaving anyone in doubt out in the cold. As Erich Fromm observed, 'It seems that nothing is more difficult for the average person to bear than the feeling of not being identified with a larger group.'[126] In Hitler's Germany, to oppose what was happening meant being a traitor to the beloved Heimatland.

For the second time in twenty-five years a genie was poised to leap out of the bottle. Belonging was about to turn pathological and Hitler was the perfect catalyst. He understood perfectly the authoritarian personality and the satisfaction the 'masses' found in domination. 'What they want is the victory of the stronger and the annihilation or the unconditional surrender of the weaker.'[127] He also knew how to harness the bonding power of oxytocin. Hitler wrote,

> If he steps for the first time out of his small workshop or out of the big enterprise, in which he feels very small, into the mass meeting and is now surrounded by thousands and thousands of people with the same conviction... he himself succumbs to the mass influence of what we call mass suggestion.[128]

At mass meetings people found they had an overwhelming desire to submit to Hitler, to annihilate the self, as well as to have power over helpless things. Hitler told them again and again that the individual was nothing and did not count. The individual should dissolve himself in a higher power and be proud of participating in its strength and glory.

To help my understanding, I watched *Triumph of the Will*, Leni Riefenstahl's film of the 1934 Sixth Reich Party Congress in Nuremberg, made for Hitler. The opening speaker, surrounded by flags and replicas of the black eagle, spells out Hitler's identification with Germany, the nation and justice. Addressing Hitler, he shouts, 'You are Germany. When you act, the nation acts. When you judge, the people judge.' At a rally for young people, the opening speaker also addresses Hitler: 'My Fuhrer, as you selflessly work for this nation, so this youth wants to be selfless. As you are loyal to us, so will we be loyal to you.' Hitler takes the floor: 'It is not the state who commands us but we who command the state. It is not the state which has created us but we who have created our state. We cannot be disloyal to what has given us strength and purpose.' At all the rallies in the film, whether for workers, youth or the armed forces, Riefenstahl shows close-up after close-up of faces transformed with joyful, directed passion. Their bodies move and speak and give the Hitler salute as one.

I sit by the fireside to watch this incendiary DVD, feeling very grounded in my own life. In fact, I waited until I *was* feeling grounded before I let myself watch it. It has an effect nonetheless. Not because I no longer believe in individual will but because suddenly I am taken over by something – I'll call it euphoria – that binds me so strongly with everybody else that there is simply no room for individual will. 'I' am subsumed into the mass – and there's relief in it, such relief. I have to remind myself by an act of will (because I *am* in my sitting room and I have seen pictures of emaciated human beings in concentration camps) that the words thrilling me so much at this moment, one people, one Reich, are blinding me to every other reality. At this moment, they sound innocent. Perhaps they don't even have meaning, they are just drum beats orchestrating my euphoria. Now I am ready to follow the Fuhrer, to do what he says, He is Germany! Germany is He! We are unified, we are one!

This is bad belonging, bad, bad belonging.

The twentieth century was an era for putting the collective above the individual. Not only Nazism but also Socialism, Communism, Fascism, and in the twenty-first century we add another – Jihadism. In June 2014, an armed group renamed itself Islamic State and proclaimed a caliphate, giving itself carte blanche to take control over the entire Middle East and beyond. 'The legality of all emirates, groups, states and organisations becomes null by the expansion of the caliph's authority and the arrival of its troops to their areas,' said the group's spokesman, Abu Mohamed al-Adnani. 'Listen to your caliph and obey him. Support your state, which grows every day.'

As with Nazi Germany, economic and social factors might explain the rise of this movement but IS leaders tell us it is all about true religion, about those who really belong – and the rest, Shi'a betrayers and the infidels, who deserve execution. IS says everyone in the caliphate must submit to Allah without question. Then greatness on earth and treasure in heaven will be theirs.

It appeals to the young: to those who have not yet made up their minds about the world; to those who find themselves tormented by doubt; to those who don't belong in the wider society; to teenagers whose hormones are running amok.

A young girl in Glasgow, a clever young girl who wanted to be a doctor, found herself overwhelmed by confusion. Her blog chronicled her journey towards certainty.[129] 'I'm sure bipolar, one day my blog will be all Jihadi blah blah and the next day I am singing. May Allah guide me.' She reflected that she had no direction any more. 'Once upon a time I used to be such a career-obsessed girl, now I have no clue. I just want another fresh start, to do it right this time.' When clarity came to her, Aqsa Mahmood, whose immigrant father was the first Pakistani to play cricket for Scotland, got on a plane to Syria, where she married an IS fighter and started blogging tips and advice to other young women who were thinking of joining the movement. Their day, she told them, would revolve around cooking and cleaning, looking after and sometimes educating children. After all, women were created to be mothers and wives...

Aqsa and other young girls who became Jihadi brides, and expected never to see their parents again, blogged not only about Jihadism but also about cute kittens, home-baked pizza and fashion. It was a way of showing their followers and perhaps themselves that they still possessed that quality so prized in the West – individuality. But belonging with people fighting a grand cause was more important. With the help of Smiley-face icons, young recruiters explained how IS would look after them. Houses were free, so were electricity, water and medical care. Monthly grocery supplies would be provided. Wrote Aqsa, 'Once you arrive in the land of Jihad [it] is your family.'

I can't help thinking that when I was a teenager, if I had been offered Jihadism instead of the Open Brethren, I might have been tempted. It's all so exciting and meaningful. You don't have to believe the atrocities, they're just propaganda by the West, the Islamic State hasn't committed a single crime. To be part of it makes you feel like a significant player in today's world, united against the West that humiliates Moslems and subjects Palestinians, Iraqis, Syrians, the list goes on, to unremitting hell on earth. Fifteen-year-old Grace blogs, 'IS has started a revolution. We are going to be the generation that made all this happen. We are going to be remembered for ages.'

When Stefan Zweig was a teenager in staid end-of-the-nineteenth-century Vienna, he and his friends loved receiving epithets like 'anarchist' or 'decadent'. 'We had the feeling that a time had set in for us, our time, in which youth had finally achieved its rights.'

Similarly, when the Halane twins from Manchester, who flew to Syria and married IS fighters, were dubbed 'The Terror Twins' in the press, the two high achievers who had once wanted to be doctors were thrilled. One of them blogged, 'I love the name because it makes me sound scary. ISIS love it when they make us sound scary because it makes us a Big Threat.' They married Jihadi soldiers, became Jihadi widows and by May 2015 were reported to be on the run from ISIS, facing execution should they be tracked down.

Instant communication. Instant belonging. Instant meaning and purpose. Through submission we are promised something greater than ourselves, that makes us feel strong, invincible even. It doesn't last. It's an invitation to unleash the unconscious primeval depths. It does not truly belong to the modern age. It is not the hope of the future.

Gabriele

The effects of Hitler's ministrations penetrated deep into succeeding generations and not only on the children of his murder victims. To learn of their parents' history has filled many with horror and a sense of revulsion at being connected with it.

Gabriele Gschwendtner came to New Zealand from Bavaria in southern Germany when she was twenty-two and, after a return visit several years later, decided to make her home here. During her visit to New Zealand, in 1989, the Berlin Wall fell. Walking the Abel Tasman Track, where news was scanty, she couldn't understand what had happened.

'There is something very heavy in Germany generally but particularly in my family history. That is trauma from the war, and I know the story – very dark, very traumatic – and it's not being dealt with by the generations that followed. I have named it and cried tears for it. I love going back to Bavaria, but it's like my parents embody the sadness and the trauma, and there is a lot of heaviness and sadness to go back to always, because they are not of a generation that goes, "Okay, I'm going to look at what this is that I'm carrying around with me and have some therapy." I think this heaviness and sadness is why I am not living in Germany. It has driven me and also my only sibling to go far away to liberate something and to become who we are.'

Leaving Germany for a less rigid culture enabled Gabriele to express her deepest sense of self. Cycling around New Zealand on her mountain bike, she felt happy and free.

'I think if I had stayed in Germany I wouldn't have dared go in for this creative life that I'm living today. I would have stayed with psychology and probably become a therapist. I wouldn't have dared swim against the current and say, I'm going to do clowning and I'm going to write music and I'm going to try to survive by being self-employed and doing whatever odd kind of work it takes.'

She created her own company, Playfool Spirit. Using Buddhist teachings on mindfulness and compassion, she took clowning into schools, rest homes and other groups. Whether she is expressing a prepared story or improvising, she tries to be totally present in the moment, letting go of thinking and her ego. At such times, she feels a deep sense of trust in herself, a deep sense of authenticity. Yet, despite her happiness at living in New Zealand, Gabriele says she will never be 'a New Zealander'.

'The older I'm getting, the more I am aware of being German, even though I have New Zealand citizenship. My roots are where I come from. Sixteen years ago, I was very happy leaving all that behind. I didn't seek out German friends where I lived on the West Coast. I was not looking for Germans and I was glad not to speak German. But that has completely changed through finding my roots again. I don't have to avoid other Germans now. In fact, I can see some good qualities in them. For example, reliability. When New Zealanders fail to pay a deposit or turn up for one of my classes they have enrolled in, I think, Oh, I must be very German because I would be reliable!'

Her parents' health is deteriorating, so Gabriele has committed herself to frequent visits to help them. She usually stays two months.

'The longer I'm there the more I speak proper Bavarian. By the end of the time I have slipped into a different identity and a different language and a different sense of humour. My first name is Ursula, so when I'm in Germany I am Uschi, but here in New Zealand I use my middle name and I'm Gabriele. So I'm really two different people, two different identities, two different lives. I like them both. I enjoy coming up the Bavarian mountains, mountains I have known for forty years. The smell of nature is different because there are flowers and herbs that don't grow here, but I love the smell of the New Zealand bush as well and so I am a little torn. But I know it doesn't really matter where I go, I can create home anywhere.

'It is a funny thing but I don't know homesickness. My brother and his wife are different. They miss their German friends from Bavaria, they miss the German education and what the night sky looks like in Germany. They are a lot more connected to the earth and they do have homesickness but I never had that. When I'm here I don't have homesickness for Bavaria, and when I'm in Bavaria I don't have home-sickness for here.'

Ethnic volcanoes

For a while it seemed as though the progression from tribe to nation came naturally to the human race. As people adapted to operating within larger and larger identity units, nations would learn to coop-erate with one another more effectively. The cataclysmic wars of the twentieth century and the capacity of modern technology to annihilate everybody, did much to concentrate minds on finding happier alterna-tives. It was time to stop marching on other people's territory and start cooperating within supra-national structures. United Nations and the European Union were born.

Is sociologist Charles Taylor right when he tells us that modern individualism doesn't mean ceasing to belong, but imagining oneself as belonging to ever wider and more impersonal entities: the state, the movement, the community of humankind?[130] What seems to be hap-pening on the ground is that, instead of nations working for the good of all their people, many are fragmenting into units based on ethnicity or religion. In a way, of course, communities have always evolved out of people sharing common language, culture, traditions, history, economy and territory, but to live in ethnic nationhood as the result of evolution is one thing; to create it by expunging those who are different is quite another. People have a natural tendency to what Freud called 'the narcissism of minor difference' – the smaller the real difference between two peoples, the larger it looms in their imagination. New Zealanders and Australians love to jibe each other, as do North and South Islanders, even Aucklanders and Wellingtonians. Accentuate the difference, claim superiority, feel good. Just good fun, isn't it?

Not in the case of the former Yugoslavia. Although that country was conceived as a single nation for all South Slavic peoples, the aspiration disintegrated after bloody civil war. Yet Serbs and Croats were not so different. Under the Austro-Hungarian Empire, they shared language and the same village way of life for centuries. When the empire collapsed, the citizens of the new Yugoslav nation needed to find their way towards civic democracy, but the effort was hijacked by invasions during World War II and separatist factions that committed crimes of unspeakable cruelty against one another. After 1945, it became a federation of ethnically-based republics. Tragically, instead of acknowledging the wounds of civil war, President Tito cracked down on civic multi-party opposition. Instead of healing, the wounds festered. After Tito's death in 1980, anyone living outside the borders of his or her ethnic republic suddenly found themselves part of an endangered ethnic minority. Nationalist politicians on both sides took the breakdown of trust as their starting point and fanned it into an explosive narrative featuring their lot as blameless victims, the other lot as genocidal killers. By 1990 the state was doing so badly at protecting its citizens that no one in a minority could be sure who would protect them. Mutual terror degenerated into ethnic hatred and a functioning nation state evaporated. Vulture warlords appeared bearing gifts – security and a solution: 'If you cannot trust your neighbours, get rid of them. We'll help you.' Ethnic cleansing got underway.

Ethnic Nationalism offered citizens the intense excitement of focusing on 'higher things', though the banality of bourgeois politics would have helped them far more. It would have enabled them to confront the facts around them – the poverty and backwardness that were preventing them taking their place in the modern world – and to start dealing with it. Now the former Yugoslavia is divided into states defined even more rigidly by ethnicity and its once-shared language is fragmenting too. People still living in ethnic minority survive in soul-destroying poverty among the ruins of what was once their home. Looking over their shoulders, they wonder if their enemies will return.

Nationalism is one of those words meaning different things to different people and different countries. In Latin American countries, discrimination on the basis of biological physical features is less prevalent;[131] for Russia, Geoffrey Hosking argues, nation never existed as a separate entity from longing for empire; Britain developed a sense of nation *before* creating an empire; the Chinese were shocked to encounter the Western idea of empire. Theirs was more a kind of paternalism based on the teachings of Confucius. It had no desire to hold extensive dominion over other countries.

Michael Ignatieff offers a definition that applies to all these variants: 'As a cultural ideal, nationalism is the claim that while men and women have many identities, it is the nation which provides them with their primary form of belonging.'[132] He points out that many tribal peoples and ethnic minorities do *not* think of themselves as nations and seek no state of their own.

I'm no nationalist. New Zealand, much as I love it, is not my most important form of belonging, just a strand, as England is a strand. If England called to me now, 'Come back, all is forgiven!', would I return? No. Though I grew up in a southern counties community bound together by common language, culture, traditions, history, economy and territory, I no longer experience England as a national – and that's fine. The UK will always be part of my identity, but each time I go back it's more like a foreign country – the density of the population (I'm going to get knocked off this footpath) and of its housing (I can't see any trees), the colours of the inhabitants (everyone else in this Underground carriage is black) – these are changes I have not been part of and I experience them as a stranger. Actually, I enjoy it more that way – I used to feel overwhelmed on my visits, torn apart in terms of belonging. Now I go back as a tourist with memories and feel proud of my many-stranded identity.

Nationhood, being an imaginary, depends on how we imagine it and our powers of imagination can persist through centuries if we so direct them. The German émigrés who left Germany 300 years ago to settle in the eastern Slavic border regions of what later became Russia, continued to see themselves as German right up until 1989, when the Berlin Wall fell and Germany, believing that nationality is in the blood, allowed them the right of return. Although their habits and mentality were Soviet and their German was, at best, a history-laden fossil, many took up the offer. Deposited in Frankfurt, they confronted a way of life so alien that a flush toilet, shower and bath presented them with unfathomable mystery, and they had to be shown how to cross the road. They were surprised by everything, but most of all by the foreigners. 'I thought I was coming to Germany,' said one, 'instead, it's Turkey.'[133] It's true, there are a good many Turks. Until recently they were debarred from becoming German citizens, though increasing numbers had been born and bred in that country. These bizarre consequences arise logically from an imaginary that makes nationality dependent on ethnicity.

Let's imagine something different. Let's locate our national belonging where we live, where it's concretely real, and jettison any idea of belonging that ignores geographical and historical reality. Let citizens participate in lawmaking and government, which is often dull and sometimes banal. Good luck to those who prefer excitement and warlords; civic nationals have time and mental space to focus on other things – beauty, nature, joy in body and intellect, love, conversation, caring for fellow man – and difference. Let our ethnic communities organise public festivals based on their traditions: Diwali, Lantern, Pasifika, Eid ul-Fitr. Joyful sharing increases the understanding and celebration of difference, and helps contain fear of the stranger at a more or less rational level.

People are feeling their way towards a new political narrative capable of replacing the old isolating and exploitative neoliberal one. Instinctively we understand that we need a new sense of belonging, such as George Monbiot explores in *Out of the Wreckage: A New Politics for an Age of Crisis.* 'Through restoring community, renewing civic life and claiming our place in the world, we build a society in which our extraordinary nature – our altruism, empathy and deep connection – is released. A kinder world stimulates and normalizes our kinder values.'[134] Monbiot proposes a name for this story: the Politics of Belonging.

TWELVE

THE GREAT BELONGING

Possession

What if we have got our basic premise wrong? What if being on earth is not all about *us* after all? What if the world only seems the way it does because of the mindset we apply to it?

We are habituated to dividing up the world in terms of ownership. Vast chunks of land, air and sea are deemed to 'belong to' – which is different from belonging. Like millions of others I acquiesce in these classifications, but while my land agent and lawyer assure me that the land I inhabit is wholly mine, this is not universally acknowledged. Like traditional Māori who believed land was unownable, various creatures of strong will, before whom my defences crumble, have taken up residence. Creepy crawlies live in the soil, butterflies lay eggs on the flowers and vegetables, aphids consider themselves entitled to the roses, while on any given day birds and hedgehogs tweet and snuffle their way across my borders. Even in the glasshouse, snails and thrips help themselves without asking, and, though I want my place to be a food haven and sanctuary for birds, cats flout my wishes.

Nor does the weather respect my land. Torrential rain deposits debris on clean, neat paths and kills trees that don't like wet feet; the sun scorches down for weeks, causing expensive plants to shrivel and die. The wind blows away my spring blossom and reduces my slender saplings to leaning towers. Tectonic forces don't give a damn either.

King Xerxes experienced something similar in 480 BC when he invaded Greece with a titanic army. Looking down at the plains covered with his regiments, he began to weep, realising that in 100 years' time all his men would be dead. Later on in Europe, people treasured paintings featuring a skull and hourglass among joyous symbols of fecundity and sensuality. They needed to remind themselves that within a few years they would lose all they possessed and that sooner or later they too would face what Robert Burns called 'the derisive silence of eternity'.

Gyan

Recently I met someone through my brother Atma who, though brought up in southern England in a Western tradition, seems to exist outside this orientation to ownership. By choice he does not own a dwelling and has no home base. Food and shelter are provided by the people he 'assists' – though this term does not really describe the relationship. An engineer by training, he is able to turn his hand and brain to many kinds of construction and he has also built a large network of spiritual institutions, ecological communities and individual people glad of his assistance. His whole being exuded a kind of ease rare in my experience. I wanted to understand how it was that Gyan's orientation to possessions – and therefore belonging – was so different from my own and that of so many other Westerners.

Jenny: Did your background predispose you to seeing things differently?

Gyan: There was no background of mendicants or homelessness. My parents and grandparents had houses. My paternal grandfather was head of a big school. My maternal grandparents had jobs in the city. There is nothing that could have predisposed me apart from the fact that my parents lived a very simple life and a very happy life, managing a small farm until I was about six. My mother cooked on an open fire so it was quite similar to a hippie kind of life, but this was in the 1950s, before hippies existed.

Jenny: You must have been aware that ownership was the expectation of a lot of people for themselves in the West.

Gyan: Luckily, from my father in particular, there was no imposition of that expectation. In fact my father has sometimes said that *I* am living the life for him. He had a dream himself in the sense of being unformatted in the material world.

When Gyan was twenty-seven he became involved with spiritual teachings, so I asked him what he had done in his early twenties.

Gyan: I travelled all around the world – three, four, five times round and round. I travelled in Asia, a little bit in Africa, a little bit in North America, but mainly in Asia with just a shoulder bag. Alone. For three years. No sleeping bag, just a sheet. I had a rule at that time – this is before I knew there was such a thing as 'renunciation' – that every Sunday I took everything out of the bag and anything I hadn't used in the last seven days, I gave away. Everything had to be immediate. If you lived in the present moment, you needed very little.

Jenny: And at this point it wasn't informed by any teaching?

Gyan: Zero. Zero teaching. I had no idea of what the Hindu people or the Sannyasa people in India call Parivrajak, which is that you don't live anywhere, like the sadhus in India who live on permanent pilgrimage – they cannot live anywhere more than three days. I didn't know that at all but I experienced it during that time.

Jenny: And did you sometimes think, What am I going to do with the rest of my life? Will I have to get a job?

Gyan: Never. Actually one of the things that I have always had from childhood is that I don't believe this socio-economic paradigm is very stable. I never believed that it was going to give me a pension. Even if I saved a lot of money I didn't really believe it would be there later on when I needed it – which has happened to some people. So I didn't find this particular paradigm very attractive. To make money, to work for a large corporation, it didn't seem like fun.

Jenny: So what brought you to spiritual teaching?

Gyan: In India I met some friends who were doing yoga. I didn't really have a big intention to do yoga but I became involved in that school and so I trained with them for twelve years. There's a rule in many spiritual teachings that the initial studies should last for twelve years and then you should leave it, so I did.

Jenny: Did your involvement in the spiritual side of things make the usual kinds of belonging unnecessary to you?

Gyan: You could look at it in two ways. You could think that the spiritual orientation provided another community or social format, like the family or like a village, which you could identify with – and that was true to some extent. But that was not the point. The main point is that you identify with your own inner stillness, space, whatever you want to call it. It doesn't necessarily have a religious context. It's an experience of being with yourself, at peace – peace is a tricky word, it has a lot of things hanging off it – 'stillness' is better, or 'darkness'. There is a sense of, What do you need if you are content to be still? That was probably part of my character but it was guided by being with some great masters.

That notion may have started from a simple life with my parents, which was after the Second World War when there was rationing and they lived on vegetables and milk. That was very attractive, because there was a bubble of euphoria – there weren't bombs dropping anymore and everybody felt really good. The sixties, the Flower Power came out of that. And then there was my sense of lack of security within the socio-economic model on offer within society – it didn't seem like it was a stable thing to place one's belonging in. And then travelling and looking at cultures and later taking on teachings. Maybe all those things came together to enhance a meditative stillness and I didn't bother.

Jenny: And so the other ways in which people often do develop a belonging, a community, a relationship like marriage or even a particular place, were they never terribly important to you?

Gyan: No. I haven't rejected them but they just weren't attractive. I helped many people, fixing their gutters, their whatsits, so it is not that I rejected, it's just that I never found those things worthy of putting effort into. Both Hindu and Buddhist teaching says that there is nothing secure. There was a contemporary Hindu master who said that in relationship (maybe he meant in marriage, maybe he meant in girlfriend-boyfriend, maybe he meant in community), there are three qualities that hold it together and they are: giving and giving and giving. In other words, the teaching says we are 'still' within our self, we have whatever we have, and we offer that to the society. So we are not dependent on it and it's not a co-dependent relationship. It's a relationship with oneself from which you then try to offer, say, help with building a hut or whatever need people may have.

Jenny: You said you bought a house once, which you had for six weeks.

Gyan: Yes, there was a house and there was a friend, a physiotherapist in Australia. We weren't in partnership or anything, we were good friends and we thought okay we'll get this house. I had finance at that time so I just paid cash for it. It was a cheap, wooden house and I only bought half of it – and I didn't like it! It was kind of a game even to buy it – no mortgage and the deposit I paid was my car.

Jenny: So ever since then have you followed the kind of life you have now?

Gyan: Yes. Offering service in different places, always connected with the teachings. Or doing something for friends. Sometimes there is a little stipend. One or two thousand dollars a year is enough to survive. That enables me to live a life in which contemplation is the major element. The work I am doing here with your brother, helping him on the land, is not different from contemplation. The physical work I do is within the practice of generosity, or at least an attempt to offer something of value to other people.

Jenny: What about your sense of individuality?

Gyan: The aim in the yoga practice or in eastern religions is for the individual ego to dissolve, for you to become less. The idea is that you remove, not your character, but definitely the obstacles and the difficulties in your character in order that... It's my lifestyle now, I can just relax with it.

Jenny: The way that individuality works in the UK, it's very much emphasised, isn't it?

Gyan: Yes, it's a cult of individuality.

Jenny: What was your feeling about that, when you were in your twenties?

Gyan: I didn't have any feeling about it. I think I joined it. I think I still am part of individualisation in the sense of being separate, in that sense of being 'I' and not 'we'. I think I am still basically the same because I came from that paradigm, but there's something that I am aware of and working on, maybe. The sense of homogeneity underneath all the phenomena, animate and inanimate.

Jenny: So the way you live heightens your awareness of that.

Gyan: Yes, it does, but it's not a *direct* process because at least in the East and with a lot of the Eastern teachings, particularly, say, with karma yoga, the purpose of the practices is to remove obstacles, to remove tensions, to remove preferences, to remove choices, to remove me making decisions all the time about what I like or don't like. So then, by becoming calm or still or spacious or in some sense empty, *naturally* your character will come out and naturally you'll be expressing yourself in a non-egoic way, in a creative and hopefully helpful way. So you don't have to *aim* for that any more. My actual belief is that true openness and stillness and contentment within the human being is a very beautiful state naturally. You don't have to put beauty there, you don't have to try to make it good, it is already good inside.

Jenny: Does that lead you away from feeling a strong attachment to emotions?

Gyan: Yes, but again you're looking at it from the other way, you see. This is the big difference between the East and the Western psychological and spiritual paradigm, that the Western paradigm is trying to find God, is trying to refine themselves, to make themselves more subtle, to make themselves closer to the image of God or universality or whatever. But the East doesn't do that, the East says, I'm already there, 'I've got lots of shit in me, I've got lots of preferences and hang-ups and imbalances, even violence or whatever, which I'm going to try and work with, and balance out, in order that what I really am comes out.' They're not trying to *make* it.

Jenny: It's like a sculptor revealing the statue.

Gyan: Exactly, that's a very good example. Michelangelo, when he made David, people said, 'What an amazing thing you've made.' He said, 'No, it was there when I received the block. I only removed the rubbish.' So the West is trying to put plaster of Paris on something in order to make a David but the East sees a universe in which everything is already formed and we just need to learn to see it.

There are between four and five million sadhus [religious ascetics or holy people] in India today, it's considered an admirable way of life, wandering around, supported by society. It's a bit like in our own times before the Industrial

Revolution, where there were mendicants, friars, travelling spiritual people, Biblical storytellers, hermits. Owners of a property like your brother's – I've actually seen this in a Victorian paper – would advertise for a hermit. They would offer a hut so they could have a little of that calm vibration on their property. It wasn't so that they could go and learn yoga from them or meditation, they just wanted to be providing a place where a quiet person could live, where they could grow some vegetables and go to the river to wash.

My Maria Stuarda moment

In Donizetti's opera *Maria Stuarda*, a young queen facing execution looks forward to joining 'the Great Belonging'. The phrase has special meaning for me because of something that happened in 2002. The upper chamber of my heart was, as usual, receiving information from the outside world to indicate how fast my heart should beat, but suddenly ceased to pass it on to the lower chamber. I had 'complete heart block'.

I only knew that I didn't feel up to a three-hour walk planned for that Saturday and that when I wanted to make a cup of tea, I was wondering if I'd get to the kitchen without fainting. Within minutes of seeing the doctor I was lying on a hospital bed watching a monitor spell out my descending pulse rate. It was down to about twenty-seven and I remember thinking, 'Oh, well, all it needs to do for me to die is keep on going down.' I took pleasure in the idea that I could now see my life's whole narrative, even though dying would rob me of achieving half the things I'd intended to. To be alive and yet see my story complete seemed to bring two halves of myself together. I and my story. Whatever my story was, no matter how inconsequential, it was mine, it was an entity in the world.

It turned out I didn't need to die after all. With a pacemaker wired to my heart, all I had to do was rely on a battery and lead a normal life. I took a week off work and spent much of the time gazing at trees. It was a big effort to drag myself back to engaging with normal daily life. From then on whenever I felt too caught up in life I could reference myself back to the day when everything nearly stopped, the day I nearly left everything. Now, even without dying, I could turn to the trees, the flowers, the rocks and stones and be one with them, let them be my centre, let them be my axis. And I retained a sense of quiet certainty that one day I would be part of that great belonging.

A scenario

Once upon a time we saw the universe in a certain way and it seemed to fit the facts. There was an all-powerful creator who put us in it to fulfil his own purpose, which we were supposed to spend our lives attempting to carry out. This gave our lives meaning and transcendence, a blueprint for living together in harmony.

But our ideas of god changed. It became impossible to believe in the old way, with the old certainty. We saw that chance played a huge part in what happened to us. The universe no longer seemed to have intrinsic purpose or meaning, but *we* still needed purpose and meaning. Without it we could not see the point in living.

From outside, God came inside. For a while we consulted him deep inside, then that didn't seem essential either. Authenticity became our salvation – 'This is how we must face the world,' we said, 'with our own authentic selves.' But something was missing, a kind of void that capitalism offered promise of filling. Its language and values were the most universal of all. Profit, self-interest, bottom line, these seemed to be all that mattered. It was like a new religion. You couldn't argue with it. Capitalist values poured into the self and set like concrete.

And yet the self was not of set form; it was fluid, plastic, continually changing in interaction with its physical and social environs. It was capable of becoming more (or less) wise, more (or less) adapted to a changing modern world, more (or less) attuned to those around it.

The Axial Age

A few years ago I studied the ideas of Buddha. I was drawn to the lack of dogma and the attempt to see the world as it is.

Having to rely on a battery for my continued existence made me a dependent creature, but Buddha offered a way to be positive. He said there was no such thing as an inviolable, permanent self. The human being was made up of non-human elements. The Vietnamese Zen master Thich Nhat Hanh put it this way:

> The great body of reality is indivisible. It cannot be cut into pieces with separate existences... Consider the example of a table. The table's existence is possible due to the existence of things which we might call 'the non-table world': the forest where the wood grew and was cut, the carpenter, the iron ore which became the nails and screws, and countless other things which have relation to the table, the parents

and ancestors of the carpenter, the sun and rain which made it possible for the trees to grow.

If you grasp the table's reality then you see that in the table itself are present all those things which we normally think of as the non-table world. If you took away any of these non-table elements and returned them to their sources – the nails back to the iron ore, the wood to the forest, the carpenter to his parents – the table would no longer exist.[135]

In Buddha's thought I saw similarities with Christianity, the faith I'd been brought up in, and then I learned that all the great religious traditions started during the same period. I saw interconnections and understood I belonged on a grander scale yet – with the whole history of mankind. I realised that the ways humans found meaning in life are all of human origin. They were not revealed by superhuman intelligences but slowly created.

A German philosopher named Karl Jaspers identified the period (a few hundred years either side of 500 BCE) and named it the Axial Age because it represented a pivotal change in the spiritual development of humanity. Before then, people did not make a clear distinction between religion and culture. Their gods and spirits were more like an early form of science than a separate religion, part of how they understood and responded to their natural environment.

During the Axial Age, major population groups in five or six areas of Asia found that their traditional ideas of human identity could no longer explain what was happening in their world. They were experiencing an unexpected and unprecedented level of violence. New technology was often a catalyst – the invention of the wheel, for instance, which enabled horse-led war chariots to cover great distances and engage in raids and major theft. Sages were much disturbed by the loss of equilibrium and a peaceful way of life. They reasoned that since events on earth always reflected cosmic events in heaven, the people perpetrating violence on earth must have their counterparts up there. Perhaps there were violent gods as well as peaceful ones? If so, then people on earth had to decide – were they on the side of order or evil? Once the sages had brought evil within the compass of the human psyche, they began to imagine an interior world. The new ideas were much better suited to peoples whose place of residence might change, who might be cast into exile and have to forge a whole new sense of identity in another place.

In her book *The Great Transformation* British scholar Karen Armstrong looked in depth at the particular peoples among whom the new ideas of spirituality developed.[136] She found that in India, Greece, China and the Middle East, most of the Axial philosophers had no interest in theological belief; what mattered was not what people believed but how they behaved.

Ritual and animal sacrifice had long provided a way of introducing humanity to a spiritual level of existence; the Axial sages substituted morality. The only way to encounter what they called 'God', 'Nirvana', 'Brahman' or 'the Way' was to live a compassionate life. Rather than relying on beliefs, you should get on with living an ethical life. Disciplined and habitual benevolence would bring transcendence.

The objective was to create a new kind of human being. All the sages preached a spirituality of empathy and compassion; they insisted people must abandon their egotism and greed, their violence and unkindness. And nearly all the Axial sages realised you could not confine your benevolence to your own people: your concern must somehow extend to the entire world. Each tradition developed its own formulation of what became known as the Golden Rule: Do not do to others what you would not have done to you.

Armstrong was a Roman Catholic nun for seven years. When she left her convent in 1969, she thought she'd 'finished with religion'. She wanted to be an English literature professor. But while working in television she was sent to Jerusalem to make a film about early Christianity, 'and there for the first time, I encountered the other religious traditions: Judaism and Islam, the sister religions of Christianity. And I found I knew nothing about these faiths at all – despite my own intensely religious background. I'd seen Judaism only as a kind of prelude to Christianity, and I knew nothing about Islam at all.'[137] Armstrong soon became aware of profound connections. She looked back in time to the Axial Age, of which the later traditions were the flowering, and found that people laid such emphasis on compassion because it worked. When they implemented the Golden Rule as a daily practice, they transcended their ego-bound existence.

But the way of compassion is difficult and despite the all-out efforts of the Axial sages, people came to equate religious faith with believing things. Egotism got in the way. People of all religious traditions developed a tendency to set themselves or their own people above others and when they wanted to go to war it was, and still is, the easiest thing in the world to say God was on their side. People learned how to live with contradictions that allowed them to ignore compassion and tolerance. We do it still: making war while we say we want peace, spraying poisons from the air while protesting our love for the environment, killing ourselves with indulgence while seeking the secret to a long healthy life.

The Axial Age did not last for ever. As the world re-stabilised, people sought to attune their spirituality to political realities. Rabbinic Judaism, Christianity and Islam represented a great flowering that in its essentials remained true to prophet Jeremiah, but individuals of all the religions of the Axial Age resorted to cruelty, superstition and exclusion of others.

Adaptations made it easier for people of a less intellectual stamp to encounter the divine. Although Buddha consistently taught against the cult of personality, in the centuries after his death icons representing him in various meaningful postures became extremely popular. The Buddha's face was fashioned to express serenity and fulfilment, helping people to understand and aspire to what a human being could become.

In our own time, we are again facing unprecedented violence and even the possibility of human extinction. The equilibrium of the world is profoundly upset – to a point where the problems and suffering seem greatly to out-perform the fun and kindness. As Armstrong says, 'One of the great tasks of our time is to build a global society where people can live together in peace.' She suggests we once again bring the Golden Rule to the forefront of how we find meaning in our lives, 'this imaginative act of empathy, putting yourself in the place of another'.[138]

We can take comfort in knowing there are millions who think as we do, who are working for change or at least who care about their fellow human being. The Charter for Compassion, Armstrong's brainchild created in 2009, brings together people of all religious, ethical and spiritual traditions 'from Seattle to Karachi, Houston to Amsterdam, in schools, houses of worship, city governments and among individuals everywhere', calling on the human race to activate the Golden Rule around the world.[139]

We are past the point where it is useful to think in terms of national or religious affiliation; the pivotal test of our time is to think in terms of the world. Through the imaginative act of empathy we can move beyond toleration towards appreciation of the other. This enables us to build our own sense of belonging and encourages the societies we live in to create political, social and economic institutions that belong to us.

Lashings of doubt

If individuality began with the Axial Age, why didn't I explore that at the beginning of this book? Why did I begin with the Renaissance and its new understanding of self, an understanding that in the hands of Luther and Calvin emphasised belief above behaviour, certainty above doubt? Maybe because the Axial Age felt too far away. Now I feel differently. Zoroaster, Socrates, Confucius, Jeremiah and Buddha – followed by Rabbi Hillel, Jesus and Mohammed – feel like real people, questing, discovering, opening up the world. They achieved insights we have never surpassed.

The questing that has gone on since then, often painful both to followers and non-followers, has also been part of the human quest for meaning and purpose. We in this age, who accept that the universe may not exist for any discernible purpose, know we have to create that purpose for ourselves and the best way may be to see ourselves as part of one entire whole. Every day we are made more conscious of how the environment and everything in it is part of who we are and how we can exist. When we experience ourselves as one inseparably within the whole, we are filled daily with a sense of belonging.

It will not always be clear to us how to do this, but the doubt that has afflicted us in the West almost unbearably for the last few centuries is also part of our modern human condition. It's the price of our individuality. Recently I heard an interview with Thomas Burstyn, a New Zealand filmmaker who goes to extraordinary lengths to get to the essence of the people he portrays. I was surprised to hear him tell broadcaster Kim Hill he was beginning to think that fiction was more honest. Hill asked if he was getting the collywobbles. Was he having a crisis of faith? 'Yes, but that never stops me from moving forward. I am always terrified but I feed on that. I like the challenge of being uncomfortable. I think it is a very creative energy.'

Good things can come from acceptance of doubt. It need not overwhelm us. Much more than permanence and certainty, it is the condition of the human race and so we should resist the urge to give away our individuality and annihilate ourselves in the group. By hanging in together on the doubt and practising the Golden Rule, we can transcend this Age of Loneliness.

ACKNOWLEDGEMENTS

A thousand thanks to my friends and family, whose encouragement gave me the confidence and stamina to keep going, and to friends and colleagues who offered professional assistance: Brian Bellett, Norman Bilbrough, Elizabeth Caffin, Brian Easton, Peter Farrell, Ray Grover, Chan Hirythach, Kahukura Kemp, Jan Logie, Gordon McLauchlan, Giles Moiser, Ruth Pink, Anna Rogers, Mary Ellen Ross, Antoinette Wilson and Quentin Wilson.

Also to those who gave so generously of their time and thoughts in interview: Glenys Anderson, Eileen Cassidy, Geoff Chapple, Julia de Bres, Gabriele Gschwendtner, Gyan, Mary Holm, Betty and John James, Janet, Todd Jenkins, Pauline Jones, Tama Moiser, Tarek, Sara and Margaret, Judith and David White.

With thanks to the following for permission to quote:

1981: The Tour by Geoff Chapple
Copyright © 1984 by Geoff Chapple
by permission of the author

Chris Else in *New Zealand Books*, Vol. 25, No. 2, 2015
Copyright © 2015 by Chris Else
by permission of the author

The Broken Book by Fiona Farrell
Copyright © 2011 by Fiona Farrell
by permission of the author

Independence Day by Richard Ford
Copyright © 1995 by Richard Ford
By permission of Penguin Random House

Man's Search for Meaning by Viktor E. Frankl
Copyright © 1959, 1962, 1984, 1992 by Viktor E. Frankl
Reprinted by permission of Beacon Press, Boston

Being Mortal by Atul Gawande
Copyright © 2014 by Atul Gawande
by permission of Profile Books

The Miracle of Mindfulness by Thich Nhat Hanh
Copyright © 1975, 1976 by Thich Nhat Hang,
Preface and English translation Copyright © 1975, 1976, 1987 by Mobi Ho
Reprinted by permission of Beacon Press, Boston

Shaken Down 6.3 by Jeffrey Paparoa Holman
Copyright © 2012 by Jeffrey Paparoa Holman
by permission of the author

Singer in a Songless Land by K.R. Howe
Copyright © 1991 by K.R. Howe
By permission of Auckland University Press

Jane Kelsey, 'Life in the Economic Test-tube: New Zealand "Experiment" a Colossal
    Failure'
http://www.converge.org.nz/pma/apfail.htm accessed 10/05/2014
by permission of the author

Michael King, *Te Puea: A life*
Copyright © 2008 by Michael King
by permission of Penguin Random House NZ and with thanks to Rachel King,
    courtesy of Michael King's estate

Marjolein Lips-Wiersma, 'The Map of Meaning'
Copyright © 2000–2013 by Marjolein Lips-Wiersma
by permission of the author

NOTES

1   Stefan Zweig, *Erasmus of Rotterdam,* Plunkett Lake Press eBook.
2   Molière, 'The Misanthrope', in Molière: Five Plays, Methuen World Classics, London, 1982.
3   Denis Diderot, *Rameau's Nephew and D'Alembert's Dream*, Penguin, London, 1966, p. 49.
4   Ibid., p. 120.
5   Ibid., p. 111.
6   Johann Wolfgang von Goethe, *The Sorrows of Young Werther and Selected Writings*, Signet Classic, New American Library, New York, 1962, pp 93–94.
7   Ibid., p. 105.
8   Jane Austen, *Mansfield Park*, Collins Classics, London, 2011, p. 324.
9   Jill Stark, *High Sobriety: My Year Without Booze*, Scribe Publications, Melbourne, 2013, p. 160. Study by Dr Nicholas Carah from University of Queensland using young *Hello Sunday Morning* participants as subjects.
10   Ibid., p. 160. Recent British study.
11   Ibid., p. 283.
12   Susan Cain, *Quiet: The Power of Introverts in a World That Can't Stop Talking*, Penguin, 2012, p. 44.
13   Ibid., p. 185.
14   Ibid., p. 217.
15   Te Rangi Hiroa (Sir Peter Buck), *The Coming of the Maori*, Māori Purposes Fund Board, Whitcoulls Limited, Wellington, 1982, p. 456.
16   J.L. Nicholas, *Narrative of Voyage to New Zealand*, Wilson & Horton, 1817, pp 271–2.
17   Augustus Earle, *A Narrative of a Nine Months' Residence in New Zealand in 1827*, Whitcombe & Tombs, Christchurch, 1909.
18   Eric Schwimmer, *The World of the Maori*, Reed Education, 1977, p. 132.
19   R.L. Stevenson, *Travels with a Donkey in the Cévennes*, Penguin Classics, London, 2004, pp 83–84.
20   K.R. Howe, *Singer in a Songless Land: A Life of Edward Tregear*, AUP, 1991.
21   *Fairy Tales and folk-lore of New Zealand and the South Seas*, Lyon and Blair in-school reader series, 1891.
22   Herbert Guthrie-Smith, *Tutira: The Story of a New Zealand Sheep Station*, A.H. & A.W. Reed, 1921, this edition 1969, p. 135.
23   Ibid., p. 217.
24   Ibid., p. 174.
25   Ibid., p. 236/7.
26   Ibid., p. 229.
27   D.H. Lawrence, *Studies in Classic American Literature*, Penguin Books, 1971, p. 12.

28   William Bradford, *Of Plimoth Plantation* – https://en.wikipedia.org/wiki/
      Pilgrims_%28Plymouth_Colony%29#Bradford_1898.
29   Lawrence, *Studies in Classic American Literature*, p. 9.
30   Ibid., p. 13.
31   William Colenso, *In Memoriam: An Account of Visits To, and Crossings
      Over, the Ruahine Mountain Range*, Napier, 1884, p. 31.
32   Grahame Sydney, Brian Turner and Owen Marshall, *Timeless Land*,
      Longacre, Dunedin 1995, p. 159.
33   Brian Turner, in *Taking Off*, Victoria University Press, Wellington, 2001.
34   Sydney et. al, *Timeless Land*, p. 158.
35   R.L. Stevenson, *The Amateur Emigrant*, Penguin Classics, 2004, pp 207–8,
      210.
36   Ibid., pp 210, 211.
37   Ibid., pp 226–7.
38   Eric McCormick, *The Inland Eye: A Sketch in Visual Autobiography*,
      Auckland Gallery Associates, 1959, p. 7.
39   Geoff Chapple, *Te Araroa: The New Zealand Trail*, Random House,
      Auckland, 2002, p. 16.
40   Ibid., p. 13.
41   Jeffrey Paparoa Holman, *Shaken Down 6.3*, Canterbury University Press,
      2012, p. 26.
42   Ibid., p. 50.
43   Fiona Farrell, *The Broken Book*, AUP, 2011, pp 66–67.
44   Geoff Chapple, on 'Tales of the Trail' TV documentary, 2015, Episode 2.
45   Martin Luther, 'The Estate of Marriage', 1522, https://www.1215.org/
      lawnotes/misc/marriage/martin-luther-estate-of-marriage.pdf p. 9, accessed
      14 July 2013.
46   Dr Rowan Williams, on 'The Protestant Revolution', TV programme,
      Tristram Hunt.
47   Luther, 'The Estate of Marriage', p. 10.
48   Emily Brontë, *Wuthering Heights*, Thomas Nelson and Sons Ltd, p. 80.
49   Richard Ford, *Independence Day*, Alfred Knopf, 1995, p. 77.
50   Honore de Balzac, from *The Inventor's Suffering*, cited in Erich Fromm's
      Fear of Freedom, p. 16.
51   Viktor Frankl, *Man's Search for Meaning*, Beacon Press, 2006, pp 37–38, 41.
52   Ariane Sherine, 'Marriage for One: Meet the Women Taking the "We" Out of
      Wedding', in *The Spectator*, 27.08.2016, p. 8.
53   James Meek, 'From Wooden to Plastic', in *London Review of Books*, 24
      September 2015, p. 25.
54   Michael King, *Te Puea: A Biography*, Hodder & Stoughton, 1977, p. 40.
55   Atul Gawande, *Being Mortal: Illness, Medicine and What Matters in the
      End*, Profile Books, London, 2014, p. 122.
56   A. Lane, O. Luminet, B. Rimé, J.J. Gross, P de Timary, M. Mikolajczak,
      'Oxytocin Increases Willingness to Socially Share One's Emotions',
      International Journal of Psychology 48 (4), pp 676–81.
57   A. Theodoridou, A.C. Rowe, I.S. Penton-Voak, P.J. Rogers, 'Oxytocin and
      Social Perception: Oxytocin Increases Perceived Facial Trustworthiness and
      Attractiveness', *Hormones and Behavior* 56 (1), pp 128–32.
58   C. Cardoso, M.A. Ellenbogen, L. Serravalle, A.M. Linnen, 'Stress-induced
      Negative Mood Moderates the Relation Between Oxytocin Administration
      and Trust: Evidence for the Tend-and-Befriend Response to Stress?',
      Psychoneuroendocrinology 38 (11), pp 2800–4
59   Shaul Shalvi, Carsten K.W. De Dreu, 'Oxytocin Promotes Group-serving
      Dishonesty', *Proceedings of the National Academy of Sciences of the United
      States of America* 111 (15), pp 5503–07.
60   C.W. De Dreu, S. Shalvi, L.L. Greer, G.A. Van Kleef, M.J. Handgraaf,
      'Oxytocin Motivates Non-cooperation in Intergroup Conflict to Protect
      Vulnerable In-group Members, *Plos ONE* 7 (11), pp 1–7.

61   On *Huffpost*, 'Megachurch "High" May Explain Their Success', 20 August 2012, https://www.huffingtonpost.com/2012/08/20/megachurch-high-may-explain-success_n_1813334.html, accessed 4 December 2014.

62   S.G. Shamay-Tsoory, M. Fischer, J. Dvash, H. Harari, N. Perach-Bloom, Y. Levkovitz, 'Intranasal Administration of Oxytocin Increases Envy and Schadenfreude (delight in the misfortunes of others), *Biological Psychiatry* 66 (9), pp 864–70.

63   Gregory Berns, *Iconoclast: A Neuroscientist Reveals How to Think Differently*, Harvard Business Press, 2008, pp 59–81. Cited in Susan Cain, *Quiet: The Power of Introverts in a World that Can't Stop Talking*, Penguin, 2013, pp 91–92.

64   Nicholas Carr, *The Shallows: How the Internet is Changing the Way We Think, Read and Remember*, Atlantic Books, 2011.

65   Maggie Rainey-Smith, from a reading at a New Zealand Society of Author's meeting, June 2013.

66   S. Stronge, et al., 'The Facebook Feedback Hypothesis of Personality and Social Belonging', *New Zealand Journal of Psychology*, 44, pp 4–13.

67   Stephen Marche, 'Is Facebook Making Us Lonely?', *The Atlantic*, May 2012.

68   Benedict Anderson, *Imagined Communities: Reflections on the Origin and Spread of Nationalism*, 1983, Verso Editions, London, p. 37.

69   Alison Gray, *Springs in My Heels: Stories About Women and Change*, Bridget Williams Books, 1991, p. 84.

70   Geoff Chapple, *1981: The Tour*, A.H. & A.W. Reed, Wellington, 1984, p. 248.

71   'It's Just a Game' (anon.) in *The New Zealand Experience: 100 Vignettes*, collected by B. Shaw & K. Broadley, Dunmore Press, Palmerston North, 1985.

72   'Urewera 4 Trial: Day 17 – Waiting for a Bit of Land', by Annemarie Thorby, *Scoop*, 9 March 2012.

73   'Tame Iti – The Man Behind the Moko', NZ On Screen documentary for TV, 2007.

74   Ibid.

75   Ibid.

76   Ibid.

77   http://www.ngaituhoe.com/Folders/Tameiti.html, accessed 7 March 2015.

78   John Ahni Schertow, 'Tame Iti and the Tuhoe Nation', in IC Magazine, 26 June 2007.

79   'Tame Iti older, wiser – and now a vegan', in *The Weekend Herald*, 2 March 2013.

80   Ibid.

81   'Police Commissioner apologises for raids', by Michael Fox, on www.stuff.co.nz, accessed 30 April 14.

82   'Tūhoe Rising', by Sam Judd, *Greenideas*, June 2014, pp 28–31.

83   'Tame Iti to Stand for Maori Party', by Michael Fox, on www.stuff.co.nz, accessed 30 August 2014.

84   'Tame Iti – The Man Behind the Moko', ibid.

85   Ibid.

86   Chris Else, 'Poppy lopping and cultural cringeing', in *New Zealand Books*, Vol. 25, No. 2, 2015.

87   Jean Jacques Rousseau, *The* Social Contract, Book 1, Chapter 8: The Civil State, 1762, Constitution Society on net, public domain.

88   Edmund Burke, *The Works of the Right Honourable Edmund Burke: A New Edition*, Vol. VIII. London: F.C. and J. Rivington, 1815, No. 1, p. 172.

89   Edmund Burke, *Reflections on the Revolution in France*, Vol. 3, p. 356.

90   Saul Bellow, *The Victim*, Penguin, 1966, p. 85.

91   Lucinda Holdforth, *Why Manners Matter: The Case for Civilised Behaviour in a Barbarous World*, Random House, Sydney, 2007, p. 4.

92   Wendy Mogel, 'The Dark Side of Parental Devotion', *Camping Magazine*, 1 January 2006, http://www.wendymogel.com/articles/item/

the_dark_side_of_parental_devotion_how_camp_can_let_the_sun_shine/
accessed
15 November 2017.

93   Keith Perry, 'One in Five Children Just Want to be Rich When They Grow
up' in *The Telegraph*, 5 August 2014.

94   Erich Fromm, *The Fear of Freedom*, Routledge & Kegan Paul, 1942, p. 10.

95   George Monbiot, 'The Age of Loneliness is Killing Us' in *The Guardian*,
14 October 2014.

96   F.A. Hayek, in an interview with Thomas W. Hazlett, May 1977, as
published in "The Road to Serfdom: Foreseeing the Fall", in *Reason*
magazine, July 1992.

97   Milton Friedman with assistance of Rose D. Friedman, 1982, Preface,
Capitalism and Freedom (originally published 1962), University of Chicago
Press, Chicago, 2002, p. xiv.

98   For the sequence of events during and after the invasion of Iraq, Naomi
Klein's illuminating book *The Shock Doctrine: The Rise of Disaster
Capitalism*, Penguin Books, London, 2008, originally published by
Metropolitan Books, Henry Holt and Co., 2007, was my main source.

99   'Billions wasted in Iraq, says US audit', Ewan MacAskill in *The Guardian*,
1 May 2006.

100   Jane Kelsey, 'Life in the Economic Test-tube: New Zealand "Experiment"
a Colossal Failure', http://www.converge.org.nz/pma/apfail.htm accessed
10/05/2014.

101   Ibid.

102   Paul Piff, in a TED talk, 'Does Money Make You Mean?' https://www.ted.
com/talks/paul_piff_does_money_make_you_mean, accessed 16 November
2014,

103   Ronald Inglehart, 'Inequality and Modernization', in *Foreign Affairs*,
Jan/Feb 2016, pp 2–10.

104   Klein, *The Shock Doctrine*, pp 421–2.

105   These figures come from a Serious Fraud Office report which was never
brought to publication, but obtained by Radio New Zealand under the
Official Information Act in 2014.

106   Jonathan Tepperman, 'Brazil's Antipoverty Breakthrough', in *Foreign
Affairs*, Vol. 95, No. 1, Jan/Feb 2016, pp 34–44.

107   Writers for the 99%, *Occupying Wall Street: The Inside Story of an Action
that Changed America*, Haymarket Books, 2011.

108   Interview on TV programme, "The 99% Occupy Everywhere", World2Be
2013.

109   Piff, 'Does Money Make You Mean?'.

110   Adam Smith, *Theory of Moral Sentiments*, Prometheus Books, 2000, p. 3.

111   George Monbiot, *Out of the Wreckage: A New Politics for an Age of Crisis*,
Verso, London 2017, p. 15.

112   Keith Jensen, Amrisha Vaish and Marco F.H. Schmidt, 'The Emergence of
Human Prosociality: Aligning with Others through Feelings, Concerns, and
Norms,' in *Frontiers in Psychology* 5, (July 2014) https://www.ncbi.nlm.nih.
gov/pmc/articles/PMC4114263, accessed 6 October 2017.

113   George Monbiot, 'How Do We Get Out of this Mess?' in *The Guardian*,
9 September 2017.

114   Geoffrey Hosking, *Russia: People & Empire*, Fontana Press, 1998, p. xx of
Introduction.

115   Roth, Joseph, *The Radetzky March*, 1932, this edition Allen Lane 1974,
p.108.

116   Ibid., p. 155.

117   Ibid., p. 236.

118   'The Game of Our Lives', *Home & Away* episode four of five-part television
series made by George Andrews Productions with narration by Finlay

Macdonald, https://www.nzonscreen.com/title/the-game-of-our-lives-home-and-away-1996, accessed 6 October 2017.

119   Charles Taylor, 'The Politics of Recognition', in *Philosophical Arguments*, Harvard University Press, 1995, pp 25–73.

120   Edmund De Waal, *The Hare with Amber Eyes*, Vintage Books, 2011, p. 117.

121   The *Deutsches Volksblatt*, editorial by a Romanian university professor from Yassy in 1908. A paper read by Hitler.

122   Adolf Hitler, *Mein Kampf*, Houghton Mifflin Co., New York, 1971 (1925), p. 57. The thoughts of Hitler in this section all come from his book.

123   Stefan Zweig, *The World of Yesterday*, Pushkin Press, London, 2009, p. 246.

124   Hitler, *Mein Kampf*, p. 56.

125   'All in the Best Possible Taste with Grayson Perry', 2012 documentary TV series.

126   Fromm, *The Fear of Freedom*, p. 181.

127   Hitler, *Mein Kampf*, p. 469.

128   Ibid., p. 715.

129   Aqsa Mahmood's blog was closed down by Tumblr in 2015, but screen shots and references to numerous parts of it can be found on the web.

130   Charles Taylor, *Dilemmas and Connections: Selected Essays*, Belknap Press of Harvard University, 2011, p. 87.

131   Richard T. Schaefer (ed.), *Encyclopedia of Race, Ethnicity and Society*. Sage, p. 1096.

132   Michael Ignatieff, *Blood and Belonging*, Vintage, 1994, p. 3.

133   Ibid., p. 75.

134   George Monbiot, 'How Do We Get Out of this Mess?' in *The Guardian*, 9 September 2017.

135   Thich Nhat Hanh, *The Miracle of Mindfulness: An Introduction to the Practice of Meditation*, Beacon Press, Boston, 1987, pp 47–48.

136   Karen Armstrong, *The Great Transformation: The World in the Time of Buddha, Socrates, Confucius and Jeremiah*, Atlantic Books, 2006.

137   Armstrong, Karen, TED talk, 'My Wish: The Charter for Compassion', https://www.ted.com/talks/karen_armstrong_makes_her_ted_prize_wish_the_charter_for_compassion, accessed 2 September 2015.

138   Armstrong, Karen, TED talk, 'Let's Revive the Golden Rule', https://www.ted.com/talks/karen_armstrong_let_s_revive_the_golden_rule, accessed 2 September 2015.

139 Text from the website for The Charter for Compassion, https://charterforcompassion.org/. accessed 2 September 2015.

BIBLIOGRAPHY

Books

Anderson, Benedict, *Imagined Communities: Reflections on the Origin and Spread of Nationalism,* Verso Editions, London, 1983

Armstrong, Karen, *The Great Transformation: The World in the Time of Buddha, Socrates, Confucius and Jeremiah*, Atlantic Books, London, 2007

Aron, Elaine N., *The Highly Sensitive Person,* Element, London, 2003

Austen, Jane, *Mansfield Park*, Collins Classics, London, 2011 (originally published 1814)

Bellow, Saul, *The Victim*, Penguin, Harmondsworth, Middlesex, 1966 (originally published 1947)

Brontë, Emily, *Wuthering Heights*, Thomas Nelson and Sons Ltd, London and Edinburgh (originally published 1847)

Burke, Edmund, *Reflections on the Revolution in France*, edited by Frank M. Turner with essays by Darrin M. McMahon, Conor Cruise O'Brien, Jack N. Rakove and Alan Wolfe, Yale University Press, New Haven, 2003 (originally published 1790)

Burrow, John, *Lord Macaulay's History of England from the Accession of James II, 1848–1861, Introduction and selection by John Burrow*, Continuum International Publishing Group, London and New York, 2009

Cain, Susan, *Quiet: The Power of Introverts in a World That Can't Stop Talking*, Penguin, London, 2012

Carey, Tanith, *Taming the Tiger Parent*, Robinson Publishing Ltd, London, 2014

Carr, Nicholas, *The Shallows: How the Internet is Changing the Way We Think, Read and Remember*, Atlantic Books, London, 2011

Chapple, Geoff, *Te Araroa: The New Zealand Trail*, Random House, Auckland, 2002

——————, *Te Araroa: A Walking Guide to New Zealand's Long Trail*, Random House, Auckland, 2011

——————, *1981: The Tour*, Reed Publishing, Auckland, 1984

Colenso, William, *In Memoriam: An Account of Visits To, and Crossings Over, the Ruahine Mountain Range*, Napier, 1884

de Botton, Alain, *Status Anxiety*, Pantheon Books, New York, 2004

de Waal, Edmund, *The Hare with Amber Eyes: A Hidden Inheritance*, Vintage, London, 2011

Diderot, Denis, *Rameau's Nephew and D'Alembert's Dream*, translated with introductions by Leonard Tancock, Penguin, London, 1966 (originally published c. 1761)

Doidge, Norman, *The Brain that Changes Itself: Stories of Personal Triumph from the Frontiers of Brain Science*, Penguin, New York, 2007.

Earle, Augustus, *A Narrative of a Nine Months' Residence in New Zealand in 1827* (originally published 1832)

Easton, Brian, *In Stormy Seas: The Post-War New Zealand Economy*, University of Otago Press, Dunedin, 1997

————, *The Commercialisation of New Zealand*, AUP, Auckland, 1997

Eldred-Grigg, Steven, *The Great Wrong War: New Zealand Society in WWI*, Random House, Auckland, 2010

Farrell, Fiona, *The Broken Book*, AUP, Auckland, 2011

Ferguson, Harvie, *Self-Identity and Everyday Life*, Routledge, London and New York, 2009

Ford, Richard, *Independence Day*, A.A. Knopf, New York, 1995

Frankl, Viktor E., *Man's Search for Meaning*, Beacon Press, Boston, 2006 (originally published 1946)

Friedman, Milton with assistance of Rose D. Friedman, *Capitalism and Freedom*, University of Chicago Press, Chicago, 2002 (originally published 1962)

Fromm, Erich, *The Fear of Freedom*, Routledge & Kegan Paul, 1942

Galbraith, J.K., *The Economics of Innocent Fraud*, Penguin, London, 2005

Gawande, Atul, *Being Mortal: Illness, Medicine and What Matters in the End*, Profile Books, London, 2014

Geering, Lloyd, *Such is Life!* Steele Roberts, Wellington, 2010

Goffman, Erving, *The Presentation of Self in Everyday Life*, Anchor Books, New York, 1959

Guthrie-Smith, Herbert, *Tutira: The Story of a New Zealand Sheep Station*, A.H. & A.W. Reed, Wellington, 1921 (this edition 1969)

Hager, Nicky, *Dirty Politics*, Craig Potton, Nelson, 2014

Hall, John A., *The Importance of Being Civil: The Struggle for Political Decency*, Princeton University Press, Princeton, 2013

Hayak, F.A., *The Road to Serfdom*, University of Chicago Press, Chicago, 2007 (originally published 1944)

Hitler, Adolf, *Mein Kampf*, translated by Ralph Manheim, Houghton Mifflin Co., New York, 1971 (originally published 1925)

Holdforth, Lucinda, *Why Manners Matter: The Case for Civilised Behaviour in a Barbarous World*, Random House Australia, Sydney, 2007

Holman, Jeffrey Paparoa, *Shaken Down 6.3: Poems from the Second Christchurch Earthquake, 22 February 2011*, Canterbury University Press, Christchurch, 2012

Howe, K.R., *Singer in a Songless Land: A Life of Edward Tregear*, Auckland University Press, Auckland, 1991

Ignatieff, Michael, *Blood and Belonging: Journeys into the New Nationalism*, Vintage, London, 1994

Jones, Jenny Robin, *Writers in Residence: A Journey with Pioneer New Zealand Writers*, Auckland University Press, Auckland, 2004

King, Michael, *Te Puea: A Biography*, Hodder & Stoughton, Auckland, 1977

Klein, Naomi, *The Shock Doctrine: The Rise of Disaster Capitalism*, Penguin, London, 2008

Lawrence, D.H., *Studies in Classic American Literature*, Penguin Books, London, 1971 (originally published 1924)

Lips-Wiersma, Marjolein and Lani Morris, *The Map of Meaning: How to Sustain Our Humanity in the World of Work*, Greenleaf Publishing, Sheffield, 2011

Maalouf, Amin, *On Identity*, Harvill Press, London, 2000

McCormick, Eric, *The Inland Eye: A Sketch in Visual Autobiography*, Auckland Gallery Associates, Auckland, 1959

Mein Smith, Philippa, *A Concise History of New Zealand*, Cambridge University Press, Sydney, 2005

Molière, 'The Misanthrope', in *Molière: Five Plays*, Methuen World Classics, London, 1982

Monbiot, George, *Out of the Wreckage: A New Politics for an Age of Crisis*, Verso, London, 2017

Nicholas, J.L., *Narrative of a Voyage to New Zealand*, Vol. 1, London, 1817, facsimile edition, Wilson & Horton Ltd, Auckland

Prochnik, George, *The Impossible Exile: Stefan Zweig at the End of the World*, Other Press LLC, New York, 2014

Rashbrooke, Max (ed.), *Inequality: A New Zealand Crisis*, Bridget Williams Books, Wellington, 2013

Reed, A.W. (revised by Buddy Mikaere), *Taonga Tuku Iho: Illustrated Encyclopedia of Traditional Māori Life*, New Holland, Auckland, 2002 (originally published 1963)

Roth, Joseph, *The Radetzky March*, Allen Lane, London, 1974, revised translation by Eva Tucker (originally published 1932)

Rousseau, Jean Jacques, *The Confessions*, translated by J.M. Cohen, Penguin, London, 1996 (originally published 1781)

Sandel, Michael J., *What Money Can't Buy: The Moral Limits of Markets*, Allen Lane, division of Penguin, London, 2012

Schwimmer, Eric, *The World of the Maori*, Reed Education, division of A.H. & A.W. Reed, Wellington, 1977

Stark, Jill, *High Sobriety: My Year Without Booze*, Scribe Publications, Melbourne, 2013

Stevenson, R.L., *Travels with a Donkey in the Cevennes and The Amateur Emigrant*, Penguin Classics, London, 2004 (originally published 1879)

——————, *Virginibus Puerisque and Other Papers*, Penguin Books, Harmondsworth, Middlesex, 1946 (originally published 1881)

Stiglitz, Joseph E., *The Price of Inequality: How Today's Divided Society Endangers Our Future*, W.W. Norton & Co., New York, 2013

Storr, Anthony, *Solitude*, HarperCollins, London, 1997

Sydney, Grahame, Brian Turner and Owen Marshall, *Timeless Land*, Longacre, Dunedin, 1995

Taylor, Charles, *Dilemmas and Connections: Selected Essays*, Belknap Press of Harvard University Press, Cambridge, Massachusetts and London, 2011

——————, *Modern Social Imaginaries*, Public Planet Books, Duke University Press, Durham and London, 2004

——————, *Philosophical Arguments*, Harvard University Press, Cambridge, Massachusetts and London, 1995

The Letters of Abelard and Heloise, translated with an introduction and notes by Betty Radice, revised by M.T. Clanchy, Penguin Books, London, 2003 (originally published 1974)

Traue, J.E., *Ancestors of the Mind: A Pakeha Whakapapa*, Gondwanaland Press, Wellington, 1990

Trilling, Lionel, *Sincerity and Authenticity*, Harvard University Press, Cambridge, Massachusetts and London, 1971

Turner, Brian, *Somebodies and Nobodies: Growing Up in an Extraordinary Sporting Family*, Vintage, Auckland, 2002

——————, *Taking Off*, Victoria University Press, Wellington, 2001

von Goethe, Johann Wolfgang, *The Sorrows of Young Werther and Selected Writings*, Signet Classic, New American Library, New York, 1962 (originally published 1774)

White, Emily, *Lonely*, HarperCollins, New York, 2010

Wilkinson, Richard and Kate Pickett (eds), *The Spirit Level: Why Equality is Better for Everyone*, Penguin, London, 2010

Writers for the 99%, *Occupying Wall Street: The Inside Story of an Action that Changed America*, Haymarket Books, Chicago, 2012

Zweig, Stefan, *Erasmus of Rotterdam,* Plunkett Lake Press eBook (originally published 1934)

——————, *The World of Yesterday*, Pushkin Press, London, 2009 (originally published 1942)

Articles

Easton, Brian, 'From Reagonomics to Rogernomics', in *The Influence of American Economics on New Zealand Thinking and Policy: The Fulbright Anniversary Seminars*, edited by Alan Bollard, NZIER Research Monograph 42, 1988

Fox, Michael, 'Tame Iti to Stand for Māori Party' and 'The Man Behind the Moko' and 'Police Commissioner apologises for raids' on www.stuff.co.nz, accessed 30 August 2014

Gere, Judith & MacDonald, Geoff. 'An Update of the Empirical Case for the Need to Belong', in *Journal of Individual Psychology*, Vol. 66, No. 1, March 2010, p. 93

Hazlett, Thomas W., 'The Road to Serfdom, Foreseeing the Fall' in *Reason* magazine, July 1992

Inglehart, Ronald, 'Inequality and Modernization', in *Foreign Affairs*, Jan/Feb 2016, pp. 2-10

Judd, Sam, 'Tūhoe Rising', in *Greenideas*, June 2014, pp 28-31

Marche, Stephen, 'Is Facebook Making Us Lonely?' in *The Atlantic*, May 2013

Meek, James, 'From Wooden to Plastic', in *London Review of Books*, 24 September 2015

Monbiot, George, 'Neoliberalism is creating loneliness. That's what's wrenching society apart' in *The Guardian,* 12 October 2016 and 'The age of loneliness is killing us' in *The Guardian*, 14 October 2014 and 'How Do We Get Out of this Mess?' in *The Guardian*, 9 September 2017

Perry, Keith, 'One in Five Children Just Want to be Rich When They Grow up' in *The Telegraph*, 5 August 2014

Sherine, Ariane, 'Marriage for One: Meet the Women Taking the 'We' Out of Wedding', in *The Spectator*, 27 July 2016, p. 8

Schertow, John Ahni, 'Tame Iti and the Tuhoe Nation', in *IC Magazine*, 26 June 2007

Tepperman, Jonathan, 'Brazil's Antipoverty Breakthrough', in *Foreign Affairs*, Vol. 95, No. 1, Jan/Feb 2016

Thorby, Annemarie, 'Urewera 4 Trial: Day 17 – Waiting for a Bit of Land', on *Scoop*, 9 March 2012

Wane, Joanna, 'Does Money Make You Mean?' in *North & South*, April 2014, p. 36

Wood, James, 'On Not Going Home', in *London Review of Books Podcast*, Vol. 36, No. 4, 20 February 2014, pp 3–8.

INDEX